Beyond Secrecy

Beyond Secrecy

The Untold Story of Canada
and the Second Vatican Council

Bernard M. Daly

NOVALIS

© 2003 Novalis, Saint Paul University, Ottawa, Canada

Cover: Christiane Lemire
Layout: Caroline Gagnon

Business Office:
Novalis
49 Front Street East, 2nd Floor
Toronto, Ontario, Canada
M5E 1B3

Phone: 1-877-702-7773 or (416) 363-3303
Fax: 1-877-702-7775 or (416) 363-9409
E-mail: cservice@novalis.ca
www.novalis.ca

National Library of Canada Cataloguing in Publication Data

Daly, Bernard M. (Bernard Michael), 1925–
Beyond secrecy : the untold story of Canada and the Second Vatican Council / Bernard M. Daly.

Includes bibliographical references and index.
ISBN 2-89507-406-2

1. Vatican Council (2nd : 1962–1965) 2. Catholic Church–Canada. 3. Secrecy–Religious aspects—Catholic Church. 4. Church and the press–Vatican City. I. Title.

BX830.1962 D23 2003   262'.52   C2003-904382-7

Printed in Canada.

All rights reserved. No part of this publication may be reproduced, stored in a retrieval system, or transmitted in any form, or by any means, electronic, mechanical, photocopying, recording, or otherwise, without the written permission of the publisher.

We acknowledge the financial support of the Government of Canada through the Book Publishing Industry Development Program (BPIDP) for our publishing activities.

5   4   3   2   1   07   06   05   04   03

To Mae
To our children, our grands and great-grands
And to all the Catholic bishops of Canada

Contents

Acknowledgments and Thanks 8

Preface 10

1. Life Before Vatican II 15

2. The First Session: 1962 69

3. Intersession: Fall 1962 to Fall 1963 101

4. The Second Session: 1963 118

5. The Third Session: 1964 149

6. The Fourth and Final Session: 1965 197

Conclusion 219

Notes 234

Index 243

Acknowledgments and Thanks

For this book, I started with personal files gathered over more than 40 years. When Vatican II ended, I had English texts or summaries of all the oral interventions of the Canadian bishops. I have checked but did not footnote each of their official Latin versions. These can be found in *Acta Synodalia Sacrosanti Concilii Vaticani II* for the dates that I note in this book. Major academic libraries also have the bishops' 1959 suggestions for council topics in *Acta et Documenta Concilio oecumenico Vaticano II apparando: Series secunda (praeparatoria)*. I note where I asked for help to go beyond my basic Latin. I also depend on and borrow from many other authors, as noted. All translations from the French are my own, as are any errors or deficiencies in them. Every workday in Rome during the four council sessions, I wrote about 2,000 words for publication. Sent to Ottawa, these articles were published by the Information Service of the Canadian Catholic Conference (ISCCC), and are kept in the CCCB Archives in Ottawa. I use them for this book as a quarry of information, examining them as cultural fossils of my own making. A special Latin jargon grew up around Vatican II – *schema* for draft text, *aula* for St. Peter's basilica as transformed into a meeting place for the council, and so on. I shunned all that jargon in this book, in favour of terms and descriptions that I hope are clearer to contemporary readers.

Special thanks to Mae Daly and our six children – Tom, Pat, Mary Anne, Michael, Teresa and Tim – for supportive endurance of my absence from home during each of the four council sessions. They also safeguarded my almost daily letters to them, a total of 70,837 words that renew memories of many council experiences. Pierrette Warwick in Ottawa typed and mailed the daily news bulletins of the CCC Information Service with my council articles, a priceless contribution to the record. Claude Ryan and Réjean Plamondon of Montreal, my French counterparts for the CCC Information Service, helped me more than they can remember. Also, thanks to Desmond Fisher of Dublin who during the council years was editor of *The Catholic Herald* in London; his personal and technical support during the council greatly facilitated my work in Rome. For work on this book, thanks to Gilles Routhier of Laval University, who has done more than any other Canadian to research and record what Vatican II meant to Canadians. I wrote an article for each of two major books on the council that he has edited, but I have drawn much more from them than I contributed. Thanks to Gregory Baum for suggesting this book and helping to outline it. To Bishop Remi De Roo for many general comments and especially for help with drawing material from the Baudoux archives. To Jan Grootaers in Louvain for files about Baudoux in the interconference group. To Brigitte Pageau-Pollock and Jean-Alexandre Charland at CCCB Archives in Ottawa. To Marc Lerman at Toronto Archdiocesan Archives and Kevin Kirley CSB at Basilian Archives in Toronto. To Metropolitan Michael Bzdel in Winnipeg for locating and translating excerpts from Hermaniuk's council journal. To Peter Clark OP in Grenada for translating Bishop Borecky's eloquent Latin *votum*. To Aloysius Kedl, Oblate archivist in Rome, for a summary of the intervention by Leo Deschatelets. To Cardinal Carter, Archbishop Spence, Bishop Borecky, Bishop O'Mara, Bishop W. Emmett Doyle, Michael Barry, Bill Ryan SJ, Bonnie Brennan and Réjean Plamondon for helpful correspondence. To John Thompson and Mary Anne Burke who helped me shape my initial outline, and to Mary Anne and Joe Burke for research help. To Lillianne Alexander, Meryl Augustine, Jacqueline Charles and Cherril Pascall who maintained the congenial work space in Grenada where I wrote the book. To Jim Creskey, for helpful editing. At Novalis, special thanks to Kevin Burns, Michael O'Hearn and Anne Louise Mahoney. And, above all, I thank God for everything, especially for giving Mae Daly her musical talents, the pursuit of which contributed so much to her happiness in Canada and Grenada while I was immersed in the lonesome solitude of researching and writing.

Preface

I did not plan – I never even could have dreamed – that one of the greatest events in Christian history would take up so much of my life. When the Second Vatican Council opened in October 1962, I had been a journalist for 14 years, writing about public events and commenting on them. The assignment to cover Vatican II came as a complete surprise early in the summer of 1962. How would I prepare for such a challenge? At the time I had a slight acquaintance with Gregory Baum, a theologian at St. Michael's College in Toronto. I knew he was one of a number of Canadians already working for the council behind the scenes in Rome. I asked him for a reading list, and devoured the five books he recommended, which described and analyzed the 20 church councils held during past centuries, and speculated about the coming one. Even with that background, however, the difficulties of writing about Vatican II were enormous. The greatest hurdle of all was the Vatican secrecy rule. With the passage of 40 years, much has come to light that was hidden from journalists during the council sessions. That is why this book can be written now about what Canadians did at Vatican II.

The opportunity to write from Rome about the work of 2,500 bishops gathered there by Pope John XXIII was worlds away from my first journalistic endeavour. When I was a child, one of the newspapers that came into our Saskatchewan farm home was *The Prairie Messenger*, published each week by the Benedictines at St. Peter's Abbey, about 300 kilometres from where we lived. Its editor at that time was a learned and kind monk, Wilfrid Hergott, who was also the "Brother Ben" who produced the page entitled *The Junior Messenger*. Each week he printed some short letters from youngsters, and added his few words of welcome and encouragement. I think I was in Grade 3 in our one-room prairie school when our mother coached my younger brother Carl and me to write to Brother Ben for the first time. We mailed off 30 or 40 words each about life on the farm and at Wanganui school, and a few weeks later were thrilled to see our words and names in print. Other similar letters followed. I went on to be the editor of *The Sonorian*, the school paper at St. Thomas College in Battleford, where I finished high school; later, I dabbled as a news reporter for *The Sheaf*, the student newspaper at the University of Saskatchewan in Saskatoon. With my newly minted Bachelor of Arts degree, I began work in 1948 as a professional journalist at the *Saskatoon Star-Phoenix*. By the time John XXIII announced in January 1959 that he was calling a general church council, I was in Ottawa editing the *Information Service* of the Canadian Catholic bishops. When I arrived in Rome in October 1962, I was used to getting out the news, but almost totally unprepared for what began to happen to me and around me in Rome.

This book is my account of Canadian participation in the council, from the day John XXIII announced it until it closed nearly seven years later. When I landed in Rome I was, like everyone else, totally unaware of what direction the council would take, but I knew it would be an important event. The Canadian bishops had sent me there to help get the story out. My press accreditation was one of nearly a thousand issued to writers and broadcasters from around the world. When Pope John XXIII met with journalists in a special 13 October audience in the Sistine Chapel, I had a place standing a few feet in front of him. I listened carefully as he, speaking in French, encouraged us to tell the world the truth about the council. I said to myself, I am a long way from that first letter to Brother Ben.

The pope that morning did not even hint at how much our work would be impeded by the Vatican policy of "secrecy always and everywhere." Covering Vatican II was going to be a challenge for journalists even with all the help we could get. On any day we might be struggling to tell about biblical events since Abraham left Ur, to summarize liturgical changes since the Last Supper or to discuss reasons for Christian divisions going back 400 years to the Reformation or 1,000 years to the East-West schism. The council topics ranged across centuries and through church history, theology, bible studies, canon law and the various sub-divisions of each topic. As it turned out, we learned that even a pope's personal wishes can be frustrated. John XXIII urged us to tell the whole truth, but others imposed secrecy. To write about the council's vast agenda for readers, listeners and viewers of Canadian media was going to be hard enough, but to make things even more difficult, we were forbidden to enter the council hall. Every bishop and theologian allowed to go in had to take an oath of strictest secrecy, with special warnings to avoid talking to journalists. How were we to find out what was happening?

In the council press office set up to serve us, the inexperienced staff was caught in a squeeze between their superiors, who were stressing the rule of secrecy, and a thousand journalists, who were demanding information. They did tell us that the first topic for study was the liturgy, the church's public worship. They described the beginning of the debate only in the most general terms. The first daily press releases were summary and vague: "Today some speakers favoured greater use of vernacular languages, while others stressed the importance of retaining Latin." No names were given. Frustrated journalists quickly resorted to reporting rumours and leaked information. Many soon gave up and went home.

The bishops from various countries gradually became aware that a new information policy was needed. Canadian bishops were among the leaders in seeking improvements. It took time to make changes, however, and they did not come into effect until during the second session in the fall of 1963. Eventually, reporters, grouped by the various major languages, received oral briefings at noon, after each day's general assembly. Speakers were named and their words summarized briefly. Written press releases later in the day confirmed the details. However, during the four sessions, each fall from 1962 to 1965, the great assembly of more than 2,500 bishops was closed to journalists, except for rare special passes to enter the hall for a day or two. These occasions gave us only a sense of atmosphere, for there was no provision for translating the debates, which were carried on in Latin. There was no council press gallery. As for the afternoon and evening working commissions, where tense struggles took place over the final wording of council texts, the secrecy rule was applied strictly. Cardinal Paul-Émile Léger of Montreal, the most vocal Canadian in the debates, generally declined to speak to journalists about the council's daily work. Other Canadian bishops and theologians also stayed within the secrecy rule, though some bishops agreed to be interviewed after they had spoken during the general debate. In addition, journalists found a dependable source of information in the many public lectures given by bishops or theologians who used these occasions to promote their views on council topics. Depending on your language skills, you could chat with Congar or Danielou, Rahner or Ratzinger, or other well-known authors, or with newcomers like Hans Küng, who was at the council as *peritus* (expert) for a German bishop.

One of Pope Paul VI's many contributions to the church was his decision to open the special Vatican II archives to researchers. Large books contain every word spoken in the general debates, along with the written notes submitted by many bishops. Minutes of what happened in the council's secret working commissions were written by their secretaries, even if not in a consistent way; these can now be studied. And, apart from the council archives, all around the world researchers can explore the personal diaries and letters written during the council by many of the bishops and theologians, including Canadians. As a result, more and more books about Vatican II are being published in many languages.

When I reread what we journalists wrote 40 years ago about Vatican II, I am impressed at how accurate and full our reports were given the difficulties we faced. However, the information now available from official and private archives goes far beyond, and sometimes corrects, what we wrote day by day. What was once secret can now be put on the public record. This book is my attempt to fill in parts of the story of Canadian participation at Vatican II that were not made public at the time of the council. There is still more to be told, I am sure.

Catholic life before Vatican II was marked by holiness and joy – and also by scruples, social habits, obedience and fear.

Scruples? The spring Mae was 11, her Catholic school, in a parish church basement in Tillsonburg, Ontario, offered prizes to pupils who attended mass and received communion every morning during Lent. She nearly lost her chance at a prize one morning when she rushed to the church almost late and very thirsty. She was about to gulp a mouthful of water in the washroom when she was frozen by a sudden question: Would she lose her prize if she swallowed? Would that break the required pre-Eucharist fast? She has a vivid memory of spitting out the water and drying the inside of her mouth with toilet paper. And she did get a prize.

Social habits? The pre-council dress code for church-going complicated our 1961 summer holidays. We pitched our "two-room" tent in the long-stay area of Lac Philippe national park north of Ottawa. We planned to attend Sunday mass in the nearby Ste-Cecile-de-Masham. That it was a French parish was no problem. The problem was how to pack the hats Mae and three daughters needed for church. They could have used head scarves, but all opted for white wide-brimmed Easter favourites! For the two weeks, the hats were under a watermelon, where the camp stove was supposed to go, inside a sleeping bag, out in a sudden shower…and worn jauntily and comparatively uncrushed for an hour each Sunday!

Obedience? Weekends were popular times for weddings, and Mae sang at many of them. She recalls in particular one in Saskatoon at which she did not sing! She thought that just singing would not break the church law against "attending" the Anglican service, but decided to ask Bishop Pocock about it anyway. His 1950s answer was no, you can't go!

Fear? One example was fear that a child would die without being baptized. Mae remembers that she both went along with the plan but also wept bitterly when our first-born was baptized a few days after birth, before she felt strong enough to go to the church for the ceremony.

1

Life Before Vatican II

As they ate breakfast on the morning of 25 January 1959, Canadians were unaware that in Rome Pope John XXIII was changing the modern world, especially for Catholics and other Christians. He was announcing the Second Vatican Council. Planning their Sunday, preparing for church as most did in those days, some of the 18 million Canadians perhaps chatted about the Cold War. Earlier in the month Fidel Castro had led his revolutionary forces into Havana. The Berlin wall would not be built for another two years, but Soviet leader Nikita Khrushchev was talking about building intercontinental ballistic missiles. Most Catholics in Canada were not aware that their bishops were preparing changes in church food rules for Lent that would be announced a year later. People in Quebec did not know that they were living the last few months of an historic political era, for Premier Maurice Duplessis would die in September and the "Quiet Revolution" would take off. Prime Minister John Diefenbaker had just announced that he would not intervene in a strike at the Canadian Broadcasting Corporation (CBC). The Supreme Court of Canada was about to decide, by a split 4–3 vote, that the CBC did not contravene the Lord's Day Act by broadcasting in Toronto on Sundays. Ottawa's Anne Heggtveit had won a combined ski title in Switzerland; the Montreal Canadiens were leading the six-team National Hockey League; and Yogi Berra, a 10-pennant veteran with the New York Yankees, had signed his 1959 contract "for approximately $57,500."

The previous October, Pope John XXIII had made world headlines when he was elected at nearly 77 years of age, but by January most people were aware that he frequently left Vatican City for short trips around Rome. His visit that Sunday to St. Paul's Outside the Walls would seem like just another such excursion until the next day's newspapers came out. The pope was back on page one. He had announced an ecumenical or general church council, along with a synod for the diocese of Rome and a revision of the Catholic code of canon law. The council was the big news! The very idea launched a wave of expectations and hopes that eventually swept up Canadians and people around the world. It also set off a struggle for control at the highest levels of the Catholic church, details of which would remain secret for years, though some Canadian bishops were deeply involved, and all of them eventually had to vote for one side or the other.

Although John XXIII announced a council in vague terms, the major news services in Rome immediately gave it a sharp focus. The United Press International (UPI) condensed both the pope's words and a Vatican press release into a blunt report, printed by the *Ottawa Journal* on page one of its 26 January 1959 evening edition. It said: "Pope John XXIII launched the Roman Catholic world today on a new offensive to win back the Eastern Orthodox and Western Protestant churches into the church of Rome." A similar report by the Associated Press (AP) added more details the next day. "Pope John XXIII," it said, "will convoke a great assembly – the 21st ecumenical council in the 2000-year history of the Roman Catholic church – to seek unity of the Christian forces in the world. Return to the fold of the Eastern Orthodox Church's 129 million members was seen as a prime object of the conclave.... Reaffirmation of the church's stand against Communism may be another major subject of the ecumenical council, the first since 1870." For its part, the Canadian Press (CP) report in the *Ottawa Journal* said "Canadian Protestant church leaders reacted with cautious interest last night to the possibility of invitations to the first Roman Catholic ecumenical council, a world gathering of the hierarchy, in nearly 100 years." Dr. W.J. Gallagher, of Toronto, general secretary of the Canadian Council of Churches, comprising

Protestant denominations, said the reaction to any overture "in my opinion would depend on the nature of the invitation." He described the pontiff's announcement as "quite surprising." "However," he added, "I believe personally that if the Protestant churches were invited to send observers to such a council, many of them probably would accept."[1]

Similarly, as early as 27 January, W.A. Visser't Hooft, the Dutch Reformed pastor who was general secretary of the World Council of Churches (WCC) in Geneva, expressed a "very special interest" in John XXIII's reference to Christian unity (and two weeks later the WCC executive committee approved his statement as representing it).[2] In Quebec's French dailies, *La Presse* carried John XXIII's announcement on page one: *Historic decision by John XXIII/ An ecumenical council at the Vatican/First in a century – Union of Christian forces.* In its turn, *La Nouvelliste* at Trois-Rivières said: *The Pope calls an ecumenical council/ John XXIII makes an historic, very unexpected decision.*[3] The day after the pope's announcement, most articles about it made page one. *La Presse* ran three items, *Le Devoir, Le Soleil* and *Le Droit* two each. I was then the editor of the English information service of the Canadian bishops' conference (CCC) in Ottawa. Our 28 January release reported that Canadian Protestant leaders had shown "cautious interest" in a Catholic council.

A lead editorial in the 27 January *Ottawa Journal* set the coming event in a global perspective. It noted that, "2,000 years after Bethlehem, Christians number less that one third of the world's inhabitants – 835,000,000 out of 2,644,000,000." The full text of the Vatican announcement of the council was published in the *Toronto Daily Star*.[4] For its part, the Toronto *Globe and Mail* in an editorial called for the Canadian government to establish diplomatic relations with the Vatican. "It is hoped," the editorial said, "that the spectacle of ecclesiastics from every corner of the earth gathering in Rome next year will not be lost on the Canadian cabinet and on other governments which do not maintain diplomatic relations with the Vatican. Vatican City is a unique world centre, in touch with the remotest parts of the globe, and Canada is the loser by not having representation there."[5]

No official Catholic reactions

Apart from the pope's brief announcement, word about Vatican II was spread first by the secular news media, not Catholic officials. This was the first time in church history that such important information was communicated to church members mainly by media not controlled by the church itself, Laval University theologian Gilles Routhier, has noted.[6] In Canada, there were no media interviews with Catholic leaders in Montreal or Quebec, and English-speaking bishops were similarly silent. Canadian bishops apparently were waiting for more and clearer information from the Vatican. It did not come for many weeks. This delay is explained in part by the power struggle that developed at the Vatican immediately after John XXIII's announcement. Another factor was the strict oath of secrecy under which Canadian and other bishops outside Rome had to work, once they began to get involved in the process a few months after the pope's announcement.

John XXIII seemed unlikely to launch the Catholic church into a continuing state of renewal and reform. He was nearly 77 when elected 28 October 1958. Many thought he would preside briefly until a consensus emerged around a younger successor to Pius XII. He began without a clear agenda for change. Much has been written, much of it only speculation, about how the idea of a council developed in his mind during the months after his election. If he consulted some cardinals or other advisors, there is no evidence that they included either Cardinal James McGuigan, archbishop of Toronto, or Cardinal Paul-Émile Léger, archbishop of Montreal, the two Canadian cardinals at the time. Much of what we know today about his announcement and what immediately followed it has come to light since Vatican II, as researchers have gained access to key archives, journals, letters and other documents. For his part, John XXIII said the Holy Spirit suddenly prompted him. However, as he told non-Catholic Vatican II observers, "I do not like to appeal to special inspiration. I am satisfied with the orthodox teaching that everything is from God. In light of that teaching I regarded the idea of a council as likewise an inspiration from heaven."

From 25 January 1959 until Vatican II opened nearly 45 months later on 11 October 1962, his plan emerged gradually. Both opposition and support developed. Behind a veil of secrecy, the pope's plan was resisted and opposed by some Vatican officials. Many of them thought that a new council was unnecessary, since the papal prerogatives of primacy and infallibility had been given authoritative approval at the First Vatican Council, called in 1869 and adjourned hastily, its agenda not completed, when Italian troops entered Rome in 1870. Indeed, they thought a new council was not only unnecessary but even a direct threat to the central position defined for the pope by Vatican I. The French Dominican theologian Yves Congar noted later,

> the hopes raised by the announcement of the council were covered over with a thin layer of ash. There was a lengthy silence, a kind of blackout that was hardly broken by one or other reassuring statement from the pope. But even these statements were rather vague, and it seemed that the pope had drawn back from his original announcement. This was noted in several quarters, even though the pope himself said publicly that he had not changed.... The impression was abroad – confirmed by people coming from Rome and reporting the latest gossip from the wretched curia – that in Rome a whole team was busy sabotaging the pope's plan. They also said that the pope was fully aware of this."[7]

However, John XXIII did not retract his decision, so Vatican officials had to deal with it. Those opposed to a council began working to focus the new council, like past ones, on reasserting accepted truths and perhaps condemning errors and defining new doctrines. The pope persisted in rejecting this approach. His council would be "a new Pentecost" and "eminently pastoral." It would rejuvenate the church, bringing it up to date so as to serve the world better and open up paths toward the reunion of separated Christians. But it was not until his address opening Vatican II that he spelled out very clearly what he meant by *aggiornamento*, or updating. He disagreed with "prophets of doom" who "keep saying that as compared with past ages, ours is getting worse." The council would focus on the only thing the church could give the world: the ancient message of the gospel. The substance of this message is one thing, the way it is presented is another, and it is the latter that must be taken into consideration, he said. Nowadays, the church "prefers to use the medicine of mercy rather than severity. She considers that she meets the needs of the present day by demonstrating the validity of her teaching rather than by condemnations." However, even this apparently clear and certain papal direction did not win all minds, and much of the drama of Vatican II would be in the struggle to decide what direction the church should take at the council.

Looking back, it is surprising that so vague an initial word produced so great "a burst of attention, interest, and, above all, expectation in the public mind."[8] Support for John XXIII's council came first from a diverse public opinion. News of it spread through world media in a few hours, greeted with attention, interest and even excitement, despite uncertain and varied expectations. Christian ecumenists responded positively. Enthusiasm mounted quickly in Catholic movements for renewal of biblical studies, catechetics and liturgy, whose leaders were facing resistance and opposition. As preparatory work continued, the pope experienced growing support from diocesan bishops outside Rome, who were asked for their suggestions. His expansive vision reflected the geniality of his spiritual and public life.

Yousef Karsh, the famed portrait photographer, found John XXIII to be "good-humored, earthy but still saint-like, gregarious and unashamedly fond of people, ... a simple, compelling, forthright human being." The pope's self-effacing sense of humour came through when he told Karsh, "The Lord knew from all eternity I was going to be pope; you'd think he would have made me more photogenic."

Catholics in Canada

To set the scene for what happened in Canada after John XXIII announced Vatican II, a brief sketch of the pre-council church seems necessary. In the 1950s francophone Catholics were an overwhelming majority in Quebec. As the decade was ending, post-war secularization was developing quickly and the church was losing influence, but this was not a common perception at the time. In the other Canadian provinces, Catholics were minority groups in the total population. There was one Catholic church in Quebec and another elsewhere in the country, one might say hastily. However, there was also over-arching unity, arising both from a common spirituality and from some important common structural elements.

As described in detail by Jesuit Terence Fay in *A History of Canadian Catholics*,[9] a common spirituality provided a deep Catholic unity across the country. Fay echoes others in calling it the "ultramontane spirituality." The term *ultramontane* – beyond the mountains – was coined in France to describe influences coming across the Alps from Rome. As Fay summarizes, "ultramontane spirituality imbued the faithful with a renewed reverence for the Chair of Peter and respect for its spiritual leadership." Ultramontane spirituality featured the triumphal piety of the papacy restored after the loss of the papal states and the Italian army's invasion of Rome in 1870. This interrupted the First Vatican Council before it completed its agenda but after it approved decrees on papal primacy and infallibility. As part of this spirituality, liturgical and devotional life in parishes all across Canada emphasized the devotions of Holy Eucharist, Sacred Heart, Corpus Christi, Benediction of the Blessed Sacrament, the Forty Hours devotions, Our Lady and the Rosary that various popes had encouraged. Canadian neo-ultramontane spirituality transmitted a religious commitment to the Roman tradition.[10] It romanized the Canadian church. Education and piety went hand in hand in the effort to restore an international Catholic culture that the French Revolution had destroyed. Because of this widespread spirituality, Catholics across Canada had much in common. Similar devotions, processions, large rallies and pilgrimages were familiar to Catholics everywhere in the country, despite some cultural and linguistic differences. As for the bishops, theologian Michael Fahey has noted that during the years from the close of Vatican I (1870) to the death of Pius XII (1958), "bishops were seen as receiving their sacramental power by papal appointment, and not through the sacramental action of ordination to the fullness of the priesthood. A fair number of bishops saw themselves as kinds of senior acolytes, clerks of the pope, serving as what Karl Rahner called a *Sprachohr* – a megaphone – for papal teaching."[11]

Bishops working together

Besides a common spirituality, another unifying factor for Canadian Catholics was the developing national association of the bishops of Canada. The Canadian Catholic Conference (CCC) was founded in 1943 because the bishops felt the need to meet each year to discuss common pastoral needs and how to address them. The terrible final battles of World War II were taking shape, and postwar pastoral problems were already discernable. Under church law at that time, the CCC was only a voluntary national association, but all the bishops in fact participated. Officially bilingual from the start, it was "an organism of vigilance, of consultation and of co-ordination which would assure the Church in Canada a stronger influence and an increase of prestige," in the words of Cardinal Jean-Marie-Rodrique Villeneuve of Quebec, its first president. It received Vatican approval for its first constitution in June 1948. From its first meeting, the CCC undertook projects that had relevance all across the country. The bishops discussed how to support Catholic hospitals as the provincial and federal governments became more involved in health care. They also worked at shaping a national organization that might represent all Catholics in charity and social welfare work.

The first pastoral office set up within the CCC was a department of social action. Its first task was to aid Catholic displaced persons from European war zones coming into Canada as immigrants. It also took on the role of teaching the concepts broadly known as Catholic social doctrine. The first CCC joint statement in 1943 tried to end a decade-old controversy about whether Catholics could support the new Co-operative Commonwealth Federation (CCF) party. The bishops declared, without naming the CCF, "that the faithful are free to support any political party, which maintains the fundamental Christian principles, which are traditional in Canada, and which favours, in the economic and social order, the necessary reforms demanded with insistence in pontifical documents."[12]

During the 19 years from 1943 to the opening of Vatican II, the Canadian bishops therefore gained increasing experience of working together as a national association. Together they were becoming aware that many items of earlier church discipline no longer suited an increasingly urbanized and industrialized Canada. For example, many traditional church holy days were becoming problematic for Catholics. Earlier, in a rural setting, they had been able to leave work for morning church services on such days, following strict rules about avoiding "servile" work, fasting, or abstaining from eating meat. Now, increasingly, even on Sundays as well as other holy days, Catholics had to go like anyone else to their round-the-clock shift work in factories or public services. Responding to earlier requests from Canada and elsewhere, the Vatican gave permission in 1949 for an individual bishop to dispense some groups of workers or other Catholics in their diocese from the church's general laws on fast and abstinence.

One response by Canadian bishops to this changing situation was a 13 October 1960 CCC statement on Sunday work. The bishops expressed grave anxiety over the growing tendency by commerce and industry to consider Sunday an ordinary working day. They said that "if this tendency should one day be confirmed by legislation or, by increasing toleration, should come to be accepted as normal in our society, then all who proudly profess the doctrine of Christ would witness the disappearance of institutions which were established through the unceasing efforts of many generations." The CCC expressed the belief "that our federal and provincial leaders will, in their wisdom, find ways to overcome our present difficulties, and even to anticipate the possible future economic fluctuations in such a way as to uphold the sanctity of the Lord's Day in years to come."[13]

Despite this protest, what Christians regarded as the sanctity of the Lord's Day nevertheless continued to be eroded in the developing industrial economy. To avoid a hodge-podge of different diocesan rules for servile work, fast and abstinence, the Canadian bishops agreed that for the beginning of Lent 1960 every bishop would enact the same regulations, so that one set of new rules would apply across the country. In a related adjustment to the new conditions of modern life, a 1958 Vatican instruction required all Canadian bishops to develop programs for changes in how Catholics worshipped. Pope Pius XII called for increased participation in church services by lay Catholics. The instruction allowed, among other things, changes in the traditional Sunday morning hours for mass to include evening services, and encouraged "dialogue masses" in which the whole congregation would pronounce the Latin prayers usually said only by altar servers in reply to the priest.

New mission projects

Another pre-Vatican II experience that began to influence Canadian bishops was John XXIII's early 1959 plan for pastoral co-operation between dioceses in Latin America and North America. When Archbishop Sebastiano Baggio arrived in Ottawa early in 1959 as Apostolic Delegate, he informed the Canadian bishops of the pope's plan. He spoke first to Bishop Albert Sanschagrin of Amos, Quebec. They knew each other from previous meetings when both were working in Chile. Sanschagrin took a lead role in shaping the Canadian response. At a November 1959 meeting in Washington, DC, attended by bishops from Canada, the US and Latin America and Vatican officials, the plan was moved forward. It had two main parts. Canadian dioceses were encouraged to send priests and lay personnel to work in matched Latin American dioceses. This was somewhat novel for diocesan personnel, for usually members of traditional missionary orders of men and women went abroad for such work. John XXIII was anticipating by this move a Vatican II teaching about the responsibility of each bishop for the welfare of the whole church, and not just his own diocese. Eventually, 27 Canadian dioceses from coast to coast would have personnel in various southern dioceses. The second part of the pope's plan called for Canada and the US to finance seminaries in Latin America. The U.S. bishops undertook one, since closed, in Brazil; the Canadian-built seminary is still operating in Tegucigalpa, Honduras. Canadian financial responsibilities for it ended in 1977.

Therefore, although some may have thought it monolithic and unchangeable, the Catholic church in the late 1950s in Canada was not entirely stable or static. Besides the changes just noted, the Catholic Action movement was an important local agent of changes that began in the Canadian Church in the late 1940s, and continued during the 1950s and up to the beginning of Vatican II. Catholic Action was centred in Quebec with outreach to French-sector dioceses across Canada. Among member groups were the Young Catholic Students (JEC) (male and female), Independent Catholic Youth (JIC) (female), Young Catholic Workers (JOC) (male and female), Rural Catholic Youth (JRC) (male and female), League of Catholic Workers (LOC) (male and female), as well as Rural Catholic Action (male, female and mixed). JEC, JIC, JOC, JRC and LOC each had a national bishops' mandate, giving their action official, public status.[14] Their counterparts that developed in English dioceses were especially the Young Christian Workers (YCW), Young Christian Students (YCS) and the Christian Family Movement (CFM), a grouping of couples that had no direct counterpart in Quebec.

Quebec also had a strong Catholic trade union sector. It had no English counterpart, but efforts were made to establish one. One example of this was a Toronto meeting in February 1944 to discuss the task of "the Christian reconstruction of Canadian society" or "building a Catholic-inspired Canadian social system," as spelled out by the Quebec priest involved in planning the study days, J.C. Leclaire of St. Hyacinthe. He and Henry Somerville, editor of Toronto's *Catholic Register*, the two main organizers, had common views on the theories about society that shaped the social encyclicals of Popes Leo XIII and Pius XI. They hoped that Catholics in English areas could build counterparts or their own versions of the Quebec Catholic Action groups. To that end, 50 delegates from Quebec were drawn mainly from the Canadian Confederation of Catholic Trade Unions (CTCC) and the Catholic Union of Quebec Farmers (UCC). English delegates met with them to discuss "Industrial Relations" and "The Rural Problem." Also invited were some representatives of so-called neutral trade unions – U.S. based unions that had no direct church links. In bilingual sessions, the delegates shared their differing views about the role of the state in labour questions, owner-worker collaboration, relations among unions, benefits under collective agreements, the possibility of reducing strikes, and "the corporative organization of society." The latter topic explored the Catholic view at that time that, ideally, social affairs should be directed and social harmony achieved by three-way collaboration of the state, associations of industrialists, and strong, responsible unions of workers.[15]

For those of us involved in Catholic Action – especially students, young workers, couples – the movement meant an awakening. We learned in small self-directed groups how to *observe* the society of which we were part in a systematic and critical way, how to *judge* world events in the light of gospel values, and how to *act* together for desired social change. This learning process resulted in Catholics who did not just follow faithfully, but instead took up creative, leadership roles that had little or no place in ultramontane spirituality. Some bishops and priests welcomed this while others felt threatened and worried.

That challenging lay vision was emerging within the framework of the much greater changes brought about by the Second World War. Its horrors, and especially the slaughter of Jews, shattered ultramontane certitudes and somewhat undermined reliance on papal leadership. How could such evil happen even in officially Catholic countries? Pius XII's personal response to fascism began to be questioned. More broadly, notions of individual rights and of democracy that had been questioned or opposed by earlier popes were now championed against the collectivist crimes of fascism and communism. Around the globe, in new nations emerging from colonialism, new churches were also emerging, with new longings to express their faith in their own cultural ways, even though they were still largely led by bishops and priests formed by Roman schools. Catholic scholars of scripture and early church writings, long held in check by ultramontane opposition, were giving leadership to movements for the reform of liturgy and catechetics in particular. It must also be said that twentieth-century popes also contributed to the stirrings of change. Examples include the social encyclicals starting with Leo XIII, the encouragement of the lay apostolate by Pius XI and Pius XII, the support of biblical research by Pius XII and his 1958 directive for greater congregational participation in the celebration of the Eucharist, leading to the "dialogue mass."

Council and Quebec

Within the larger framework of a changing world, Canada itself was changing. The Second World War massively increased industrial growth. In Quebec especially, but throughout the country, this growth was accompanied by a movement of people from the land to the cities. There, Catholics were influenced less by their home parishes and more by ideas from the new communication media, especially radio and the movies and, after 1952, from national television. A growing class of young professionals wanted a greater voice in education, health care, welfare services, labour unions. A huge debate swept Quebec during the late 1940s and the 1950s about the balance to be sought between confessional (i.e., church-related), non-confessional and neutral organizations. Routhier has shown that questions about how the changes in Quebec schools, hospitals and welfare services, and not preparations for Vatican II, dominated the meetings of the Quebec bishops from the time the council was announced until it opened. All this change we now refer to as "Quebec's Quiet Revolution," that took off after Premier Duplessis died in September 1959 and the new Lesage government took over in 1960 under the slogan "Time for a change."

News of the council came, then, at a time when widespread debate had already begun in Quebec about how the church should relate to social changes there. In Quebec, as across the rest of Canada, news of the pope's call for *aggiornamento* or updating would give new impetus to fledgling movements for reform in biblical studies, liturgy, catechetics, the lay apostolate and church unity efforts. At the time, there was a vast network of pious associations promoting popular devotions. Many were centred in Quebec but well represented across Canada. Associations such as the Leagues of the Sacred Heart and Holy Name Society dominated Catholic parish life for laity. And there were similar associations for the clergy. A membership of 300,000 "Leaguers" was reported in the 1940s, and their *Messager Canadien du Sacré-Coeur* printed 75,000 copies in 1959. Shrine magazines, promoting pilgrimages, flourished. *L'Oratoire* at St. Joseph's Oratory in Montreal had a circulation of nearly 140,000 in 1959. *L'Annales de la Bonne Saint-Anne de Beaupré* had nearly 170,000, and the *Revue Notre-Dame du Cap* reported 238,000 French and 12,000 English copies in 1959. These publications were intended to sustain the devotion of Catholics while also instructing them in moral and doctrinal matters. The anti-communist talk that had marked the pontificate of Pius XII, and the church's resistance to atheist ideologies formed the backdrop of the editorial line of most of them. The unquestioned authority of the pope was a rampart on which they sought support. They were soon surprised to learn that the pope was going to convoke a huge church assembly, with debating and voting. Editors of these magazines found themselves poorly equipped to interpret a church event that did not fit with the image of the church of which they were the source. They also lacked information. In their publications, the council at first had a slightly timid echo, but interest increased towards the opening of the first session. The council was first presented as an important event, but an affair of the pope, bishops and religious superiors, for which people should pray. However, after initial hesitation, council themes found a place in the devotional magazines between 1959 and 1962. [16]

Even though ideas about the council itself made slow progress at first among Quebec Catholics, Routhier concludes that Quebec Catholics in general and their bishops in particular lived through an intense process of preparation for the council from 1959 to the fall of 1962. This was because the Quebec church was involved from the late 1940s and into the early 1960s in an open, far-ranging debate on two questions that would be central to Vatican II. One was religious liberty. The other was freedom for diversity and debate within the church itself. The religious liberty debate was about whether schools, hospitals, trade unions and similar institutions could be allowed to "deconfessionalize," that is, to develop outside church control. That debate showed deep divisions that were open and public. This led to the second question, how to handle freedom of speech within the church.

An idea of the intensity of the debate in Quebec can be gained from the case of Archbishop Joseph Charbonneau of Montreal. A former vicar-general in Ottawa, he was named archbishop of Montreal in 1940. A Franco-Ontarian, he was seen by some to have been parachuted into Montreal; for others, he was not a strong organizer and administrator. Still others, however, welcomed him as a man of large vision – populist and ecumenical, and neither nationalist nor ultramontane. As historian Jean Hamelin records, "His attitude towards socialism, his stand in favour of non-confessional projects, the autonomy he gave to leaders of Catholic

Action marginalized him among Quebec bishops."[17] His support of workers in industrial disputes won him no friends around Premier Maurice Duplessis. Who or what sealed his fate is still a debated matter, but some facts are clear. Late in 1949, Charbonneau was informed he should either resign or accept the appointment of an administrator for the diocese; people were told early in 1950 that Charbonneau had resigned "for health reasons." Montreal received a new archbishop, Paul-Émile Léger, but the swirl of debate about social changes affecting the church raged on.

Later, under Léger, a pivotal and very public issue was what to do about the book, *Les Insolences du Frère Untel*. The author, though supposedly anonymous, was soon found out to be a Marist religious brother. In earlier years, his outspoken public criticism of much about church-led life in Quebec probably would have led to him being officially silenced and his book banned. The record of their long debates shows that Quebec bishops were divided on what to do about Frère Untel. In the end the moderate views of Léger, and of Archbishops Roy of Quebec and Lemieux of Ottawa, and others, prevailed. Reprimand was kept internal to the Marist Brothers. The tumultuous debate simmered down with no public censure, and no censorship.

Claude Ryan, then general secretary of L'Action catholique, summed up these events by noting that in Quebec in the months after the council was announced, the church in Quebec experienced the same division and debate that later occurred in the council itself. In particular, Léger experienced a personal transformation.

> Arriving in Montreal after the forced resignation of Archbishop Joseph Charbonneau, Léger had to resituate the Montreal church on a more traditional path wanted by those who had wanted his predecessor to leave as his orientation was judged to be too liberal. At the end of several years marked by outstanding success, he noticed however that the applause he got came mostly from those already won to his cause, and that his message hardly touched those who most needed to be reached. This was the beginning of a process that led him to try to draw closer to those distanced from the church, to revise many judgments, and often to take innovative decisions giving witness to a prophetic detachment from the privileges that the institutional church long

had enjoyed. Considered at the start of his episcopacy to be very tied to the conservative wishes of the Roman Curia, Léger showed himself at the Council to be one of the figures at the lead of Vatican II's marching wing. Faced with the changes that developed, Léger's colleagues in the Quebec episcopate also showed a sincere openness to the aim of the updating of the Church sought by John XXIII, but in less spectacular ways than Léger did. Even if, in general, the perception they had of the changes coming in Quebec remained well short of what did happen, they saw them coming without arrogance, and with fitting discretion and humility.[18]

The Rest of Canada

For Catholics in English dioceses outside Quebec, news of the coming council did not arrive in the midst of a transforming, all-inclusive debate about church-secular relations and freedom in the church, as it did in Quebec. Instead, there was slowly increasing interest and activity in fledgling church reform movements that were given new impetus by John XXIII. The liturgical movement is a prime example of changes already under way in 1959. Catholics going to Sunday mass in the early 1950s experienced a Latin service that had hardly changed for centuries. If someone like Samuel de Champlain could have walked into a 1950s Catholic church, he would have felt pretty much at home: the priest at the altar with his back to the people, the Latin, the incense, the sanctuary bells. There was something awesome about being part of a culture that seemed to stand outside time. It was also somewhat unreal. Therefore, specialists, especially in some European monasteries, were calling for some renewal, based on new studies of the scriptures and early church writings. Partly in response to this research, and also at the urging of some bishops, Pius XII issued his 1958 instruction on liturgical reforms. It opened the way for changes in holy week ceremonies, evening masses, dialogue masses in which the entire congregation was encouraged to speak the prayers formerly said only by altar servers, and some changes in the daily breviary prayers the clergy were required to say. This led to considerable activity at the local level. The week after John XXIII announced the council, there was news that Halifax priests met to discuss how to increase liturgical participation.[19]

A few weeks later Archbishop Skinner of St. John's, Newfoundland, said in a pastoral letter that "the training that is necessary (for the 'dialogue mass') can best begin in our schools, where Latin and the simple Gregorian Chant should be taught." Illustrating the current Romanist view, Skinner added: "I am prompted and indeed obliged to do so by an Instruction from the Sacred Congregation of Rites."[20] In Toronto in June McGuigan noted "it is the wish of the church that the laity become more active in participating with the priest at Mass."[21] In August Archbishop Philip Pocock announced that observance of Pius XII's instruction would begin in Winnipeg the second Sunday of October.[22] In the Saskatoon diocese, more active congregation participation in the mass began on November 29 on the instruction of Bishop F.J. Klein.[23] The next month, education and the liturgy were the theme of a three-day Toronto conference sponsored by the Ontario English Catholics Teachers Association.[24] Speakers included Benedictine Godfrey Diekmann from St. John's Abbey in Minnesota, who later would have a prominent role in council revision of the liturgy."Gradual restoration of the almost lost art of liturgical assistance at mass, rather than revolutionary change, is the mind of the church," Bishop Thomas J. McCarthy of St. Catharines said as guest speaker.[25] Similar liturgical renewal events continued during 1960, 1961 and 1962, in London, Nelson, Fredericton, Vancouver, Kingston. Just a month before the council would open in Rome, a major liturgical program was launched in Toronto by Pocock, who by then had been transferred from Winnipeg as designated successor to Toronto's ailing Cardinal McGuigan.[26] Of special interest is the fact that Pocock invited the US scripture specialist, Barnabas Ahern, to be a major speaker at the Toronto workshops. Less than two months later in Rome, Ahern would be a guest lecturer invited to inform Canadian bishops in Rome about the latest methods in biblical studies.

Regarding Unity

Looking back on the 1950s and earlier, Fahey noted that

> The Canadian bishops, as most of the Catholic faithful, were largely disinterested in the growing phenomenon of ecumenical co-operation in the first half of the 20th century. The efforts of Faith and Order movement to involve Roman Catholics at its first meeting in Lausanne had been countered by the papal encyclical *Mortalium animos* (1928) that disparagingly described ecumenism as "pan-Christian" leveling of true doctrine. *Humanae generis* (1950) warned of the dangers from false irenicism between Catholics and non-Catholics.[27]

All the more remarkable, then, is the extent to which news of the council was followed by increased ecumenical activity by Canadian Catholics. In Toronto, less than eight months after John XXIII's announcement, a new approach to Protestantism was outlined in September 1959 to the twelfth annual Seminarians Conference at St. Michael's College.[28] Contemporary Protestantism had developed a character distinct in some ways even from its own tradition, explained Jesuit Gustave Weigel, later a council expert, prominent for his work in bringing about a greater understanding between Catholics and Protestants. The essential characteristic of modern Protestantism was the immediacy of the individual's personal experience with God, Weigel explained to seminarians from many parts of North America. He charged Catholics to master the medium or "language" of modern Protestantism and bear witness to the truths of their own faith. Other church unity events soon followed. Before year-end, Pocock in Winnipeg was lauding the desire for unity among religious colleges at the University of Manitoba.[29] A few months later, McGuigan in Toronto praised ecumenical dialogue and hoped "that the pattern set by these men of religion may be repeated by other men of goodwill in other walks of life, before our civilization destroys itself through perverse ignorance and want of charity."[30] As 1960 was ending, the Anglican primate of Canada, Howard H. Clark, said in an interview in *WEEKEND* magazine that "our aim should be the union not only of Protestants, but also with Orthodox (that is, the Eastern)

Christians, and even, far away and difficult as it seems, with the Roman Catholic Church."[31] To begin 1961, Latin and Greek Catholic parishioners in Saskatoon were among the 2,000 canvassers who went to 24,000 households in a city of 90,000 to ask questions about religious affiliations, preferences and practices of adults, the information to be made available to the different religious organizations in the city.[32] In Toronto, an inter-denominational workshop on religious broadcasting was held in June 1961, in co-operation with Toronto broadcasting stations and the Ryerson Institute of Technology. It paralleled a workshop in Moncton, New Brunswick, a few months earlier that marked the first time in Canada or the United States that a group of priests, nuns and ministers assembled to study radio and television productions.[33]

Six months before the council opened, meetings of Catholic and Protestant clergy were organized in the Bathurst diocese by the Legion of Mary.[34] About the same time, the only Canadian consultant on the Vatican's Secretariat of Christian Unity, Toronto theologian Gregory Baum, was preparing for a public lecture tour. Talks on "The Second Vatican Council: The Church's new outlook on the World" were scheduled for Saskatoon, Edmonton, Vancouver, Calgary, Regina and Winnipeg.[35] By then, Archbishop MacDonald had given Edmonton Catholics the signal to respond to any invitation from non-Catholics to discuss church unity. He said Catholics should bear in mind that their aim was to explore the points that separate Catholics and non-Catholics as well as those points each had in common. He said Catholics "should offer a welcoming hand and make it easy for anyone" to discuss these matters.[36] Also in Alberta, just before the Council opened, a display at Alberta summer fairs featured the ecumenical theme. The Edmonton Catholic Centre with the Legion of Mary sponsored a trailer display on "Christian Unity and the Ecumenical Council," presented through posters, charts, pictures and clippings.[37] This Alberta initiative paralleled a project at the Central Canada Exhibition in Ottawa. Members of the Legion of Mary staff said an increased number of requests were received in 1961 for literature about the council from people passing through the Catholic Information booth. There also was more interest in learning about the Catholic attitude towards Jews.[38]

Meanwhile, the secular media also took up the Christian unity theme. An editorial in the *Ottawa Citizen* for 1 January 1962 noted "the desire of Christians to come closer together ... is a theme that is more pronounced now than in a number of centuries.... As expressed by an English-speaking Catholic bishop in New Delhi recently, 'dialogue has replaced diatribe.' ...The archbishop of Canterbury visited Pope John during the past year. Organic mergers of Protestant faiths have taken place from North America to South India. The new mood can also be seen at the community level." In similar vein, an editorial in the *Toronto Telegram* noted that the year 1961 had "witnessed major steps in the search for the unity of all Christians.... Now when the hopes of multitudes centre around a co-operative internationalism instead of a continuance of chaos and anarchy, the classic Christian treatment of human relationships in the twelfth and thirteenth chapters of St. Paul's first letter to the Corinthians is receiving emphasis. He saw a basic fact of life – that all men are co-operating members of one another and that only one quality, love, can keep such members from catastrophe."[39] An editorial in the Toronto *Globe and Mail*, for its part, related the unity theme to the coming council. "The Ecumenical Council is not expected to produce church unity overnight, or even in the foreseeable future. It will achieve its purpose if it promotes a greater spirit of tolerance, greater respect for the sincerity of those holding different views and a greater awareness of the basic tenets on which the Christian religion was originally founded."[40]

Lay apostolate

Spiritual movements featuring large rallies, processions and organized public protests were still part of Catholic life in the late 1950s. In June 1959, a rally of 6,000 Holy Name Society members from all the parishes of the Kingston archdiocese was told that Catholic laymen "must be the instruments through which the reign of Christ will be brought about."[41] Similarly, there were 20,000 participants in a September Marian Day rally in Hamilton.[42] On May 1, 1960, in Windsor, while 35,000 spectators watched, 40,000 Catholics marched in Canada's only May Day parade – called Windsor's Mary's Day Parade.[43] Still later, a resolution deploring "the growing tendency of not observing the precepts of abstaining from servile work on Sunday" was adopted by the annual Ontario convention of the Daughters of Isabelle in Niagara Falls.[44]

However, even as such rallies continued, a different kind of social role for lay Catholics began to be emphasized. In September 1959 McGuigan stressed in his regular Saturday column in the *Toronto Telegram* that every worker co-creates with God and co-redeems with Christ, "and it is only by seeing work in this light that we shall realize that it is not an evil but a good."[45] Léger in Montreal similarly called on laity to go "where priests cannot go," saying that the sacraments of baptism and confirmation are like degrees of the priesthood of Jesus."[46] In Saskatoon later in 1960 Bernard De Margarie, a young chaplain for the Christian Family Movement (CFM), stressed that "by God's will, laymen are in charge of the temporal order," and it is their responsibility to reconstruct and harmonize the world so that "it may sing God's glory."[47] Students at St. Paul's College in Winnipeg heard a similar message. They were told by Hugh P. Kierans SJ, the college rector, that the task of the lay person in the world involves above all else engagement in the events of the world and a sense of personal responsibility for this engagement.[48] These insights – in Toronto, Montreal, Saskatoon, Winnipeg – read today as prophetic forerunners of teaching on the laity that would be contained in Vatican II texts still four or five years away in the future.

Consultations with laity

A special feature of Canadian preparation for Vatican II was an extensive program for consultations with the laity. Some bishops also asked diocesan priests in a formal way for their suggestions, but these exercises were not as novel as lay consultations and therefore attracted less attention.[49] Sessions with the laity involved Quebec Catholics in particular, but there were interesting events elsewhere. After Easter 1962 the small parish of Wisehart in the Regina archdiocese held its own "council" based on what was then known about the coming Vatican council. It was organized by the parish priest, Emil Kutarna, and parishioners to study needs in their parish.[50] A few months later, pastors in the diocese of Sault

Ste. Marie began asking laity for opinions and suggestions regarding the council, to be brought to the attention of Bishop Alexander Carter on 24 September when he met priests for a pastoral day.[51] And, later, there was the *Brief to the Bishops*, a collection of essays by lay women and men mainly in Toronto. Six of them presented a 48-page brief to Pocock just before he left Toronto for the opening of the council.[52] A much expanded collection of 34 essays on church topics related to Vatican II was sent to the bishops in September 1964, before the council's third session. These essays were published as a book in the spring of 1965.[53]

By far the most extensive pre-council consultations with lay church members took place in 12 Quebec dioceses. Writing in the Paris-based *Informations catholiques internationales*, journalist José de Broucker reported at the time that "this pre-council dialogue took on in Quebec an extent that was completely unknown elsewhere."[54] The first consultation was in Montreal in October 1961. Cardinal Léger presided. Panels of lay leaders discussed a variety of topics and reported their conclusions and wishes to the cardinal that day. This consultation was followed by others in Joliette diocese (Jette) early in January 1962; St. Jean (Coderre) at the end of January; Montreal again, for a different group, in March; Quebec (Roy) later in March; St. Anne de la Pocatière (Desrochers) in April; St. Jerome (Frenette) in May; Amos (Sanschagrin) in late May; Sherbrooke (Cabana) in June; Rimouski (Parent) in early July; Nicolet (Martin) in September; and in Ottawa (Lemieux), French and English sectors, late in September.[55]

The idea to organize these meetings came from L'Action catholique canadienne. Until then, bishops were asking the laity to pray for the success of the council. At the first such consultation in Montreal in October 1961, Léger noted that "the church is an hierarchical community of free persons in which dialogue is as much a duty as obedience." Claude Ryan replied that "it's as if the church is our business once again. We are required to speak and discuss. We are questioned. Our advice is sought. And all that eventually could come to bear on decision-making."[56] Lemieux said at the outset of the French-sector consultation in Ottawa: "It is precisely because I am aware of my mission as witness that I feel the need for closer contact with people of my diocese. As I am preparing to study today's major issues, I need more than ever to have information and suggestions from lay Christians. So I thought of consulting the laity, to ask them to give me their suggestions for the council."[57]

Numbers participating and the formats for each consultation varied, with about 250 representatives of parishes and organizations at each of the two Ottawa sessions. The bishops listened to a wide range of opinions. In Quebec City, Roy heard lay views on religious education of children, confessional schools, the parish and liturgy, Catholic action and the apostolate, Catholicism and contemporary ideologies, Catholicism and modern culture. Questions about family life, including birth control, were raised in some Quebec dioceses.[58] From the Ottawa English sector Lemieux also heard many wishes that were not directly related to the coming council but called for changes in the local church. Recommendations by the liturgy group included the establishment of parish liturgical committees and of a diocesan committee on sacred art and architecture. Parents should be given more responsibility for preparing children for the sacraments, and communion should be given under both species occasionally. A small majority favoured greater use of the vernacular in place of Latin. Another group recommended more information about parish and diocesan administration, and a greater lay voice in the church's temporal affairs. Another suggested more teaching about Catholic social doctrine in all educational institutions "since Catholics as a whole are not sufficiently aware of the critical movements of the day and so are not active enough in fields such as labour, co-operatives and politics." Also, there should be clearer understanding of the difference between fundamental and incidental obstacles to Christian unity. Other panelists recommended top-level diocesan programs in public relations, education in the use of the mass media, and development of church-sponsored broadcasts, each committee to include lay and clerical experts and artists.[59]

Bishops overly optimistic about openness

In the midst of these consultations, the Canadian bishops issued a 25 April 1962 joint statement about the coming council. It recalled that in a 5 June 1960 statement the pope attributed his decision to call the council to an inspiration of the Holy Spirit:"An inspiration, the sudden spontaneity of which struck us like a sudden and unexpected blow, in the humility of our soul… a thought which suddenly came to us like a full-blown flower of an unexpected springtime."The council's most pressing topics, the bishop added, again quoting John XXIII,"will be those which concern the spread of Christian standards of morality, the revival of Christian standards of discipline into closer accord with the needs and conditions of our times." They foresaw that "while clarifying and developing what is fundamental and unalterable in the church, the council will make opportune changes in certain other aspects. The eternal truths of revelation do not change and can never become antiquated, but their human expression and their concrete presentation must be adapted to the language and customs which change over the years." John XXIII echoed this point when he opened the council six months later. The bishops added that the church in itself is unchangeable and immutable in its basic constitution founded by Jesus Christ, but in certain details such as liturgical customs or methods of administration there may be elements now out of date which it would be better to change. They quoted John XXIII's 13 November 1960 address, that the church's "earthly pilgrimage across the centuries is yet far from the moment when she will attain her triumph in eternity. This is the very noble intention of the ecumenical council – to pause and to make an affectionate study of the aspects of her most ardent youth and to recompose them in such a way as to reveal her strength to the modern mind." They also reflected on how the council could be a step toward Christian unity. Regarding relations with the world, they said the church "needs to define the attitudes and the means by which she intends that Christian principles may be established among men in all aspects of their lives – familial, civic, economic, political and social." It would not be a question of defining a particular point of doctrine; rather, the whole approach to life would be considered.

To participate better in the council, the Canadian bishops added, Catholics "should strive to know more about it, by learning about the preparations and about accustomed council procedures."They quoted an October 1961 remark by Léger, that "this is the first time in the history of the world that it is possible for all Christian people to be fully informed almost instantaneously about the activities and concerns of the council. If the great media of communications rise to the high level of accomplishment of which they have proved themselves capable, it could happen that all the members of the church and indeed all men will feel that they are sharing, really and directly, in the council." In this regard, the Canadian bishops were overly optimistic. They wrote without taking into account how Vatican officials later would do their utmost to keep all council business secret. The bishops concluded "the best preparation for the council, as well as the simplest and at the same time the most difficult, consists in living from now on with deeper convictions in accordance with the demands of Christian principles," and added "prayer to the Holy Spirit will likewise be the first element of all serious preparations."

Vatican developments

While various pre-council events were making news across Canada, a vast enterprise was under way at the Vatican behind the veil of strictest secrecy. Immediately after John XXIII's initial announcement, Canada's news media showed lively general interest in the coming event, but there was little or no news about later work in Rome. Even from Canada's Catholic bishops there was only silence for months. One explanation is that the bishops were soon involved in work that they had to do under a solemn oath of secrecy. Almost four months following the pope's initial announcement, an "antepreparatory" (pre-planning) commission was set up at the Vatican. Significantly, the pope made this known on Pentecost, 17 May. Its members were 10 clerics from Vatican offices, headed by Cardinal Tardini who had been named earlier by John XXIII as his secretary of state. The Tardini commission had a three-phase task. It was to consult the world's bishops, Vatican offices and leading Catholic universities on subjects to be discussed at the council. It was then to review these suggestions and sketch an agenda for the council – a task that the pope concluded a year later with a 5 June 1960 statement. Thirdly, the Tardini commission was to suggest names for 10 preparatory commissions to draft texts for discussion.

This was uncharted work. No one involved had ever prepared a general church council.

The pope asked Tardini to prepare a communication to all the bishops of the world to invite them to send their suggestions for topics to be studied by the council. The first draft reflected the curial view that the new council should follow traditional lines, reinforcing existing teaching and perhaps declaring new doctrines and condemning errors. It would have asked the bishops to indicate their views on such matters. John XXIII rejected the text, and asked Tardini to prepare instead a simple letter to ask the bishops, and major Catholic academic institutions, for suggestions.

Consultation of bishops

Tardini's letter was dated 18 June 1959. It was nearly the middle of July before some of the Canadians received it. They were to respond by 1 September, so they had only six or seven weeks of summer holiday time for consulting and drafting their responses. Theologians and other professors at Catholic universities, colleges and seminaries were not readily at hand to help with ideas or drafting. Besides, the bishops already had some important domestic preoccupations. As we have seen, they were in the midst of efforts in their dioceses to apply the 1958 Vatican instruction on liturgical changes. They were preparing the CCC statement opposing servile work on Sundays. They were developing their plan for co-ordinating diocesan regulations for fast and abstinence across the country at the beginning of Lent 1960.

Tardini's letter to the bishops said John XXIII regarded their views as "highly important," and asked them to reply "with complete freedom and honesty." They could "make discreet use of the advice of expert and prudent churchmen." The letter also said "the subjects for the council can be points of doctrine, the discipline of the clergy and Christian people, the manifold activities of today's Church, matters of greater importance with which the Church must deal nowadays, or, finally, anything else that Your Excellency thinks it good to discuss and clarify." Researchers analyzing the replies from all the bishops have wondered how different they might have been if Tardini had made no suggestions in his letter.

Both by their high response rate – about 89 percent – and what they wrote, the Canadian bishops showed themselves to be interested in the council and concerned about the pastoral care of their people.[60] In all, 60 Canadian sets of suggestions from 62 bishops were received in Rome. (Four Catholic centres of learning – the Pontifical Institute of Mediaeval Studies in Toronto, and theology faculties in Laval, Montreal and Ottawa universities – also sent suggestions.) Archbishop Duke of Vancouver and Martin Johnson, his coadjutor (designated successor), sent a joint reply. So did Bishop Alexander Carter of Sault Ste. Marie and Auxiliary Bishop Jette of Joliette, who mailed their shared suggestions from Paris. Tardini told the bishops they could consult, but few indicated in their replies that they did so. Maurice Baudoux in St. Boniface consulted the most extensively, setting up a panel of 19 priest specialists and sending a questionnaire to parishioners – but he ignored the first deadline and submitted his report only in March the next year. Only a few Quebec bishops set up consultations, among them C.E. Parent in Rimouski, Maurice Roy in Quebec and M.-J. Lemieux in Ottawa. Georges Cabana of Sherbrooke wrote that he worked with Albertus Martin of Nicolet, but their texts had few common points. Joseph O'Sullivan of Kingston and Joseph Ryan of Hamilton listed the same concerns but used different words to express them, and did not refer to any collaboration. Five of the 16 points listed by John Cody of London coincided word for word with five of the 12 points submitted by William Smith of Pembroke – but Msgr. Michael Barry of Pembroke, Smith's secretary at the time and during the Council, insists that Cody and Smith did not collaborate in their replies.[61]

No replies were sent by St. Peter's Abbey in Muenster, Saskatchewan, and five dioceses: Amos (Joseph A. Desmarais); Antigonish (vacant); Chicoutimi (Georges Melançon); Joliette (J.A. Papineau); Kamloops (Michael A. Harrington); and Toronto (Cardinal McGuigan). Most conspicuous in this short list is McGuigan, Canada's senior cardinal at the time. His health was declining and a stroke in 1965 prevented him from attending the council's fourth session, but in 1959 he was still in charge of the archdiocese. Pocock, his designated successor, was not transferred from Winnipeg to Toronto until 1960. Retired bishop John A. O'Mara, who was McGuigan's priest secretary at the time and until his death in 1974, suggests a reason for McGuigan's silence:

> When Pope John XXIII called the council in January 1959 there were 50 Cardinals in the church. Cardinal McGuigan knew most of these especially those resident in Rome through the meetings of the congregations of which he was a member and especially the congregation for Bishops and that for the propagation of the faith. He perceived that most of the Curia Cardinals were surprised and concerned by the announcement since they saw no need for such a vast undertaking. In their opinion the First Vatican Council had given all the directions needed so that the Pope could rule the church. I believe that this influenced Cardinal McGuigan who participated fully in the preparations and the deliberations of the council but he did so in a reserved fashion. Moreover he carried strong memories of the power of the Roman curia because of the dismissal of Archbishop Charbonneau in 1950 and the transfer of Msgr. Montini to Milan in 1954. Both of these events I believe contributed to his hesitation in responding to the initial questionnaire concerning the council.[62]

There is no doubt about McGuigan's disagreement with curial officials over Charbonneau's forced resignation early in 1950. McGuigan had mounted a stout defence of Charbonneau when, in 1947, the Apostolic Delegate to Canada and Newfoundland, Ildabrando Antoniutti, asked McGuigan in a 2 July 1947 letter for his opinion about the debate in Quebec over "Neutrality, Confessionality and Non-confessionality." Antonuitti wrote that he particularly wanted McGuigan's advice "on the question in general and on whether or not it would be appropriate to issue some statement as to the line of conduct to be followed. I would furthermore be obliged to Your Eminence if you could add your judgment concerning the attitude adopted in this matter by His Excellency the Archbishop of Montreal."[63] McGuigan's long 31 July reply showed his deep understanding of the social changes then beginning in Quebec and the accompanying debate that was dividing Catholics there. He urged that the Vatican should say nothing more about the situation. He concluded pointedly:

"Therefore, I think before God that the Archbishop of Montreal should in no way be condemned by the Holy See even if some bishops, inspired perhaps unconsciously by a nationalistic spirit, disapprove of him; rather should he be guided and encouraged in the very great and momentous task which is his as the Archbishop of Montreal at this time when the French Canadian people are undergoing an evolution of thought in regard to their educational and social destiny."[64] Nevertheless, an array of church and civil opponents forced Charbonneau to resign early in 1950. By May that same year, McGuigan had written to Charbonneau at least three times and received two letters from him.[65] In a heart-rending handwritten note to McGuigan in August 1950, Charbonneau noted that, "From the very beginning, with a Christ-like charity, Your Eminence was the first among our many colleagues to attend to my bleeding heart and assuage the feel of my deadly solitude. This I will never forget…."[66] It would not be surprising, then, if McGuigan still had negative feelings about some Vatican officials when he received Tardini's letter in the summer of 1959, just a few months before Charbonneau's 19 November 1959 death in Victoria at age 67.

Most of the Canadian replies to Tardini were a page or two in Latin. French replies were sent by Léger, Coudert in Whitehorse, and Blais, then recently retired after more than 20 years as bishop of Prince Albert, Saskatchewan, and serving in Montreal as an auxiliary bishop when he wrote his reply. With only a few exceptions, Canadian bishops showed themselves to be open to change, seen as necessary pastoral updating. "One does not find (in the Canadian response), as one finds in that from the US or Latin America, observations on the corruption of contemporary society or dechristianization and the dangers of false philosophies, or efforts to condemn Marxism, materialism, relativism or hedonism. This line of thought simply isn't present."[67] For example, Pocock, then still in Winnipeg, wrote just three short paragraphs to ask that both central Catholic teachings and necessary disciplinary norms be restated in positive language that would appeal to today's people "without anathemas and condemnations," and that something be said that might increase appreciation and esteem for diocesan priests.

It should be no surprise that the lists from all regions of Canada were dominated by items about regulations concerning servile work on Sunday and related fast and abstinence rules, which were listed in at least 27 of the 60 Canadian replies. As we have seen, at the time the bishops were planning new cross-Canada Lenten regulations on these matters for 1960. The bishops, who were also implementing a 1958 Vatican directive on the liturgy at the time, identified liturgical questions as their second major area of concern. In general, they wanted changes to suit modern times, simplification of some rites to make their meanings clearer, and (with only few exceptions) greater use of the language of the people. Opponents to change from Latin included Cabana in Sherbrooke; Douville in Ste Hyacinthe; Pelletier in Trois-Rivières; LeBlanc in Bathurst, New Brunswick; Leverman in Saint John; O'Reilly in St. George's, Newfoundland; and Skinner in St. John's, Newfoundland. (McGuigan in Toronto shared this view, though he did not reply to Tardini.) Several wanted to cut the concluding prayers at the end of mass that Pope Leo XIII had ordered, and to simplify the formula used at the distribution of communion. Roy alone asked that when they met in large gatherings priests should be allowed to concelebrate mass, rather than each say an individual mass. Several bishops asked that priests be allowed to administer the sacrament of confirmation if an unconfirmed person, usually a child, were in danger of death. Years later in his study of the Canadian replies, Laval University theologian Gilles Routhier noted that Lemieux was almost the only one to refer explicitly to the liturgical movement then gaining strength in Canada. However, he added, "if this group of (Quebec) bishops was not profoundly nourished by the liturgical movement, it was at least favourable to the reforms undertaken by Pope Pius XII (Holy Week, breviary, evening masses, vernacular) and willing to pursue them."[68] Some bishops in every province suggested changes in the breviary prayer for priests. It had been compiled in the first place for use in monasteries by groups of monks following a common schedule each day. It no longer suited the varied and unpredictable schedules of busy priests in modern parishes. Bishops wanted it simplified, to emphasize morning and evening prayers without mandatory mid-day prayers.

Also, they argued, Canadian priests would benefit by being able pray in their own language, rather than in Latin.

Recomposing unity

The problems of recomposing Christian unity were dealt with by some as a matter of the return or conversion of Protestants to Catholicism. Others stressed the need to reaffirm articles of Catholic faith in language that Protestants could easily accept. Misunderstandings often arose from lack of knowledge, prejudices or false notions of Catholicism. The most extensive comments about Christian unity came from Blais, who had retired earlier in 1959 from Prince Albert, Saskatchewan, and was in Montreal by the time he wrote his 27 August 1959 reply, and from Coudert of Whitehorse. Blais noted that he was still bishop of Prince Albert when John XXIII announced the council. He had spent a total of 25 years in western Canada "where only 23 per cent of the population is Catholic" (only 17 per cent in his former diocese). He recalled "when John XXIII announced his intention to hold an ecumenical council at which the union of all believers with the Roman Catholic church would be treated, I could see that this invitation by His Holiness pleased the non-Catholics in Prince Albert diocese." Many of them, he said, "are well disposed to unity under the aegis of the Roman Catholic church. But writings and speeches by many Protestant ministers spread many objections, prejudices and errors." And, in these same circles, "many Catholics have not been taught well enough, or are not sufficiently apostolic, to explain what they believe and why they believe, to reply to objections and put an end to prejudices." These Catholics, with their schoolbook knowledge, needed "to learn their religion with the head of an adult." Therefore Blais proposed that "a massive campaign of religious instruction should be launched, organized with a view to preparing for joining with the church of Christ, and even to offset the opposition that Protestant ministers could organize." He proposed that "official communiqués" could be launched from the Vatican to the whole world by press and radio, "setting out the truths we believe: Communiqués clear, brief, positive...." Catholics and non-Catholics, he concluded, "are very interested in what concerns this ecumenical council, and very attentive. In these circumstances, official communiqués of the church on its fundamental teachings could attract more attention than ever."

Similarly, Coudert in Whitehorse recommended education programs especially for Latin-rite Catholics and Russian Orthodox faithful. His concerns reflected Catholic-Orthodox contacts in parts of the Yukon continuing from the time when Russian Orthodox missionaries were active in the area before Russia sold Alaska to the U.S. in 1867. Coudert urged education for Catholics, first of all, "to give them a better understanding of the position of dissident churches, especially the Orthodox churches (Greek, Russian, etc.), their doctrine, their rite, their fear of being Latinized, etc." He recommended parallel programs "organized with tact and discretion among members of the Orthodox churches to let them know the sincere desire of Roman Catholic faithful to see them return to unity of Christian faith, without for that reason imposing on them the Latin rite or particular devotions in use in the Latin church, such as public exposition of the Blessed Sacrament, recitation of the rosary as we have it, novenas that are popular in Latin countries, etc." He recommended that Orthodox leaders be invited to participate in Vatican II or its preparatory sessions, and that some eminent theologians should be sent to the World Council of Churches in Geneva to present the Catholic position and find out what they saw as obstacles to Christian unity. Coudert also wanted liturgical changes, including more use of vernacular languages, to encourage greater participation in the eucharist, though he thought the priest at mass should continue to use Latin "to keep the truly Catholic character of the offering of the holy sacrifice." He recommended that the clergy everywhere should be allowed to wear more modern clothing, such as black suits with Roman collars. Also, there should be more specific and severe norms for the clergy "to limit their *active* participation in worldly amusements, such as golf or *prolonged* hunting and fishing parties with laity." However, priests should have two or three weeks of vacation each year, with a possibility for missionaries to accumulate time, "but not over more than five years or for longer than three months," unless the bishop decided otherwise for special reasons.

Léger also raised a number of practical Christian unity issues in his French reply, the longest by far by any Canadian, taking up 19 pages in the official council record. His longest section dealt with "suggestions to help Protestants to understand the Catholic church better." For Léger, many Catholic-Protestant controversies were futile because each side argued from starting points the other side did not accept or perhaps misunderstood. "To establish an atmosphere of reconciliation among baptized Christians," he listed "the obstacles that prevent Protestants from accepting the Church" under two headings, doctrine and practice. Doctrinal difficulties started with questions of authority in the church, including the relationship of the papacy to the body of bishops, the nature of obedience, and questions of religious tolerance. Dogmatic definitions caused difficulties, and Léger urged "a prudent reserve" regarding new definitions concerning Mary. Differences also arose, he noted, because "after three centuries of separation, Catholics and Protestants today hardly speak the same language" to present the faith. He recommended courses in Catholic seminaries about Protestant theology and church life, and urged efforts "to express Catholic teaching in a non-scholastic language that would be better understood by Protestants."

Regarding misunderstandings about private revelations and popular devotions that arise from them, Léger proposed "a strong affirmation, spread abroad by a major publicity effort, on the fact that the divine revelation of faith necessary for salvation ended with the death of the last of the apostles, would do a lot to dissipate false ideas." Regarding church practices affecting Christian unity, Léger noted that "appeals expressed in general terms inviting people 'to submit' and 'return to the one true cradle' could often do more harm than good. In Catholic liturgy, non-Catholics often were more impressed by what was done than what was taught. Because of that, more dialogue masses and greater use of vernacular languages "would certainly increase Protestant understanding and love of the Catholic liturgy." He regretted the Catholic policy of granting dispensations for mixed marriages but not allowing them to be solemnized in churches. He also questioned "the policy of conditionally rebaptizing everyone without distinction" even in cases where there was a morally certain proof of valid baptism. He noted that some converted Lutheran pastors in Germany had been allowed to remain married after being ordained Catholic priests, and favoured extending such a policy to other countries. He also encouraged restoration of the permanent diaconate, including for married men. He urged that non-Catholic observers be invited to the council, that the Vatican should have an official corps of experts on ecumenical questions, and that provision should be made for good press coverage of the council, for "the eyes of all Christians will be fixed on Rome during all its sessions."

Léger also said that he wanted the breviary prayer said daily by priests to be "reduced and better balanced," with parts in the vernacular, so it would become "a better instrument for prayer." Referring to the proliferation of public clubs like the Kinsmen, Kiwanis and Lions, he asked: "What attitude should we take when these clubs fund Catholic projects and invite Catholics to discuss questions that belong to our church?" He proposed that there should be uniform fast and abstinence rules throughout the world, presented as exhortations and not prescriptions. Abstinence should be only on Fridays, fasting only on Ash Wednesday and the Fridays of Lent

Léger's second major concern was about the section of church law that dealt with relations between a local bishop and members of religious orders in his diocese. He urged that the law should set down as a first principle that "religious are subject to the bishop." He complained that members of religious orders often stressed a second part of the law, which described situations in which they were "exempt" from the local bishop's authority and subject to their own religious superior. He reported that travel agencies were building up a business in pilgrimages to various famous European shrines, without taking enough care to make them truly religious experiences. It was not enough just to include a priest in the group. Léger wanted such pilgrimages "to be organized by the local bishops or with their approval." And, in a more radical proposal that revealed one of his quarrels with religious orders, he recommended "that religious not be allowed to go to Europe without the permission of the (Vatican's) Sacred Congregation for Religious."

Eastern-Latin tensions

The replies from western provinces showed the continuing influence of an earlier major expansion of the church in Canada. At the end of the nineteenth century, it had to adjust to the arrival of the first large wave of Catholic immigrants who spoke neither French nor English. The migration of a large number of Ukrainians from the Austro-Hungarian Empire posed a particular challenge. Many Italian Catholics were arriving at the same time. They too required services in a third language, but at least they belonged to the familiar Latin rite. In contrast, many of the Ukrainians were eastern-rite Catholics, descendants of people who in 1595 broke from Orthodox ranks and agreed to recognize the primacy of the pope. They had their own liturgy using Old Slavonic instead of Latin, and favoured different devotional and liturgical practices and even different architecture in their churches. Most troublesome to Latin-rite bishops in the US and Canada was the fact that many Ukrainian priests were married. US bishops led the pressure on the Vatican for decrees, in 1894 and 1897, which banned the ordination of married men in North America and made celibate eastern-rite priests subject to Latin-rite bishops. The Ukrainians rightly resented such efforts to "latinize" them. The Austro-Hungarian government appealed to Rome on their behalf. The Russian government, in turn, made funds available to Orthodox communities in Canada for efforts to win over Ukrainian Catholics.

A number of Canadian priests, especially the Oblates, made special efforts to help them by taking steps to become bi-ritual, allowed to lead services in either the Latin or eastern rite. Provision of adequate services for Ukrainian Catholics became better organized with the naming of Ukrainian Catholic Bishop Budka to Winnipeg in 1912, with the same status as his Latin-rite colleagues. By the time John XXIII announced the council, Winnipeg was a Ukrainian metropolitan see, equivalent of an archdiocese, and there were three Ukrainian dioceses (eparchies) centred in Edmonton, Saskatoon and Toronto.[69]

The replies that went to Rome in the summer of 1959 from both Latin-rite and Ukrainian bishops in western provinces reveal the pastoral tensions they still experienced. At one level there was harmony. I remember as a youngster in Saskatchewan being taken to a eucharist celebrated by a visiting eastern-rite priest at the farm of Ukrainian neighbours. As often happened, there was no service that Sunday in our regular Latin-rite parish, and my parents somehow knew that the unfamiliar Ukrainian home liturgy was equally valid for us and "satisfied our Sunday obligation." Still, this sense of community with the other rite was a rare experience. More typical was the difficulty faced by young lovers, one Latin-rite and the other eastern, when they decided to marry as Catholics. From the point of view of church law, inter-rite marriages were only a little less complicated than Catholic-Protestant "mixed" marriages. Priests of both rites disliked the paper work involved. Eastern priests often had an additional complaint when they knew their young parishioners were being pressed to join the Latin majority by changing rites – another complicated legal process. The extent to which these matters spilled over onto the desks of bishops is evident from the replies they sent to Cardinal Tardini.

Among Quebec bishops, only Martin (Nicolet) mentioned the eastern rites. He asked that the council affirm them clearly and without equivocation, so that the Orthodox could envisage a return to the Roman church without fear of their rites being "latinized."

However, 12 of the 16 replies from bishops in the three western provinces expressed the hope that the council would sort out canonical problems between Latin-rite and eastern Catholics, especially over baptism, marriage and change of rite. Latin bishops wanted it made simpler for an eastern-rite Catholic to transfer to Latin. With even greater insistence, Ukrainian bishops ardently opposed any such easy "latinizing." Ukrainian Bishop Roborecki of Saskatoon hoped that the council would help preserve the eastern liturgy and win esteem for it. Latin priests should be educated about the eastern rite and should respect it. He also reiterated the wish of Ukrainian Catholics that their church would be formally named a patriarchate.

Ukrainian Bishop Borecky in Toronto sent Tardini one of the most eloquent and closely argued of all Canadian replies. It would be most desirable, he urged, that Catholic teaching about the church, interrupted at Vatican I, "should at last be completed and defined." In doing so, expressions and terms about the church, often used in different senses – such as its "soul" or its "body" – should be clarified, along with "that most famous adage, 'No salvation outside the church'." He emphasized that "the ancient name" for the church of Christ is the Catholic church, without added words like "Roman" or "western" or "Latin." He argued "it is extremely useful, especially for future union of dissident churches, that the equality of rites in the Catholic church should be solemnly proclaimed and emphasized" in the council. He lamented that "in practice the preeminence of the Latin rite over other rites is frequently urged and applied." Members of eastern rites "are granted permission to transfer to the Latin rite for whatever reason, even the most superficial. This unfortunate practice constitutes a grave scandal to members of the eastern church, especially for those as yet not united to the Holy See, and causes them to recoil from union with the Catholic church." In missionary lands, he added, what is the reason for new Christians "being necessarily obliged to receive the Catholic faith according to the Latin and western form of worship?" It would seem more rational and useful for such people "to celebrate the liturgy in their own language, indeed to create some form of rite which would be more adequate and familiar" for them. New rites would be no risk for church unity. Unity in faith, governance and communion is needed, he argued, but "unity in liturgy, ritual and discipline is neither essential nor always fitting and desirable for the unity of the Catholic church." Regarding church union, he added, "not only Catholics but also dissidents of Orthodox churches whole-heartedly long for the reunion of the churches.... However, the Orthodox are exceedingly scandalized when future reunion ... is considered by Catholics as being 'the conversion of schismatic Orientals'. And rightly so, since Orthodox Christians are in no way pagans needing to be 'converted' to the church of Christ. Our discourse should be about union or reunion of churches rather than about the conversion of schismatics."

In general, he said, "the Orthodox are ready to recognize the primacy of jurisdiction of the Roman Pontiff in the whole church, but not according to the extension that it enjoys today in the west, but rather according to the norm, concept and praxis in the east at the time of the seven ecumenical councils." He concluded with general remarks about adapting church discipline to modern times.

Officials in Vatican offices should include members of eastern churches who know their situations. Care should be taken to avoid "a false uniformity, protectionism, even nepotism" in deciding issues concerning eastern rites. "The present time requires that in church legislation and discipline respect be shown to the conditions, ethos, character and circumstances of various peoples or, rather, of various ethnic churches. It is not necessary for Catholic church unity that the same discipline should obtain for the clergy and people in different parts of the world. ... The good of the Catholic church and its progress are not always helped by excessive centralization or by juridical authority being reserved to the Roman curia."

Birth control discussion absent

Conspicuously absent from the Canadian replies was the matter of birth control. Paul VI later would remove this question from the council agenda and assign it to a special commission, leading in 1968 to *Humanae Vitae*, his most controversial encyclical. However, when the bishops were writing their replies in the summer of 1959, the contraceptive pill and planned parenthood were front-page news. It is striking, therefore, that only Baudoux asked that regarding population growth and birth control the church should "clarify and express a clear firm mind ... according to the present situation of medical, social and economic science." The aim of such clarification, he added, should be "to demonstrate that the church has constantly had a teaching in keeping with the natural law, and to protect the rights that flow from that law, for the common good of human beings both on earth and supernaturally." Martin in Nicolet who referred in a general way to "artificial fecondation" was the only other bishop to broach such questions. Yet, since 1955, Montreal-area Catholic couples had been developing their Service de régulation des Naissances (SERENA), widely publicized by Hélène Pelletier-Baillargeon's 1959 book about the movement. The bishops therefore ignored both a widespread question and a creative solution to it being developed by couples in their midst. On social questions in a more general sense, the only direct reference to social doctrine of the church was by Martin and Langlois. Martin raised the question of communism, socialism and capitalism. He mentioned psychoanalysis, atomic weapons, sterilization, war and its impact on civilians. He also raised the question of a theology of work, of earthly realities and history, as well as the relation of psychology to spirituality. Roy mentioned the question of the dignity of the human person, and the need to attain temporal well being, justice and true freedom, and the need to deal with theories of evolution. Coderre raised the question of hunger and under-nourishment.

Little Vatican impact

In general, Canadian suggestions were not retained by the Vatican commissions that drafted texts for council study. For example, a number of Canadians suggested the vernacular should replace Latin in parts of the mass and in the breviary. Such ideas had no place in the first drafts, but they came to the fore when the council began to discuss the liturgy as its first topic. In this way, many Canadian bishops eventually heard some of their ideas raised by others, or they took the microphone to present their own suggestions to the assembly. This happened in particular to the ideas developed before the council by Léger, and by Baudoux and his team of 19 priests. Two of these were named as bishops during the council – Remi De Roo (1962) and Antoine Hacault (1964) – and joined Baudoux in teamwork in Rome.

Baudoux introduced his 1960 suggestions to John XXIII with a crucial general principle: That the primary purpose of all council undertakings should be "concern for that essential unity that is beyond the contingencies of times and places, following the example of the multiform unity manifested in God and in Creation." Regarding doctrine, he wanted the council to stress that the church is a living body in which humans can progress in both supernatural and natural endeavours. This would counter the view that being a Christian limits personal growth in sciences, arts and social evolution, or that religion has meaning only in certain actions and not the whole of life. Similarly, he made a general suggestion regarding the reform of church discipline. The council should aim at "laws which will make the apostolate more effective and efficacious among both Catholics and non-Catholics." On the broad question of unity, Baudoux wanted the council to "clarify the degree of incorporation into Christ of all human beings." Regarding "separated Christians," he suggested that the council "a) promote those matters on which they agree with the church; b) reiterate and clarify the respect the church has for Christian people and their manifestations of church life; c) explain the church's understanding of the practical questions involved in the return of these communities; d) show more clearly the will of the church to do everything to expedite their return to the flock of Peter."

Preparatory Commissions

After the bishops had sent their suggestions to Rome, the next major news from the Vatican came nearly a year later. On 5 June 1960, Pentecost once again, the pope announced the formation of ten preparatory commissions and three secretariats, to which 15 Canadian bishops and 11 priests would be named. On the central preparatory committee (CPC) were McGuigan of Toronto, Léger of Montreal and Gaspé's Archbishop Paul Bernier, who was Canadian Catholic Conference (CCC) chairman when named. Members of the theology commission included Roy of Quebec and Maxim Hermaniuk of Winnipeg, metropolitan for Ukrainian Catholics in Canada, and Auxiliary Bishop Lionel Audet of Quebec. Canadian priests named to the same commission were Marcel Bélanger, vice-rector of Ottawa University, as consultant, and Léo Laberge, an Oblate working in Rome, as a member of the commission's secretariat. Bishop Pelletier of Trois-Rivières was named a member of the commission for bishops and dioceses, and Lemieux of Ottawa a consultant. Members of the commission for religious were Archbishop George Flahiff of Winnipeg and Father Gommar Van Den Broeck of St. Bernard de Lacolle, Quebec. Two Canadian Oblates in Rome were also named: André Guay as consultant and Joseph Rousseau as secretary. Archbishop Pocock of Toronto and Bishop Douville of St. Hyacinthe were consultants for the commission for clergy and people. Auxiliary Bishop Bélanger of Montreal was a consultant for the commission on sacraments, along with Franciscan G.M. Brisbois, a Canadian teaching in Rome. Retired missionary Archbishop L.J. Cabana was named consultant for the missions commission. Bishop Alexander Carter of Sault Ste. Marie and Msgr. G.E. Bourgeois of Trois-Rivières were consultants for the lay apostolate commission. Theologian Gregory Baum of Toronto served as consultant for the secretariat for promoting Christian unity. Bishop Frenette of St. Jerome and Father J.M. Poitevin PME were consultants for the secretariat for media questions. Only two preparatory commissions – for seminaries and for eastern churches – had no Canadian members.

"Conceived in the sin of clericalism"

The participation of Canadians in the work of the preparatory commissions from the second half of 1960 until early 1962 has not been fully documented. McGuigan's health declined during the 1960s, and Pocock assumed responsibility for the archdiocese of Toronto in March 1961. Still, McGuigan attended three or four of the seven meetings of the central preparatory committee. Any comments he made on the schemas were given orally at these meetings and were not recorded.[70] For Hermaniuk, a member of the theology commission, one highlight, as noted in his personal journal, occurred at a meeting on 6 March 1962. That day he proposed for the first time that a new "apostolic college" should be set up to allow bishops to share leadership responsibilities with the pope. He reintroduced that idea during the council. Bishop Alexander Carter was a member of the preparatory commission for the lay apostolate. There is no record of his reactions at the time, but he later told the council that the commission's text "was conceived in sin – the sin of clericalism." During the pre-council work, he explained, the president and many members of the preparatory commission "… were conscious of the fact that it was absurd that the commission on the apostolate of the laity should be composed solely of clerics… but nothing was done about this. Then, when several men and women were invited to make a contribution after March 1963, the great part of the commission's work was already done. They were introduced too late and their contribution remained minimal – a case of 'too little and too late,' as we say in English."

One of John XXIII's most innovative acts during the preparation period was creation in 1960 of the secretariat for promoting Christian unity, led by Cardinal Bea, a renowned scripture scholar. The pope assigned it equal rank with the congregations of the Vatican curia, but Bea faced a daily struggle to maintain that place among other offices with much longer experience in moving ideas through the Vatican bureaucracy. Toronto theologian Gregory Baum, a specialist in ecumenism, was chosen as a consultant of Bea's secretariat soon after it was established. Because strict secrecy was imposed on all such work at the Vatican, a long report Baum wrote to Pocock in Toronto in November 1961 is a rare document. It gives a luminous behind-the-scenes insight into pre-council work.

> I wish to inform you of the work we are undertaking, under the presidency of Cardinal Bea, in the Roman Secretariat of Christian Unity. Since you are a member of a preparatory commission, I am free to speak to you about our projects. The Catholic press has been wondering about the range of our responsibility, but since we are bound by a secret, we cannot explain our work in full. At the same time, it is the wish of Cardinal Bea that we write and speak as much as possible in order to create a public opinion which is favourable to Christian unity and to stir up Catholics to pray more ardently for the healing of our tragic divisions.
>
> The first purpose of the council, as you well know, is the renewal of Catholic life and practice. Unity is only a secondary aim. It is precisely this inner renewal initiated by the council which, in the eyes of the Pope, is the great contribution of the church to Christian unity. The role of the secretariat in this is to study various areas of ecclesiastical life and to make propositions to the council regarding changes and adaptations which will be of benefit to Christian unity. This is not the only view point in determining changes in ecclesiastical life, but it is the one which we are to study and defend.
>
> Our Secretariat has formed several subcommissions, each comprising one or two bishops and several theologians, which are to prepare reports on such subjects as *De Membris, De Hierarchia, De Laicis, De Liturgia, De Verbo Dei, De Libertate Religiosa et Cooperatione cum Acatholicis, De Judaeis* [church members,

hierarchy, laity, liturgy, word of God, religious liberty and cooperation with non-Catholics, and the Jews] and some others. In each report we present Catholic doctrine (or suggest Catholic practices) with a view to removing some of the obstacles in the way of unity and to make the church appear more truly catholic.

How does the Secretariat understand the ecumenical movement in the church? We define ecumenism as an activity within the church bringing to light her latent universality especially in regard to dissident Christians and their authentic traditions. As the missions make the church more truly universal in regard to other cultures and peoples, so will ecumenism make the church more truly ecumenical in regard to the various ways of worship, schools of theology, ascetical practices, spiritualities, etc., which are compatible with Catholic Christianity. Thus perfecting the church's catholicity (or ecumenicity), the ecumenical movement makes her a more luminous *motivum credibilitatis* [credible witness] of the Gospel and renders her more faithful to her vocation as mother of the nations.

In the report *De Membris* we examine the relation of separated Christians to the Catholic church. We insist above all on their real and supernatural *ordo ad Ecclesiam* [status as church] which demands that we regard them as Christians, as men truly reborn in Christ, even if they have not reached the fullness of sacramental and ecclesiastical life to which they are destined. In my study on papal doctrine, called *That They May Be One,* I have shown that this theology has already found expression in Roman documents. However a clear statement that men who believe in Jesus Christ as Lord and God and have received the baptism of the New Testament are, in the eyes of the church, Christians would be of importance – for dissidents as well as Catholics. We append to our report a number of practical suggestions: to be more consistent in official ecclesiastical language regarding dissidents, to acknowledge their positive patrimonies, to widen the interpretation of the law forbidding *communicatio in sacris* [worship together] and to respect more than is customary in many countries their baptisms. (There are regions in the Church where even Orthodox Christians entering the Church are conditionally rebaptized!)

The report *De Hierarchia* is a long theological document in which the christological aspects of the church's structure – her unity, her visible head, her hierarchy – is (sic) duly emphasized. We are often accused by Protestants that we have only defined jurisdictional power and hierarchical office *canonically*, but that we have no *theology* of these ministries. The report also stresses the apostolic power of the bishops in their own dioceses, and their function acting *in solido* [together], in order to set the primacy of the pope in its proper ecclesiological context. We show forth that the church universal is truly a family of apostolic churches under a supreme visible head, leaving room for great diversity in administration and custom in its various branches. This is the longest report, about 50 pages, erudite, highly theological, replete with practical suggestions. This work has been done under the chairmanship of Archbishop Jaeger of Paderborn (Germany).

De Laicis is a smaller document. Seeing that Protestant Christians accuse us of being a divided church, divided into hierarchy and people, we must set forth our doctrine, and regulate our ecclesiastical life, in such a way that the unity existing in the church of Christ, the presence of the Spirit in each member, and the truly ecclesiastical responsibility of each Christian be more clearly manifested. The report is a master-piece. The episcopal chairman of the subcommission was Bishop de Smedt of Bruges (Belgium). The bishop has published the report, in a simplified form minus the practical suggestions, as a pastoral letter called *Le Sacerdoce des Fidèles* [Priesthood of the Faithful], the English translation of which will soon appear in print.

The report *De Liturgia* was prepared under the chairmanship of Bishop Martin of Tours (France). It treats a variety of areas of our liturgical life where shortcomings have been widely criticized by conscientious Protestants and where obstacles to unity could easily be removed to the benefit of the whole church. We touch upon the role of the scriptures in the liturgy of the mass, and we advocate rotating cycles of epistles and gospels throughout the year so that the people get to know a larger part of scripture. We emphasize the proper role of the sermon, the suitability of allowing communion in two kinds on certain occasions, the vernacular in the texts which are proclaimed to the congregation, a shortening of texts in the hope of initiating a new ecclesiastical practice of reading them slowly, a better proportion between eucharistic liturgy and peripheral devotions, a christological emphasis in our veneration of the Blessed Virgin and the saints, etc.

De Verbo Dei is a beautiful document setting down the theology of the Word of God in the church, (such a theology has been neglected by us since the days of the Reformation); the Word of God as a way of grace and divine action in the church, redeeming and judging, comforting and condemning; the Word of God as it is present to us in the Scriptures, the liturgy and the sermons of bishop and priest. We show that a true celebration of the Word does not place the sacraments in the shadow, but on the contrary throws more light on them. Though the Word is primary, Word and sacrament belong inseparably together. If we understand the Word of God as divine-revelation-working-our-redemption, then the church must be said to be under the Word of God. Protestants say that the church pretends to be above the Word. This is wrong. The church does not judge God's Word, though she does judge human interpretations of that Word.

The report *De Libertate Religiosa* deals with the civic toleration of all religions, in agreement with the views of the great majority of modern Catholic theologians, against the theory which was quasi-traditional for a long time. We propose that the council make a definite statement in regard to religious liberty. The world expects this from us; and if nothing else happened in the whole council, the contribution to Christian unity and to the world's better understanding of the true nature of the church would be great indeed. We also summarize Pius XII's doctrine of Catholic cooperation with non-Catholics in the domain of civic society (which is not yet appreciated in all parts of the church) and discuss an area more properly religious and supernatural where cooperation is at times, under certain circumstances, permitted and even required.

In a report *De Judaeis* we set down theologically the church's relationship to the Old Covenant, her link to the Jewish people now, and the faith of St. Paul (which is the Catholic faith) that all of Israel shall be saved at the end. Conscious of the errors in much of Christian preaching in former centuries and the imprecisions which made their way into our catechisms, we make suggestions of how our liturgical and doctrinal texts be made more faithful to the true teaching of the Church.

There are a few other reports. We are preparing a longer document on Catholic ecumenism, its aims, methods, principles, etc., which may either be published before the council or handed to the bishops at the council. The only ecclesiastical document of ecumenism, *Ecclesia Catholica* of 1949, though incomplete and rather negative in tone, indicates that we are at the beginning of a new development.

Whether these reports will actually influence the council is another question. The procedure is here by no means clear. The documents will have to be submitted to the central commission, where Cardinal Bea is our able advocate; but even if they are accepted for discussion, it is by no means clear how our material will be integrated into the documents of other commissions which often deal with the same subject from another point of view. We believe however that even if the reports should not be discussed, they will appear in the *Acta Concilii* [official council record] and may be the starting point of developments in the church after the council.

May I close this report by remarking that the Catholic press in Europe has been rather pessimistic in regard to the council for the last few months (fall of 1961). The Roman Synod was a great disappointment to all, since it neither gave freedom of speech to the men who took part in it (everything was prearranged) nor did it tackle the problems which appear essential to clergy and people. A few other pronouncements coming from the Vatican, not from the Holy Father, have restrained the enthusiasm of the responsible Catholic press in Europe. I understand that many bishops are now in favour of postponing the council for a considerable time, since they feel that the new movements in the church, liturgical, biblical, catechetical and ecumenical, etc., have not yet touched a large part of the Catholic world.

If you give me permission, I would like to send you significant documents from time to time, (such as the pastoral letter of Monsignor de Smedt on the laity). It would help me if I knew whether reading French is a burden to you.[71]

Montreal study and petition

By far the most detailed and critical Canadian study of the preparatory work for Vatican II was done under Léger's leadership. It culminated in an urgent 1962 petition to the pope. As a member of the central preparatory commission, along with McGuigan and Bernier, Léger was well placed to follow the preparations for the council. The period from 1960 to the summer of 1962 was for him what the first session of Vatican II would be for many other bishops: a time of stocktaking and of intellectual and spiritual change. He was moved by the discussions and exchanges with other cardinals, and many meetings with John XXIII.

In the spring of 1962, Léger launched a team in Montreal to study the texts discussed in the central commission and intended to be submitted to the council a few months later. His closest collaborator was Fr. Pierre Lafortune, vicar general of the archdiocese, who accompanied Léger as *peritus* (expert) from the beginning of the preparatory period in 1960 until the end of the council in 1965. Working closely with Lafortune was André Naud, a Sulpician who had been teaching philosophy in Japan, returned to Montreal in 1962, and was in Rome with Léger as theological expert for the last three council sessions. Also involved in the Montreal team were theology professors at the University of Montreal and some diocesan priests, along with Phillipe Delhaye, a Belgian theologian invited to Montreal. This team worked on the preparatory documents during the spring and summer of 1962. Their critical study, in which Léger shared, amounts to more than 100 pages of comments in the Montreal archdiocesan archives. This work remained unknown until 1994 when a detailed analysis of it by Gilles Routhier, theology professor at Laval University, was published.[72]

By August 1962, one thing was clear to the Montreal group: the draft texts did not reflect John XXIII's vision and did not meet the high expectations that people had for the council. The team's overall judgment was that "without profound changes, these schemas will not only do no good for the church. They will do it harm, and do nothing for its prestige. They give no help in the work of rejuvenating the church and in the updating that is as necessary in theological thought as in other areas." There was a risk of profound disappointment. The texts did not agree with the orientation John XXIII had proposed for the council from the moment he announced it. In the text on the deposit of faith, the main preoccupation seemed to be "to defend the revealed deposit against errors that threaten it." While a defence of the faith is sometimes needed, "such a preoccupation with checking errors cannot be the basic outlook." It did not allow for a fruitful meeting between the church and today's people, and it "contributed to giving the world an overview of the Christian message that is not authentic."

The main concerns of Léger's team were to have the council address the contemporary world in language today's people would understand, and to assure that the council would help the church announce to the world the real message of the Gospel. They observed that, by giving free rein to the hunt for errors, the drafters "have given us, especially in the schema on the moral order, a description of the Christian message that is scarcely recognizable and would have no attraction for non-Christians." There is "an error in perspective" that misrepresents the Gospel, not only regarding "how to do things," but also in the preoccupations taken up, especially by neglecting the Gospel's main and dominant teaching: the theme of love. Hence, they formed the severe judgment that "these schemas present the Gospel in a false way," not in the sense that they teach something contrary to the Gospel, but in the sense that in them one finds neither the style nor the spirit of the Gospel, nor its essential message: charity. Indeed, "for someone reading the Gospel, this is not how the Christian moral order looks. The main preoccupations of the Gospel are not those of the schemas." Hence the conclusion that "the schema on the Christian moral order seems not only incomplete but in a certain sense false."

The hunt for errors and many condemnations in the text compromised any attempt to dialogue with the world. It ended up portraying the church's attitude as one of rejection, fear, warning, and condemnation. Left mostly in the dark was the fact that the church, through the council, wanted to have an attitude of sympathy, openness, and participation in a large and loyal research effort. Such sympathy was not to be found in the proposed texts. On the contrary, suspicion reigned. "Scornful language" is used for those who do not adhere to church teaching. "Bad intentions are attributed" to them, and their thought is "deformed or over-simplified." No effort is made to "get inside" how others think. They are "judged from above."

Positively, Léger's analysis proposed another "way of doing it" that would lead to "a totally other way of presenting the thought of the Church." It would aim at (1) meeting the worries, cares and aspirations of today's people in a way that would build on their preoccupations; (2) base itself on the contributions of contemporary thought; and (3) respect the ideas of others, doing justice to what is true in them, and moving forward from this truth. "Rather than condemning everything globally or hardening the church's position – sometimes even distorting it – thought should be given to the concerns of today's people, with eagerness to discern the real values in what they think, values that, sometimes, perhaps, are authentically Christian values that too many of us have forgotten." The Montreal study suggested that the church did not have all the truth, that it could be enriched by contemporary thought which has "real values," perhaps authentic but forgotten Christian values that were set aside or obscured, and "real richness," even if hidden under error. Twice the study stressed that there were "acquisitions" in contemporary thought. It spoke, too, of "authentic enrichment." The church should even profit from "the progress in philosophical and theological reflection" and not turn its back on these contributions. The sense of modesty that should mark the teaching of the church was stressed. It must not only enrich itself by contacts with others, but also remain aware "of the precise limits within which the church has competence to speak." Therefore nothing should lead, *a priori*, to a collision between the thought of the church and of today's people. An attitude other than condemnation must be adopted. When the church does not dialogue with people of our time, they are cast out, often with misunderstanding, and none of their preoccupations finds a place in the church. Nothing of what they have to bring is really taken up. That widens the gap between the church and contemporary people because, over all, repeated recourse to condemnations "gives an inaccurate image of the church's attitude toward what people today are asking for."

An urgent appeal to John XXIII

In the light of this study, Léger decided the situation was urgent and the stakes high: "Something extraordinary must be done." He decided to write to the pope about his concerns. His appeal to John XXIII is a 12-page letter that spelled out Léger's understanding of the kind of council the pope wanted, and outlined the mainly unsatisfactory nature of the proposed texts. Drafted in Montreal at the beginning of August, the letter was send to Cardinal Frings of Cologne for initial approval. He cosigned it and sent it to Doepfner, Koenig, Alfrink and Suenens. Later, Liénart would sign it. Montini also was asked to sign. The letter was sent to John XXIII on 11 September, the day of the pope's major radio address. Montini informed Léger on 19 September that he thought the letter "untimely" after the pope's address, which took up ideas from Suenens' plan for studying the church *ad intra* and *ad extra*. (Suenens, seconded by Montini, introduced this plan at the end of the first session, and it gradually emerged as the guiding principle for council documents.)

Léger began his letter by developing the theme that the church needs renewal. He explored three reasons for this: The church is a human society, it is a group of sinners, and it must be missionary. Since the first days of the church, human life had changed astonishingly, and the speed of change seemed to be increasing. Christ set down no specific forms for his message, and did not prescribe the institutions and structures that the church developed in its long history. The holy church is also a society of sinners, marked by the sins of individuals, false tendencies that can enter the lives of Christian communities, administrative errors, and acts of infidelity to the gospel, so that in the church weeds are always growing along with good grain. But, above all, the commandment to "go teach all nations" both invites and obliges the church to renew itself constantly.

Léger outlined two norms for renewal in the church: fidelity to Christ, and concern for humanity. This "double fidelity," he argued, pointed to some particular orientations for the council. In Christ's message and in church teaching it was highly important to distinguish the absolute from the relative, and universal and timeless values from what is said or done only by people of a particular time or place. Secondly, concern about preserving the original purity of Christ's message should be accompanied by total openness to all authentic human values. He quoted St. Ambrose's assertion that "all truth, no matter who expresses it, comes from the Holy Spirit." Léger then made an indirect but unmistakable reference to the Catholic theologians, exegetes and others who were being criticized and restricted by some Vatican officials at that time. "This attitude of welcome for true values found outside the church," he said, "will also extend to truths that arise even inside the church and are expressed in various schools of theology or spirituality, in different and valid ways of worshipping God, or in some other form. It is this state of mind that will lead to legitimate changes or adaptations that reflect the diversity of times and peoples. Naturally, it also will assure an attitude of respect for all, even those in error or who have only a partial grasp of a truth."[73] Regarding the council as a time of church renewal, Léger said he had both hopes and worries. By showing great charity and better understanding, John XXIII had created a climate favourable to dialogue among Catholics and changed relationships with other Christians. This spirit, Léger said, was reflected in the draft texts on liturgy, the lay apostolate, religious liberty and relations between bishops and Vatican offices. "However, many schemas that deal with matters of extreme importance for the church today are not sufficiently inspired by a spirit of renewal. ... Some look upon the church too much as a besieged institution that the council must defend, and do not see clearly enough its radiating deposit of salvation to be shared. The church is made to look like a body that is more juridical than missionary. The texts have not dared to turn frankly towards the real world, with its needs and its new and legitimate demands.

Instead, the thought seems to be that it is enough to repeat, more insistently, without any deepening of teaching, the old formulas that the world no longer knows how to hear. There seems to be a belief that loss of faith, weakening of morals and setbacks for the apostolate have no other causes than people's lack of attention or the malice of the age, without asking if some things are not equally caused by the obsolescence of some forms of the church's thought or action."

The letter went on to note that, while "an astonishing and admirable" amount of work had been done in a very short time, Léger was worried about the council. The theological texts, with a few exceptions, showed "a disturbing lack of vigorous theological thought and awareness of the world's problems." The church's teaching was "proposed too exclusively as a deposit to be conserved and too little as a truth to be propagated." The text on "the teaching church" proposed security and conservation rather than announcing the Gospel as the first responsibility of teaching. The text on the media was "typical of that moralism that serves the church so poorly and too easily avoids direct knowledge of the realities that it wishes to Christianize." Léger summed up the aim of his letter by saying that the council should study only texts that "represent real gains for the church and treat the problems of today's people in terms that suit our times." He urged John XXIII to stress once again the need for the council to undertake a work of renewal "in which the church will once again find the purest marks of its youth."

There is no record of a written or oral response from the pope to Léger; they met many times in the following weeks. John XXIII's radio address on 11 September and his opening address to the council a month later reflect what the letter urged, but it cannot be argued that this was in response to Léger's letter. At the very least, Léger's letter signed by the six European cardinals assured the pope that he had their support for the direction he set for the council's work. Besides these more general considerations, however, the work done in Montreal during the summer of 1962 is important for three main reasons. It demonstrates the kind of effort that some Canadians put into study of the early draft texts for Vatican II. Similar work was being done in places like St. Boniface under Baudoux's leadership. Secondly, the Montreal documents, including

Léger's letter to the pope, show that in the last few months, as the opening drew closer, Léger joined the leading diocesan cardinals in Europe in a shared critical approach to the preparatory texts. Suenens at the same time also was developing an alternative council work plan which Alfrink, Doepfner, Frings, Koenig, Liénart and Montini supported. Léger's letter dealt with attitudes and outlooks more than with strategies, and was signed by these same European cardinals (except Montini, whose personal papers still are not public). Thirdly, the 1962 work in Montreal settled Léger's mind for the work of the council. The 24 interventions he made all reflect the spirit and line of thought that he expressed in his letter of John XXIII.

That this group of cardinals who headed dioceses outside Rome was collaborating so actively just before the council opened was not known at the time. Much has been written about what a surprise it was when Lienart, seconded by Frings, moved at the start of the council's first working day to reject the lists of names proposed by curial officials for the council's working commissions, and, instead, to let all the assembled bishops elect members. That event takes on a different light in view of what is now known about the collaboration of these non-curial cardinals in the months leading up to that historic morning.

Benediction of the Blessed Sacrament was one of the devotions that declined in popularity after Vatican II. Benediction was usually a late afternoon or early evening ceremony. The sacrament in the form of a large white host, an altar bread, was exposed in the small glass case that formed the centre of the sun-burst design that was the main feature atop the monstrance, a high-standing vessel used only on such occasions. We sang a few Latin hymns everyone seemed to know by heart, especially the "*O salutaris hostia* – O saving host." The presiding priest wore a long cope instead of the fiddle-back chasuble worn for mass. Another shawl-like cloth was draped over his shoulders and around his hands when he stood to take the monstrance from the altar in front of him, turn to face the people and trace a large sign of the cross, the actual moment of the "benediction of the blessed sacrament." The only sound at that moment was the small hand-bell rung by an altar boy. Except, that is, the afternoon we attended with two children. A deep hush fell over St. Paul's cathedral in Saskatoon as the priest rose from his knees, mounted the altar steps and took the monstrance in his draped hands. He began to turn to bless us, the bell rang … and a three-year-old announced at the top of his lungs: "Uh-oh, someone at the door!"

2

The First Session: 1962

The high drama of the council's first workday caught all Canadian participants by surprise. Nobody anticipated that the cardinals who headed Vatican offices would be challenged so directly and so soon. Even Léger, whose petition a month earlier to John XXIII allied him with the thinking of the cardinal archbishops of major European dioceses, was not party to a predetermined strategy. The 26 Canadians – 15 bishops and 11 priests – involved in the preparatory commissions were aware of tensions in them between John XXIII's vision and that of some curial officials, but nobody was sure what might happen once all the bishops met. A great ceremonial opening had been planned, down to the last triumphal detail. The spectacle that unfolded was indeed magnificent, enhanced by the fact that this was the first time in history more than 2,500 bishops gathered with the pope.

For council meetings, the centre aisle of St. Peter's basilica had been transformed into a tiered high-tech assembly hall the length of a football field. Excellent acoustics. Electronic ballot counters and other modern facilities. The opening ceremony in the transformed basilica was an orgy of colour, projected to the world by television and photo magazines. An historian has described the general mood: "Great expectations, then, a lack of preparation, little experience, and, for most of the bishops – despite the impatience that showed in some of their *vota* – the habitual basic attitude that the *causae maiores*, the most important matters, were to be left to Rome, because it was thought that people in Rome saw the general problems of the Church more clearly and in a broader perspective. Well, it was Rome, the Pope, who had decided to call the bishops to a council!"[1] Nobody had foreseen that one of the crucial turning points of the entire council would come during the first few minutes of the first workday. As one result, the Canadians had to scramble to change direction on an agreement they had reached not long before leaving home.

At their final plenary meeting in Ottawa before going to Rome, the Canadian bishops' conference made two decisions regarding the council. They would not open a Canadian secretariat in Rome. They would send English and French journalists to represent their Canadian Catholic Conference (CCC) Information Service and to help inform Canadians about the council through the news media. On the first point, they assumed mistakenly that their national conference would have no part to play at the council. On the second, they foresaw accurately that the news media would have an important role. The CCC was one of the first conferences to open its own information centre in Rome for the council. If there were divisions among the bishops over the second decision, there is no record of that. Regarding a Canadian secretariat in Rome, however, the exchange of views at the Ottawa meeting revealed how the CCC operated in the years prior to Vatican II. Sanschagrin recorded the event in his journal:

> At the last general meeting of the bishops of Canada before the council ... I thought of seeking approval for setting up, at the Canadian College in Rome, a secretariat to serve the bishops. I spoke about it to Baudoux, conference president, and to several other bishops, who encouraged me to present a motion. I found a "seconder" among the English-speaking bishops. Who would not see the usefulness, the need of such an office for the Canadian bishops at the council? So I rose with confidence to ask that it be organized. All the time I was speaking, Cardinal Léger was making large gestures: NO, with a deep frown on his face. (The cardinals sat *ex officio* on the executive of the CCC. The executive faced the rest of us. The cardinal's reactions – and he had some – influenced the bishops.) When I finished, my Anglo confrere, who was supposed to second me, did not have the courage to do so. And when the president asked if my proposition had the support of another member, nobody dared to rise.[2]

As a result, largely because of Léger's assumption that the conferences of bishops would have little or no role to play, no Canadian secretariat was organized in Rome for the opening of the council. However, the need for one became imperative in the first few minutes into the council's work. That day began with a call for an immediate vote on the list of names prepared by Vatican offices for the council's working commissions. Cardinal Liénart of Lille, seconded by Frings of Cologne, immediately made a counter proposal, which was accepted with applause by the majority of bishops. The prepared lists were abandoned, and each national conference of bishops was asked to produce a list of nominees from among its own members to serve on the 10 council commissions. An improvised Canadian secretariat had to be organized in a hurry. It was part of the scene in Rome from then until the end of the council.

Before the opening

Eighty Canadian bishops traveled to Rome during the week before the council's formal 11 October opening. They checked into 19 hotels and religious houses in Rome. They joined 2,460 other bishops, abbots and religious superiors in the elaborate opening ceremonies. About their arrival, I wrote at the time:

> *This ancient city had a warm, cloudless welcome for the Canadian and other prelates coming here for the opening of the Second Vatican Council. Pope John had called the council a "new Pentecost," and whereas the first Pentecost had been marked by unity in the miracle which enabled the apostles to speak to all men, this "new Pentecost" began with the successors of the apostles sharing a vast common experience. The "fathers" of the council began to arrive in Rome in numbers the weekend before the formal Thursday opening. The experiences of the Canadians had been those of all, one felt. There had been the tense and fatiguing pressure of getting last-minute things done before leaving home. Travel to Rome was by aircraft or ocean liner, with word of his arrival usually running ahead of the bishop so that he would be met by a representative of the travel company and helped in avoiding customs and immigration lineups.*

Cardinal McGuigan of Toronto and Cardinal Léger of Montreal were honored by a send-off reception at the Dorval airport the Saturday evening of their departure, and were met in Rome the next day by a party which included airline officials and a delegation from the Canadian embassy here, led by the Canadian ambassador to Italy, Jules Léger, brother of the Cardinal.

The bishops came to various houses and hotels in Rome: Cardinal McGuigan, as he usually does here, staying at the convent of the Sisters of the Precious Blood; Cardinal Léger at the Canadian College; others concentrated especially in two hotels, the Fraternité Sacerdotal hostel and (for members of the community) the Oblate Fathers' general house. The pre-council weekend was one of relaxation for most: unpacking, greeting new arrivals, looking after such affairs as arranging for a place to offer mass each morning, walking and sightseeing in the streets of Rome — many recalling the changes in the city since their student days, when the streets had more men with carts than roaring little motor vehicles, or when all cars had to sound their horns, or when.... The newsstands they passed were filled with reminders of the coming council, most weekend papers featuring the event. Yet it was possible to meet individual Romans who asked: "What council?" The international press commented extensively on the council. "This ecumenical council," wrote Patrick O'Donovan in the London Observer, *"is different from any other. It is not called to condemn or even to promulgate new doctrine. It is domestic in purpose, positive rather than negative, pastoral rather than doctrinaire." "No one with a sense of history can fail to be moved by the imminence of the great council of the Roman Catholic church," said the lead editorial in the Monday* New York Herald Tribune. *"Whatever else the Second Vatican Council may mean... this sense of continuity, of stability, in a world of violent change is perhaps its most universal aspect." Monica Furlong in the Sunday* London Times, *commenting on the council as a "new frontier" along the "long road to unity," concluded on a note which involved the entire world in the affairs of the council. "But what will matter most," she wrote, "what will show that there really is a living Spirit at work among Christians, and that it is a spirit of truth and love, will be when the laity, Roman Catholic and Anglican, Presbyterian and Congregationalist, Baptist and Methodist, speak to and about each other with unfailing gentleness, sympathy and affection. Doctrinal differences, though they must be argued out thoroughly and honestly, may conceivably matter less than we think. But love may matter more...."*

Amid their weekend diversions, word spread informally among the bishops that their first item of business would be registration at a counter in the lobby of a large new building on the street leading up to St. Peter's, at the very edge of the great rising plaza; and the first days of the week found the bishops making their ways there. After filling in a card indicating his name, diocese and Rome address, each bishop received a few basic documents, such as the schedule of meetings for October, the general rules of the sessions and a booklet of council prayers. Since the press office serving the 1,000 newsmen present for the opening was located in the building, it was usually after he had registered that a bishop found himself confronted by a pencil and notebook, or a portable microphone. The entire world was represented in these friendly, informal meetings. Photographers of Paris Match and Life magazine. Reporters for the Copenhagen Lutheran daily paper, and for the London Daily Express. The Cardinal of India. The Cardinal-Primate of Portugal. Black-skinned bishops from Nigeria, Basutoland and Tanganyika. Lighter-skinned prelates from Kerela. A bearded, turbaned bishop from Lebanon. These encounters meant little in the way of "hard" news from or for anyone. They were, rather, part of the common experience of the eve of this "new Pentecost" – impressions to be gained, bearings to be found, perplexities to be sorted out, facts and reports to be checked: the common experience of any convocation of people, multiplied in this case for the "fathers", as for those aiding and observing, by the numbers involved. And in the foreground of their field of vision and their thoughts: St. Peter's, into which the news representatives were admitted on the Monday afternoon before the council – the second of the three occasions on which the Basilica was opened before the council, after being closed September 27 following the finding of the makings of a fire bomb.

Given almost free run during their visit, press people tried the chairs the council fathers would use, visited the first aid room, saw the electronic ballot counters and the ballot cards, and surveyed the long tiers of seats — separated by only 18 feet of floor space but extending the length of a football field. In a triumph of planning, all was disposed in a fashion that left to the great basilica its grandeur, its dignity and its central beauty. And outside, as the fountains spilled down over aged stones and visitors stopped to gaze, the barricades were being placed for control of the live Rome, expected in its hundreds of thousands for the council opening.[3]

The opening ceremonies

For Canadian and other bishops, the first days in Rome were taken up with ceremonies. At the formal opening, even more remarkable than the splendor of the occasion was what John XXIII had to say. He heralded a "future without fear." He emphasized pastoral concern about how to present ancient doctrine to modern people, with charity towards those who err, and an urgent desire for the unity of all humanity. He spelled out the kind of updating he had in mind when he spoke about *aggiornamento*. He disagreed with "prophets of doom" who "keep saying that as compared with past ages, ours is getting worse." The council would focus on the only thing the church could give the world: the ancient message of the gospel. The substance of this message is one thing, the way it is presented is another, and it is the latter that must be taken into consideration, he said. Nowadays, he said, the church "prefers to use the medicine of mercy rather than severity. She considers that she meets the needs of the present day by demonstrating the validity of her teaching rather than by condemnations." There is ample documentation to verify John XXIII's claim to have written the address "with meal from his own sack," that is, entirely on his own.[4] His message was greeted with overwhelming agreement by the Canadians present that morning.

Representing the Canadian government at the opening ceremony and the next day at Pope John's audience with diplomats was Jean Bruchesi, then Canadian ambassador to Spain and

Morocco. At the audience, the pope chatted with the delegates from 78 countries, after urging them to do "something decisive" for peace. Bruchesi showed the pope a postcard dated 1929 and signed "Msgr. Roncalli." The pope looked at it uncomprehendingly for a moment and then exclaimed with delight: "That's me!" Bruchesi had kept the card as a memento of his earlier encounter with the then papal nuncio in Bulgaria. Later that day, Bruchesi and his wife were hosts for a reception in the 75-year-old Canadian College, residence for Canadian priests studying in Rome. Guests included ten cardinals from Vatican offices, along with McGuigan and Léger and the other Canadian archbishops and bishops, Sebastiano Baggio, apostolic delegate to Canada, Canadian representatives of religious houses in Rome, and the Canadian ambassador to Italy, Jules Léger.[5]

John XXIII meets the media

There was a scattering of Canadian journalists present when John XXIII met media representatives the morning of 13 October in the Sistine Chapel at the same time as the drama of the first workday was unfolding in the nearby council hall. Jovial and smiling as he addressed us in French, he could not have been aware how ironic I found his words as I thought about the difficulties we were having getting any information at the council press office. There, great efforts were being made to maintain strict secrecy. Here, the pope was saying that prejudices about the church "rest most often on inaccurate or incomplete information." The council was a fitting occasion, he said, "to establish contact with the life of the church and to gain information from responsible sources" which clearly reflect the thought of the bishops and of the universal church here assembled. "You could make it known," he added, "that there are no political machinations afoot. You will be able to see and to report the true motives which inspire the church's actions in the world, and bear witness to the fact she has nothing to hide, that she follows a straight path without any deviations, that she wants nothing so much as the truth, for men's happiness and for a fruitful concord between the nations of every continent." Despite papal joviality and openness that morning, journalists soon knew that there were some "machinations afoot," as well as energetic efforts to maintain secrecy that made it very difficult for us "to see and to report the true motives which inspire the church's actions...."

First workday

While the pope was chatting with journalists, the council was deciding to begin work by abandoning prepared lists, and instead ask each conference of bishops to nominate some of its members for possible election to council commissions. Immediately, the Canadian bishops faced a major task for which they were not organized. Members of the Canadian Catholic Conference (CCC) living in 19 different locations around traffic-jammed Rome had to be consulted. They now had to improvise the services they would have had in their own secretariat if Sanschagrin's proposal had been approved at their meeting before leaving Ottawa. This task fell mainly to Baudoux, then CCC president. Sanschagrin's journal records his impressions of the process: "We have no one to call us together and we live in the four corners of Rome! As best we could, we managed to meet on Monday, 15 October, at the Canadian College, and to prepare our list of eventual commission members, not without bishops complaining that we had not foreseen to organize a secretariat. Baudoux told me on 17 October that an office was set up at the Canadian College."

First Canadian Office

As Baudoux began his task of consulting fellow CCC members that Saturday morning, he had only his own briefcase for an office. He soon had the use of a rented car. The driver was Cyrille Contant, who had come to Rome as secretary for Bishop Rosario Brodeur of Alexandria, Ontario. During the weekend, Contant drove Baudoux around Rome. A Monday meeting was organized at the Canadian College. There it was decided to propose 12 Canadians for the 10 commissions, in general listing those who had served on preparatory commissions. The Canadian list was ready the next day – a single page of which 1,655 copies were made for distribution to other bishops or groups of them. That hastily improvised CCC secretariat remained in business after the list making was completed. As soon as possible, a telephone for use by the bishops was installed in the room of Bernard De Margarie of Saskatoon, then living at the Canadian College while completing studies for a theology doctorate. Other Canadian priests who helped in the improvised office from time to time during the first session included James M. Hayes of Halifax, Michael J. Barry of Pembroke, Cyrille Couture of Quebec and Gilles Raymond of St. Jean, Québec. Part of its task was to arrange for Wednesday meetings of the Canadian bishops at the college.

For the 1963 second session, Raymond Limoges, CCC French general secretary, came from Ottawa for the first half of the session, and John Carley, his English counterpart, for the second half. They were both in Rome for the CCC general meeting at mid-session. Hélène Masson of Chicoutimi, who had been working in Rome, was recruited as secretary for the two-room office at the Canadian College. At the beginning of the third session, Carley located and organized two large rooms just three blocks from St. Peter's. Nora Smith and Marie Clusiau from the CCC Ottawa staff came to Rome as secretaries. A young Roman with a motor scooter was hired to run errands. Late each afternoon he went to every hotel or house where Canadian bishops lived to bring them mail, council information, and draft texts of planned interventions for which one or another of the bishops sought comments or supporting signatures. Charles Mathieu, the new French general secretary, joined Carley for the CCC general meeting at mid point in the session and stayed on to close up the office when the 1964 session ended. Mathieu returned for the final session, joined by John Shea, director of the CCC social action department in Ottawa. Shea was substituting for the newly named English general secretary, Gordon George SJ, who would take up his duties at the end of 1965. Two Canadian secretaries, Marie MacNeil of Ottawa and Thérèse Rainville of Montreal, were sometimes joined in office tasks by several local helpers.

Canadians on council commissions

After the hasty list making of the first days, the bishops voted on 16 October for members of the 10 working commissions and three secretariats. Each commission was to have 16 members elected by council members and eight named by the pope. This process developed in two stages. The elections and nominations by John XXIII during the first week in 1962 were followed by another round late in the 1963 second session, after Paul VI had succeeded John XXIII. At the end of these two steps, eleven Canadian bishops were elected and two named to the commissions and secretariats. Canadians comprised about six per cent of the elected commission members although they made up just over three per cent of the total participants in the council.

Léger and Roy were elected, and Pelletier of Trois-Rivières named, to the theology commission. They had served on the precouncil commission with similar responsibilities. The theology commission's subject matter gave it a central role, and it gained added significance because it was headed by Cardinal Ottaviani, who insisted his commission had authority to judge the work of all other commissions. This put the theology commission the centre of all major council disputes, and Léger, Roy and Pelletier had some part in them. Bishop Paré of Chicoutimi and Bishop Cody of London were elected to the commission for seminaries and Catholic education. Bishop Martin of Nicolet was elected to the liturgy commission where he would play a major role during the first two council sessions. Lemieux of Ottawa was elected to government of dioceses, Pocock of Toronto to discipline of clergy and people, Flahiff of Winnipeg to religious, and Auxiliary Bishop V. Bélanger of Montreal to sacraments. In the second round of voting in 1963, Baudoux of St. Boniface was elected to the commission for eastern churches, and Hermaniuk of Winnipeg to the secretariat for promoting Christian unity, where Gregory Baum of Toronto had been named as a consultor soon after the secretariat was set up in 1960. One Canadian priest, Léo Deschatelets, superior of the Oblates of Mary Immaculate, was named by John XXIII to the missions commission. Only the commission responsible for both the lay apostolate and the communications media had no

Canadian member. Others served in other capacities, however. Bishop Routhier of McLennan-Grouard, Alberta, was appointed to a special 14-member committee for council media relations.

Discussion begins

The first topic for council debate was a text on reform of the liturgy, the church's public worship. Léger was the first Canadian to join the discussion. Behind the scenes, at a meeting of the bishops at the Canadian College, an incident showed that other bishops felt somewhat ambivalent about the Montreal archbishop, who tended to be a lone star more than a team player. In general, other Canadians supported his views, but not always on his terms. The bishops met at the Canadian College each Wednesday afternoon, to discuss council topics or other shared concerns. Sanschagrin's council journal describes a key incident at one of these meetings:

> We Canadian bishops met many times during the four years of the council. One of the first of these was rather tumultuous. Very early, some bishops had risen in the aula [council hall] to speak in the name of the bishops of their country. Cardinal Léger wanted a "carte blanche" to speak in our name. This did not please the bishops too much. Especially since in the years before the council the cardinal had taken some rather reformist pastoral positions, after having started his career in Montreal in a conformist style. The bishops present did not dare affront the cardinal. The one who dared do so was Archbishop Cabana of Sherbrooke, who proposed that the cardinal circulate his intervention texts among the bishops, who would give him their support or not. Then the cardinal could speak in the name of 10, 25 or 50 Canadian bishops. There was a lively enough exchange. The conciliator was Archbishop Pocock of Toronto, who seconded Cabana's position. In fact, Léger did not speak in the name of other Canadian bishops.[6]

How many bishops?

The first ecumenical council, in Nicea in 325, traditionally called "the great and holy synod of the 318 fathers," in fact had barely 220 present. Vatican I opened 8 December 1869 with 642 with the right to vote. An official Vatican report put those with the right to attend Vatican II at 2904, although only 2449 (89.34 per cent) were present....A definitive list is hard to establish, but the Bologna data base of the Instituto per le Scienze Religiose puts the complete number at 3054, some only at the beginning and others only at the end. Of these, 2443 took part in the first session, and only 1897 in all four.

Debating begins

Léger spoke for the first time on 23 October, the second day of debate. The general principles for liturgical reform were being discussed. By the second day, two main questions had surfaced: Who would have the final say in liturgical changes? What would become of Latin? Underlying each question was another: Would there be flexibility? Some argued that the pope alone must remain the only judge and final decision maker. That would mean continuing control by officials in Vatican offices. Others contended that local bishops were best informed to judge the pastoral needs of their people, and that the bishops' conference in each country therefore should be given more say in the matter. As for Latin, some argued that it should be kept as a sign of unity, and others that modern languages should be introduced to increase understanding and participation.

Léger favoured increasing the competence of national hierarchies to decide liturgical reforms, and expanding the use of modern languages. His general point was that greater adaptability and flexibility should enter the church's Latin rite, and that decisions therefore should be made as close as possible to the local level. His view thus incorporated two central but hotly disputed principles, collegiality and subsidiarity. (McGuigan about this time submitted a written intervention for retaining Latin for the mass. He was concerned "that introduction of the vernacular in the celebration of the mass would break down the sense of mystery surrounding our encounter with God in this sacrament." He wanted the breviary in English and the sacraments as well but he felt strongly that the mass should remain in Latin.)[7]

Six days later, on 29 October, Léger returned to the microphone during detailed study of the eucharist. In support of communion in the form of both bread and wine on occasion, he stressed the "sign value" of this form of eucharistic meal. This was considered "the way *par excellence* through which the word of Christ and the voice of the church could be heard." He also argued that mass concelebrated by a number of priests has special meaning as a sign of unity and mutual charity. On this point, he was presenting an idea that Roy of Quebec had included in his 1959 suggestions, the only Canadian to raise the matter at that time. Léger used examples from the eastern rites, and went on to stress that the mass is not a priest's private devotion but a public action of the entire church joining to worship God. Two days later, Lemieux of Ottawa had the honour of being the first Canadian invited to celebrate the council mass that opened each workday. He followed the Dominican rite as a member of that religious order, using some ritual variations from the standard Latin mass.

According to the council rules, a working commission was responsible for each text being debated. The plenary workday ran from 9:00 AM to 12:30 PM in St. Peter's. The commissions met in the afternoons or evenings in smaller Vatican halls. Their first task was to study comments made about their text during debates, and to decide how to deal with each remark. The liturgy commission with Martin of Nicolet a member was therefore responsible for handling remarks made about the first text studied. It did not start work on the text until 5 November because of delays in the council secretariat in compiling and organizing comments about the text. The commission then set up 13 sub-commissions. Martin was named to chair the sub-commission responsible for comments on the introduction and articles 1-9 of the first chapter. These set out the principles for liturgical reform. Martin had a high profile job until the liturgy text went through the final voting stage during the second council session in 1963.

When Léger next spoke about the liturgy on 7 November, he supported the idea of allowing priests to recite the divine office in their own language instead of Latin. He also asked that these breviary prayers be reorganized and simplified to suit the life and needs of modern priests. He was reiterating points he had made in his 1959 reply to Tardini. He argued that for priests active in pastoral ministry, as distinct from monks, it was impossible to pray at regular hours throughout the day. The quality of prayer should be preferred over its quantity. The final document on the liturgy echoed Léger and a number of others on this point. It affirmed the importance of this change for the prayer-life of priests, and established the competence of national bishops' conferences to decide on the translations, to be confirmed in Rome.

After the rules for press coverage of the debates were somewhat eased as the second session opened, bishops felt somewhat freer to share their feelings, but they were very reticent to do so during the first session. Once again, Sanschagrin's journal gives a sense of what went on behind the veil of secrecy in the debate about using vernacular languages instead of Latin. He entitled his journal entry for this topic, "From the Council of Jerusalem to the Second Vatican Council." He recalled that "we were lost" during a morning mass according to an unfamiliar eastern rite, and Léger remarked "that is what we ask of our people." Sanschagrin wrote that the debates about Latin were "passionate."

> The strongest impression was left by a bishop from Japan, who showed us that by using Latin in the liturgy the Catholic religion appeared even more Western to the Japanese. ...He spoke in the name of all Japanese bishops. ...I remember that intervention as if it were yesterday. ...(It) led other Fathers to rally to their own vernacular language and culture in each country. ... (He said) we thank St. Francis Xavier and others for bringing us the faith. But we wonder if respect for our language and culture would not have made us more open to the gospel. The Second Vatican Council faces the same problem as the one that was resolved at the Council of Jerusalem. The problem then: These pagans, must we make them Jews first, to make them Christians afterwards? Our problem: Out of the Japanese that we are, must we first make Latins so that we become Christians? ...His argument turned all of us upside down. Latin was given the *coup de grace*.[8]

Events outside the council

Busy as they were with council business, the bishops sometimes participated in other events. Late in October, Léger, with a number of other Canadian bishops also present, consecrated a new Roman parish church dedicated to Our Lady of the Blessed Sacrament and the Canadian Martyrs. It is in the area of Rome near the Canadian embassy. Its builder, Robert Fortin, a member of the Priests of the Blessed Sacrament, had promoted the idea of an Italian parish church that would also be known as the Canadian national church in Rome, like other so-called national churches. A few days earlier, in sadness, Léger and other Canadian bishops participated in a requiem mass for Charles Omer Garant, 63, auxiliary bishop in Quebec, who died suddenly in Rome on 21 October 1962, the day before the opening council debate on the liturgy began. (At later sessions, there would be similar ceremonies. Archbishop Bernier, 58, bishop of Gaspé, who was CCC chairman when John XXIII announced the council, died suddenly while entering the council hall 21 November 1964; and Bishop Coudert of Whitehorse, 70, died in Rome on 15 November 1965 as the end of Vatican II approached.)

Message from non-Catholics

The council was less than a month old when the Canadian Council of Churches sent a message to John XXIII and "Reverend Fathers and Brothers." It said:

> The Canadian Council of Churches now assembled in Yorkminister Park Baptist Church, Toronto, sends you greetings in the name of our common Lord, Jesus Christ. We rejoice at the signs of the Holy Spirit's presence and ministry in your Second Vatican Council. We note your concern for the renewal of common worship and for the universal mission of the church as God's apostolic people in every nation and every realm of human existence. Like you, we are in the midst of an exhilarating revival of bible study and theological exploration. In a manifest climate of increased love, concern, and trust, God is helping you and us to know and understand one another. We believe that

through the ongoing high-priestly work of Christ Jesus the ascended Lord all these things will assuredly minister to the healing of the nations and the gathering together in one of the scattered children of God. Let us pray for each other as did the Apostle Paul for his fellow believers at Colossae: May you be strengthened with all power, according to God's glorious might, for all endurance and patience with joy, giving thanks to the Father, who has qualified us to share in the inheritance of the saints. He has delivered us from the dominion of darkness and transferred us to the kingdom of His beloved Son, in whom we have redemption, the forgiveness of sins. He is the image of the invisible God, the first-born of all creation; for in Him all things are created, in heaven and on earth, visible and invisible, whether thrones or dominions or principalities or authorities – all things were created through Him and for Him. He is before all things, and in Him all things hold together. He is the head of the body, the church; he is the beginning, the first-born from the dead, that in everything He might be pre-eminent. For in Him all the fullness of God was pleased to dwell, and through Him to reconcile to Himself all things, whether on earth or in heaven, making peace by the blood of His cross.[9]

Formation of Informal Groups

In an important but unforeseen development, some bishops organized into a number of informal groups that met afternoons or evenings when there were no council meetings. Individual Canadians were attracted to some of these groups.[10] However, formal Canadian participation was limited to a gathering variously known as Inter-conference, Conference of the 22, or Domus Maria Conference. Only official representatives of the various bishops' conferences were members of this group. Baudoux represented Canada as chairman of the CCC, and continued to do so after Flahiff succeeded him as CCC head late in 1963. These meetings of conference representatives made it easy for them to share information and plan council strategies. This group owed its existence in part to the council's 13 October decision to reject the prepared lists for commissions and, instead, vote later on lists of names prepared by the bishops' conferences.

After their involvement in that vote, conferences no longer felt as much controlled by curial limitations on their role in the church. First, some general secretaries of conferences met informally for an exploratory discussion 25 October at the African secretariat that had just been set up. At a first meeting of bishops on 9 November at Domus Maria, Baudoux was one of 18 representatives of 13 conferences. The group came to be called the "Conference of the 22," even though the number of conferences represented could vary from meeting to meeting. Beginning with the second session, they met every Friday evening at Domus Maria, a well-known Roman location for conventions of church groups. Each conference was to send one delegate, and only delegates could attend. Grootaers credits two strong personalities and two organizations as the source of energy for the first meeting. The personalities were Pierre Veuillot, then coadjutor archbishop of Paris, and Roger Etchegaray, assistant secretary of the French bishops' assembly. The two organizations were CELAM, the council of Latin American conferences of bishops, and the Canadian Catholic Conference. The CCC had particular importance for bishops of other countries who were just setting up their conferences. The Canadians had 19 years of experience as an organized conference, and theirs was functional and up to date. A constitution first approved by the Vatican in 1948 had been updated by the Canadians and approved by Rome in 1955.

The inter-conference group, with Baudoux present and active, met four more times during the 1962 session: 13, 20 and 27 November, and 4 December. Besides information sharing, four themes dominated these meetings. 1) The possibility of developing a mechanism for rejecting a text if a majority found it unsatisfactory after a first round of discussion. This need arose from the fact that Vatican officials kept insisting that the texts they had prepared before the council opened had been "approved" by the pope and therefore could not be dismissed. (John XXIII and, later, Paul VI would show that they did not share this curial view.) 2) The conference representatives wanted the bishops to have quick and easy access to the list of topics coming up for discussion. At that point in the first session, the bishops had no clear outline of future work, so they had difficulties preparing for discussions and debates. 3) On a related point, the first council session was drawing to a close and they wanted to know with certainty what topics they should study during the coming break between sessions, so they could prepare for the second session. They recommended a plan whereby the bishops would be sent the texts with instructions to send back written comments. This was foreseen as a means to reduce the number of oral interventions on minor points at future sessions. 4) They urged the setting up of a "special secretariat" to be responsible for the church's interests in social and international questions. (This request later would be part of the council's discussion of the text on the church in the modern world.)

The group's concerns about unsatisfactory texts and future topics related directly to what was going on in council debates at that time. The bishops were nearing the impasse that developed in the third week of November over the text on "the sources of revelation" drafted before Vatican II opened. Council rules at the time did not enable the bishops themselves to handle the matter, and it took direct intervention by John XXIII to send the text to a special joint commission for extensive redrafting. The third point, about work between sessions, was discussed extensively at the fourth and fifth inter-conference meetings on 28 November and 4 December. They developed a detailed plan. They recommended that the various commissions shorten draft texts of minor importance, and do so according to "the mind of the council," that is, with renewal clearly in mind. Their plan also called for the setting up of a "continuation council" that would direct and manage the study of texts during the period between sessions. When John XXIII later issued his instruction for work between sessions, these ideas from the inter-conference group were clearly reflected.

Similar work by the inter-conference group continued during the second, third, and fourth council sessions. Paul VI was kept informed of the results of their meetings. Discussion of ways to improve the functioning of the council was always a priority. However, members of the various conferences of bishops were also concerned to aid in the development of conferences, as such. For this reason, at its 18 October 1963 meeting, Baudoux made a major presentation on the constitution and operation of the Canadian conference. Its 1955 constitution was subsequently used as a model on which other groups of bishops based plans for their own national conferences.[11]

Liturgy debate continues

Baudoux made the first of his council interventions on 13 November, to talk about what the liturgy text said about church furnishings and the place of music in worship. A church building could be made beautiful without great cost, he argued. The "splendour of worship" could be enhanced without excessive cost by using some of the products of modern technology along with the natural elements traditionally used in church buildings and furnishings. These furnishings needed to be adapted in accord with renewal of the liturgy and of sacred art. In the document's section on liturgical music, he wanted more emphasis on the participation of people than on the use of Latin. Congregational participation was essential to authentic solemn worship, but Latin was not. Baudoux also wanted more emphasis on the need for agreement between the singing and the meaning of the liturgical action. By this stage in the debate, many bishops knew where they stood on liturgical reforms, and wished to vote on the text so the council could move on to another topic. A note in Pocock's personal journal catches this mood. He wrote: "Archbishop Baudoux has just spoken, suggesting several minor revisions of the text. This was prepared by Card. Léger. I am glad I did not accept the request to read it. The Fathers are exasperated by this attention to detail. Yet, due to some strange compulsion, the same ones who are exasperated step up to the microphone and perpetuate this incompetent procedure."[12]

Post-debate work on liturgy

When the theology commission met 12 November, it heard a six-page report by Martin's sub-commission on comments about the introduction. It was apparent that his sub-commission, which had met 8 November, had reasonably disposed of the most important objections to the introduction. Then, on 14 November, the commission reviewed Martin's report on articles 1-9. On 17

November, at the 21st general assembly, Martin gave an overview of the corrections that had been made to the introduction and the first four articles. The council approved this work by more that 2100 votes in favor to fewer than 30 opposed. At the 30th congregation on 30 November, Martin presented the other changes made by his sub-commission, which once again were approved. After this process of voting article by article, the whole of the introduction and first chapter were put to a vote 7 December, with 1992 in favour, 11 opposed, and 180 in favour but with some further suggestions for changes. By this vote, the first session defined the basic principles for liturgical renewal, and set the guidelines for final work on the remaining chapters during the second session.[13]

Second Topic: Divisive Dogmas

With its second topic, "The sources of Revelation," the council took up a topic even more divisive than the liturgy had been. Now it faced a strictly dogmatic topic, and one that was the subject of a still unsettled debate in Catholic theology: the relationship between oral revelation (the preaching of Christ) and its subsequent transmission (tradition), on the one hand, and, on the other, the New Testament. It also involved the role of the ecclesiastical magisterium, the teaching authority of the church. The period from 14 November to 8 December, and especially the week of 14–21 November,

> ... (marked) the turn from the church of Pius XII, which was still essentially hostile to modernity and in this sense the heir to the nineteenth-century restoration, to a church that is a friend to all human beings, even children of modern society, its culture, and its history. This period proved decisive for the future of the council, not because the council fathers already knew all the decisions they would make later, but because in it the council took possession of itself, its nature, and its purpose and attuned itself to the intentions of John XXIII, an attunement that had largely been impeded by the work of the preparatory commissions, especially the theology commission. The turn was no sudden flowering, but something that had been long desired and awaited during the decades after World War I and especially

since things had begun to open with Pope John's announcement of the council."[14]

As Vatican II began, most Canadian Catholics knew little of the intense discussion about holy scripture among bible specialists. A high-level debate had been going on for years and now came to a climax in the council. Several broad lines of questioning were involved. One had to do with the vitality of revelation itself: Were the truths of Christ's teaching just a collection of dogmas handed down from the past, which people should memorize and believe? Or was God also always speaking to his people through the truths in which they believe? A second discussion had to do with the source of these truths. Were they partly in scripture and partly in the church's tradition? At the popular level, this particular question was reflected in the idea that Catholics, unlike other Christians, believed that scripture alone was not sufficient. Another line of questioning probed whether the bible is literally true in all its details. Are some passages to be understood as literary forms used by the writers to convey truths not immediately apparent?

The first chapter of the text presented for discussion was devoted to "the twofold source" of revelation. It referred to the scriptures and to tradition "counterpoised" as two originating fountainheads of revelation. It also said "that tradition alone is the way in which some revealed truths become clear and are known." The second chapter dealt with inspiration, inerrancy and literary composition of the scriptures. Chapter 3 was on the Old Testament. Chapter IV "defended the historical truth of the 'deeds' of Jesus narrated in the gospels and the substantial fidelity of the words they attribute to him." The final chapter set out criteria for reading the scriptures by the faithful and by exegetes who were obliged to follow "the analogy of the faith, the tradition of the church, and the norms set forth by the apostolic see on the subject."

On 13 November, the day before debate began, there were several initiatives regarding what to do about the text. For two hours in the afternoon, the theology commission, with Léger, Roy and Pelletier members, held what has been called a "troubled meeting." The discussion was described as confused and not without acrimony. The secretary reported on comments by 160 bishops who had submitted written comments about the draft text. Two alternative texts were being circulated, one drafted by Karl Rahner and Joseph Ratzinger, the other by Edward Schillebeeckx. According to one report, the discussion then turned in a disorganized way around 1) the right to propose new drafts; 2) the freedom to speak in the council; and 3) the relationship between the theology commission elected by the council and the original preparatory commission for theology. Ottaviani maintained that the new commission had a duty to defend the old commission's text in the council. This would have blocked all interventions by commission members not supportive of the prepared text. Léger threatened to resign from the commission if being a member meant not being free to speak in the hall.

That evening, the representatives of bishops' conferences, including Baudoux, gathered at Domus Maria for their second meeting. At their first meeting they had talked about problems of procedure, hoping to speed up interventions and also preserve freedom of speech, and had touched on the revelation text. On 13 November, regarding the text on the sources of revelation, Germany, Japan, India and Ceylon, the Philippines, Africa and CELAM declared their opposition to it. France proposed that it should be discussed and then voted on. The bishops of Canada, Mexico and Burma were reported to be still divided. Italy refused to voice an opinion."[15]

As the revelation debate opened on the following day, Léger proposed that the text should be completely revised. The council, he said, was hoping for a text that would positively point the way to fruitful biblical renewal in the church. Instead, "we have a text which, even though it contains some good articles, reflects such a mentality that in my opinion the council cannot lend it its solemn authority." It expressed only one way of thinking, and "one single theological school should not be substituted for the variety of theological thought in the church." He criticized the draft for speaking as if it were agreed that scripture and tradition were two distinct sources of God's revelation. Also, there was danger of creating distrust about the work of biblical scholars. Careful reading of the text showed, he said, that "the mentality which inspired the whole text is a dread of 'creeping' errors." Certainly, error must be avoided; but the church could speak about all things with calmness, without aggressivity, with trust, with optimism, without losing the smallest particle of truth.

O'Mara notes that while McGuigan did not speak in the council he followed the daily discussions, read all the reports and suggestions and voted through each of the first three sessions that he attended. He was especially concerned about the controversy on the nature of biblical inspiration during the first session discussion of revelation. The Canadian Jesuit R.A.F. Mackenzie, who was rector of the Biblical Institute, came for supper with McGuigan several times and the conversation would "address this issue and the acrimonious conflict between the Biblical Institute and the Lateran University."[16]

Cardinals who echoed Léger's attack on the text included Liénart, Frings, Koenig, Alfrink and Suenens (all of whom had signed Léger's petition to the pope), as well as Ritter and Bea. Those who took an opposite view and supported the draft included Ottaviani, Ruffini, Siri and Quiroga y Palacios. Unknown until years later, John XXIII wrote in his diary for 14 November: "That disputes will arise can be foreseen. On the one hand, the draft does not take into account the specific intentions of the pope in his official discourses. On the other hand, a good eight cardinals, relying on these discourses, have discredited the main point of the draft. May the Lord help us and make us one."[17] Heavy debate on the revelation text continued for a week. In the midst of it, the Canadian bishops heard as guest lecturer an American scripture specialist who led a workshop in Toronto only a few weeks earlier. I wrote about the occasion in my 18 November letter home:

> *Went to Hotel de la Ville this morning to hear lecture for Canadian bishops by Fr. Barnabas Ahern, U.S. biblical expert, on modern thought about the bible, and whether it is exact history. He used a good example to show how a manner of speaking can be true, but not exactly historical. A man can be said to be "brave" or "to have the heart of a lion." In both cases the same idea of the man's courage is conveyed; but only the first is literally true, since obviously a man doesn't have a lion's heart. The scholars have to look at the bible in the same way, trying to decide whether in certain instances the writer intended the words to be taken literally (he is brave) or only figuratively (he is lion-hearted). In fact, there are two schools*

of thought on the question— or perhaps three, to be more exact: (1) favoring a literal approach; (2) those favoring a figurative interpretation; and (3) those saying that since both (brave and lion-hearted) can mean the same thing from a different point of view, let's just agree both have merit, and keep on studying. I must say I found it absolutely thrilling to see how eagerly the Canadian bishops hear and discuss these new ideas from the great scholars. And the scholars in turn (as one of them told me) are very much taken with our Bishops, who are by no means unnoticed men in this council. Undoubtedly your sacrifices and prayers (O Mary, Help of Bishops, Pray for them) have helped to bring things to the present state of optimism.

On the morning of 20 November, as debate continued on the revelation text, Cabana of Sherbrooke was one of the listed speakers. Before he began, it was announced that a vote would be taken at once on whether to keep or reject the much-criticized draft. Cabana was one of the last to speak before the result was announced. He made two main points. From his experience as bishop in St. Boniface and Sherbrooke, "dioceses where many separated brethren live," he believed that the text supplied what bishops and priests needed for their pastoral ministry with Catholics and non-Catholics. It should not be rejected. Besides, time was flying. The council was nearly six weeks old and still discussing only the second of 70 items on its agenda. The text should be approved for detailed study. Amendments could be made where necessary, he argued.

Avoiding a major crisis

The end of that morning's session marked the start of one of the most dramatic episodes of the entire council. A clear majority of 1,368 to 822 voted against the draft, but the opponents of the text fell short of the two-thirds total needed to reject it under council rules. Therefore, debate was to resume the next day. After that close vote, there was a mood of disappointment and frustration among the majority who had fallen just short of their goal. This included most of the Canadian bishops. Nevertheless, the Canadians left the hall at noon looking forward with some sense of anticipation and joy to a major event set for later in the day. That evening it would be their turn to be received as a group in a special audience by John XXIII.

During that audience, Léger took an initiative that leads historians to credit him, along with Bea, with helping the council to avoid a major crisis. Diary entries by both the pope and Léger show that the cardinal asked for and received permission to speak to John XXIII in private during the audience with all the Canadian bishops. Giuseppe Ruggieri, basing himself on the two diaries, describes what happened as follows: "At this meeting, the Canadian cardinal, it seems, presented a written request, which the pope would later remember as a 'letter,' and spoke to him 'frankly about the situation.' However, Léger received the impression that the pope had not decided to intervene, even though he admitted that the majority's vote to reject the schema had faithfully interpreted his own thinking." It may be impossible to measure just what influence Léger had. It is certain that the next day Léger received from the pope the gift of "an old but valuable episcopal cross" with a letter that said in part: "I was thinking of our meeting yesterday evening, of your very gracious letter, and of the conversation which followed."[18]

Whatever influenced him, overnight John XXIII decided that the wish of the majority for a new text should be respected despite the two-thirds rule. Therefore 21 November began with the announcement that John XXIII, "yielding to the wishes of many," had decided that the revelation text should be referred to a mixed commission made up of some members of both the theology commission headed by Ottaviani and the unity secretariat headed by Bea. Léger, Roy and Pelletier, the three Canadians on Ottaviani's commission, were named members of the new mixed commission, and Baum, a consultor with Bea's secretariat, was named a consultor also of the mixed commission. Their work on a new text would not return to the floor for debate until the council's third session in 1964.

As the morning session of 21 November therefore began with no new topic to discuss, the presidency decided to continue that day and the next to hear those who had been prepared to talk about the rejected revelation text. It was in an atmosphere of anticlimax, therefore, that Hermaniuk made his first intervention on 21 November. He proposed that the text's title should be simply "Divine Revelation" – the form eventually used for the final version. Such a title would speak more clearly about God being the single author and unique source of revelation. Then, when speaking about how revelation is transmitted and preserved, scripture and tradition could be distinguished. He also questioned a passage which he said tended to make too sharp a distinction between the "living preaching" of the apostles and "their preaching which under the inspiration of the Spirit is committed to writing" in holy scripture. To distinguish these was partly true but not entirely so, "because this preaching of the apostles before it was committed to writing was also a living preaching." It should also be noted, he said, that the later church's task of faithfully guarding and authentically interpreting revelation was accomplished "not only through the preaching of the church as such but also by other means, for example, in monuments, writings, and the life of the church."

Media of communication

During the somewhat confused situation after the revelation text had been sent for rewriting by John XXIII's decision, the text about the media of communication came on the floor. Two Canadians spoke about it: Sanschagrin (23 November) and Léger (24 November). Even before discussion of it began, the bishops were informed that the three major texts on church unity, the Blessed Virgin and on the nature of the church itself would follow shortly. The media text therefore was given only brief treatment, less than three full days. Most noteworthy, perhaps, is the fact that for the first time in church history a council was dealing with a temporal issue of this kind. Sanschagrin took up a practical point that several bishops had mentioned in pre-council suggestions. Why were the modern media not being used for faster communications within the church's administration? He argued that bishops should be informed about decisions and statements by the Holy See before news of these was released through the general press. If available media were used, it should be possible to inform the bishops in advance. That way, the local bishop would be prepared to give clarifications and interpretations when chancery offices and parishes began to receive questions prompted by news reports. To illustrate, Sanschagrin pointed out how the term *socialization* in John XXIII's 1961 encyclical *Mater et Magistra* had sometimes been misused by the press as praise for socialism. It took weeks for the bishops to find out what the encyclical really said. However, his point, with which many bishops were known to agree, did not find a place in the short decree promulgated at the end of the second session. A later commentator found there was "something tragicomic" about the fact that at the moment when the press was complaining it could get no information in Rome, bishops were complaining that the press was being given information before they did.[19]

Léger urged that the council should stress the church's concern about the right of everyone to receive truth through the media. The church's particular rights should not be over-emphasized. Also, there was no point, he said, in trying to insulate people from these powerful, all-pervasive media. Instead, the church should adopt them without fear, "putting an end to the negative type of criticism characteristic of so many churchmen in the past." Léger also underlined the importance of the communication media for the welfare of the church, but like other bishops he found that the document was too juridical in nature and placed too much emphasis on the rights of the church. He preferred that emphasis be placed on the church's pastoral concern. The debate ended in its third day. The text was acceptable in principle, but had to be rewritten and shortened. Practical details, it was also decided, should be outlined later by the pontifical commission for the media. Bishop Coderre of St. Jean, Quebec, was later named a member of this commission. Lucien Labelle, a priest of the St. Jean diocese, director of the national Catholic centre for the media in Montreal, was named a consultant, along with J.M. Poitevin, a Canadian priest working in Rome as director of the secretariat of the International Catholic Office for Cinema.

Unity debate begins

Hermaniuk, on 30 November, was the only Canadian to speak when the first session discussed Christian unity. Three statements on this subject had been drafted for the beginning of the council. One by the preparatory commission for eastern churches dealt with reunion of Catholics and Orthodox. A second by the theology commission referred mainly to Protestants. The Christian unity secretariat, in its turn, wrote about the general principles of ecumenism. The first session took up the first of these, entitled "That All May Be One." The eastern churches' commission had prepared it without consulting either the theological commission or the unity secretariat. While its formal purpose was to point to ways that would lead to the reunion of Catholics with the Orthodox church, it also brought up the status and significance of the "uniate churches," the eastern rites already united with Rome. Hermaniuk said that the text seemed to come too close to identifying the Catholic church with the Latin rite. He offered a "vision" of a reunited Christendom. It would amount to the start of a new era in world history. At the practical level, he stressed the importance for unity of working out an explanation of collegiality, the collective responsibility of bishops under the authority of the pope. This was to be a recurring theme for Hermaniuk. With other eastern-rite bishops, he shared a deep understanding of the problem of papal authority in the minds of the Orthodox. The Latin-rite traditions of church government, these eastern bishops argued, could be somewhat modified to incorporate some eastern traditions. The first session did not get into details of these, however. Debate ended 30 November; the next day, there was a vote that the council should approve the decree on the unity "as a document which sums up our common faith, and as a pledge of remembrance and good will toward the separated brethren of the east." However, it added that after the proposed changes had been taken into account, the decree was to be combined in a single document with the decree on ecumenism composed by the unity secretariat and with the chapter on ecumenism in the draft text about the nature of the church. This proposition was approved: 2068 for, 36 opposed, 8 void.

Debate on the church

The debate on the final document of the first session, about the nature of the church, lasted for a week, until 7 December, when the session closed. Preparation of this document had been marked especially by disagreements between the theology commission and the unity secretariat. The commission favoured a juridical conception of church as a society reflected in identification of Catholic church and Mystical Body of Christ. The secretariat looked at the church more as a mystery than a society. Regarding church membership, it started from the efficacy of grace found even outside the Catholic church and claimed a real, even if incomplete, membership in the church for non-Catholic Christians. The theology commission allowed for only an "orientation" of non-Catholic Christians to the church. There was agreement on the sacramentality of episcopal ordination, but the theology commission made the pope the source of a bishop's power of jurisdiction, while the secretariat connected it with ordination. Regarding church and state, theology stood by the view that the state was obliged to support the Catholic church and oppose (not tolerate) others, but enforce tolerance when Catholics were a minority. Unity pressed for recognition of religious freedom based on charity. At the same time as discussion of these matters began, some alternative texts about the nature of the church were being circulated or prepared, especially one by Philips working with Suenens, and others by Schillebeeckx and Rahner. These would come into play later.

Meanwhile, Léger (3 December) was the only Canadian to address the final topic of the first session. If an opinion poll had been taken at the time, it probably would have shown most ordinary people to be bored or baffled by a debate about the nature of the church. How could so many church leaders sit in solemn assembly to discuss fine theological distinctions? In a sense, Léger addressed this question. He called the text on the church the "hinge" of the entire council. There was a tendency at that time to feel discouragement. The bishops were tired. The council had been sitting for almost two months, with nothing to show in the way of finished texts. Only one chapter of the document on liturgy was ready for final voting. Léger stressed that the months of discussion had shown beyond question that John XXIII had been right in calling for renewal of the church through the council. The work must go on. The time required must be devoted to the task of rethinking and rewriting draft texts. Léger, who had played an important role in the solution of the difficulty raised by the vote on the sources of revelation, stressed the need to support the pope's desire for renewal and to plan the work of the intersession. Drawing ideas from the Vatican secretariat for extraordinary affairs, he proposed a coordinating committee that would guide the future work of other commissions. Léger's intervention therefore did not deal with the text on the floor but concentrated on the procedural problems of future council work.

The next day, 4 December, Suenens presented the plan that had been drawn up with the accord of the pope before the beginning of the council, and had then been circulated informally. He proposed a council focused entirely on the church, with two main parts, one on the church in its inner life (*ad intra*), the other on the church in its relations with the outside world (*ad extra*). On 5 December, Montini stated his agreement with Suenens, and signaled an open distancing of himself from curial circles. The workday ended with reading of the pope's work plan for the future, including the setting up of a commission, presided by the Vatican secretary of state, to coordinate and direct future work, much as Léger had suggested two days earlier.

Work on revelation text

While the council discussed the texts on unity and the church, the new mixed Ottaviani-Bea commission began work on a new revelation text. It held five meetings between 25 November and 7 December. At the 5 December meeting, Léger reported as co-chair of the sub-commission on the chapter about scripture in the church. The new text urged the utmost veneration for the Old and New Testaments, and aimed to promote, among other things, accurate translations that would give everyone access to the scriptures. The discussion that followed Léger's report caused no tensions in the group. However there was tension the afternoon of 7 December when Ottaviani and Bea were presiding over discussion of the relation between scripture and tradition. The two co-presidents disagreed. Bea proposed that the question be left open to leave theologians free for further work, but Ottaviani disagreed. Bea attempted a formula that ended with a vote of 19 for, 16 against and six abstentions. That did not settle the matter, so the mixed commission's final meeting concluded in unresolved disagreement.[20] John XXIII, however, closed the first session on a positive note on 8 December. He praised the hard work done to achieve consensus, especially on the question of liturgical renewal, a happy first choice for the council's study. The session had shown the whole world the holy freedom of the children of God, he said. He urged more hard work during the intersession to prepare for a second session, then set for early the next September, and spoke of his hope for rich fruits from the council.

From my first steps along them, the streets of Rome fascinated me. Nearly every block had a church, many of them dedicated to saints whose names brought back childhood memories.

God was a prominent figure at home when I grew up. Jesus had little place except as the infant at Christmas and as the youngest member of the Holy Family. Mary and Joseph were much more in my mind than the Holy Ghost who, true enough, was third person of the Holy Trinity in my catechism answers but never much mentioned otherwise, that I remember. I thought frequently about the saint I was named after, and also the saint whose name I took for confirmation. My guardian angel was very real to me, and so were other angels, and archangels, and even cherubim and seraphim (whatever they looked like). The fallen angels and especially their leader, the devil, were also very much part of our spiritual world. And, not forgotten, were all who had died, from Moses to Columbus to the grandparents I never met. The damned (nobody I was sure of) were in Hell, infants who died unbaptized were somehow safe in Limbo, some "souls of the faithful departed" needed our prayers so they could leave Purgatory, and join "all the saints" in Heaven. In comparison, most of my schoolmates were Protestants whose heavens seemed like a deserted place. I tended to agree later when I read an anthropologist's observation that Catholics and the Amerindians were somewhat alike in seeing the spiritual world as densely populated. And many from this vast throng had their names along the streets of Rome.

3

Intersession:
Fall 1962 to Fall 1963

Canadian bishops came home from Rome in December 1962 with a sense of excitement that they had important stories to tell. All of them also had assigned homework: to study draft texts and send back their comments. The 13 bishops who were also members of council working commissions had additional duties that would call them back to Rome for meetings to prepare texts for study at the second session set for September 1963. All this however was work for the future. For most bishops coming home in December 1962, the story telling came first. They were not downcast that during the first session no text received final approval, or that they still did not know the exact direction the council would take in the future. John XXIII had been named as *Time* magazine's "Man of the Year." That alone meant a great deal, and there also was much more to talk about.

Church unity was a major topic at a home-coming press conference by Archbishop Anthony Jordan of Edmonton and Bishop Lussier of nearby St. Paul. The fact the council was held, and that 40 non-Catholic observers attended, brought church unity closer to reality, Jordan affirmed. Lussier added that "even though the desired union is not for tomorrow, yet it is closer than ever before. On both sides a big step forward had taken place."[1] Farther north at McLennan, Alberta, Henri Routhier, vicar apostolic of Grouard, stressed that church unity is not a matter of the Catholic church triumphing over non-Catholic churches. In a pastoral letter, he urged prayers that "we be all deeply united to Christ, and that thus we come closer together eventually in perfect unity of love, doctrine and under one vicar of Christ."[2] In his Christmas message, Bishop Leverman of Saint John, New Brunswick, also stressed the importance of participation by non-Catholics. He called it a "coming together in prayer and discussion undreamed of a few years ago."[3]

At Christmas midnight mass in Nelson, British Columbia, Bishop Emmett Doyle spoke of being deeply moved by Vatican II as a "gathering of men from all nations.... We met the hierarchy of the whole church, and came to realize the extent and variety which makes up the mystical body of Christ."[4] Doyle was echoed in Winnipeg where Flahiff said in an interview "the organic unity of the church is what impressed me most at the council.... This was the topic under discussion when the council was interrupted 8 December, and it will be resumed when we go back to Rome in September." To an ecumenical audience of Winnipeg clergy, Flahiff also called the council "an eye opener and a mind-opener."[5] For Andrew Roborecki, the Ukrainian bishop in Saskatoon, the council was helping "to clear the air and resolve quite a number of problems" in the church's relations with the separated Orthodox communion, and also with the main Protestant groups."[6] And in Windsor, Ontario, Auxiliary Bishop G. Emmett Carter predicted in an interview that changes resulting from the council would be "mainly in the areas of attitudes and ideas.... Their effect may not be felt for many, many years." The strongest advocates of a change in attitudes were the bishops of France, Germany, Holland and Belgium, he said. "We North American bishops were surprised at how outspoken they were." Carter added "many of us were not satisfied with the council news service. We felt the secrecy observed at previous councils was no longer necessary, and that newspapermen should be allowed in the sessions."[7]

Differing views expressed at the council were like spotlights on a many-faceted diamond, Baudoux said in St. Boniface. The illumination "came at times from the teachings of the early Greek fathers of the church as echoed by their countrymen, the eastern-rite bishops. At other times it came from scholastic theology or doctrine developed largely in the Latin church since the Middle Ages, and vigorously supported by a phalanx of western bishops.... And again at other times the light came from a growing demand for the revitalization of the importance of scripture through modern exegetics, or a renewed and more independent study of the sacred texts, asked for by the majority of council fathers. Further light came from the search for better means of presenting the teachings of the church, with a common determination on all sides to preserve these intact."[8] For his part, Hermaniuk told 400 representatives of all Winnipeg's Ukrainian Catholic parishes and organizations that the council was simply "a miracle." He said John XXIII was justly named *Time*'s Man of the Year, because in his short pontificate he had made manifest the great truth that all peoples, whether Christians or not, are in common children of God. It is only with the pope's good will that this had been brought about. The council was "a miracle" because the fundamental attitude taken by the church to all modern problems has changed radically and a new spirit was generally evident in relations of Catholics with non-Catholics. The purpose of the council was not to condemn anyone, but to bring the truth of Christ to bear in everyday life.[9]

Immediate Canadian responses to the council's first session were not just fine words. One new initiative was a diocesan council composed of lay church members for Sault Ste. Marie diocese. Bishop Alexander Carter said, "the church is not the bishop and priests. If a bishop is going to fulfill his role he must be in close contact with his people.... He must know the laity's needs, views, grievances, joys and anxieties. Only in their lives will he be able to help them spiritually.[10] " Within a month, Carter also named eight priests to a new diocesan ecumenical committee, to which laymen would be added later.[11] By then, a commission on unity for Toronto archdiocese had been named by Pocock "to aid us in fostering the spirit of unity within the diocese at every level and to encourage and co-ordinate useful dialogue with our separated brethren." Members were six priests – Gregory Baum, Gerald J. Cochran, Stan Kutz, John E., Moss, William J. O'Leary – and two laymen – Donald F. McDonald QC and Robert G. Fitzpatrick.[12] Another new project of a different kind announced in the first month after the council's first session, was *The Ecumenist*, a bi-monthly journal for promoting Christian unity, to be published by Paulist Press in collaboration with the Centre of Ecumenical Studies at St. Michael's College in Toronto. Designed to support and advance the ecumenical movement, it would be edited by Gregory Baum.[13]

One early newspaper's assessment of the council's first session was an editorial in Montreal's daily *Le Devoir* signed by Claude Ryan, who had been in Rome for the council's first month. He wrote:

> The council made possible a lively and free confrontation of the main lines of opinion in the church today. Lately, the discussion among the different schools of thought had been pursued in the calm and discretion of seminaries and scholasticates, theology faculties, scientific publications and Roman congregations. The official church maintained the stern and rather rigid image of a unity which outsiders too easily took to be monolithic. The bishops gathered in Rome have shown that they are not simply administrators, nor mere repeaters of directives received from the supreme authority of the pope, but rather apostles influenced by their surroundings and respective cultures, and very aware of modern currents of thought. Above all, they have given the world an unexpected picture of the great variety of views that are possible within the Catholic unity. The memory of this first session will have a profound influence for generations to come on the intellectual life and modes of action of authority in the church.... A second fact emerges from this first session: the ecumenical wind that blows in the church at present is stronger than even the most optimistic observers thought.[14]

From Montreal also come more troubling news. Léger had to spend the second week of 1963 in hospital. He was treated, his office said, for "a coronary insufficiency – a diminution of the flow of blood to the heart muscle...."[15] Léger returned to his residence the evening of 14 January. To those who knew how hard he had been working, his collapse came as no surprise. In the previous six months, he had developed his far-reaching critical analysis of the pre-council draft texts and written his September petition to John XXIII; he had addressed the council six times, while behind the scenes he also was one of the most active members of the theology commission, the centre of the most intense debates of the first session; and in the first session's last two weeks he more than doubled his work load after being named to the special mixed commission to rewrite the revelation text, with extra responsibility as chair of one of its sub-commissions.

Perhaps at no time during Vatican II did emotions run higher than at the five mixed commission meetings on the revelation text at the end of November and beginning of December 1962. One analyst of the record of those meetings said they were "violent discussions ... conflicts that left the participants bruised and exhausted."[16] After all that, Léger returned to Montreal for the usual swirl of pastoral ceremonies for Christmas and the start of the new year. One of his first public acts after leaving hospital was a message for church unity octave. An irreversible impulse has been given, he said, to all who desire Christian unity. "The events that have occurred in the past two years are a sign that the Spirit of Christ is working in our midst and is moving us more and more profoundly in our quest for unity. The unforgettable opening days of the first session of Second Vatican Council, the tone and direction of the discussions in the daily meetings of all the bishops, were a constant reminder of the ardent desire for unity which animates the entire church."[17] In less than a month Léger was back in Rome for meetings of the theology commission and the mixed commission on revelation. Once again he had to cope with two sets of important meetings over the period of a few days. The theology commission met on 21 February, and the mixed revelation commission on Saturday, 23 February, for the first time since December 1962.

Secret battles to promote texts

The period from the end of first session in December 1962 until the opening of the second in September 1963 is called the council's "second preparation." Only texts written during this period or later made it to the floor for study and debate during the council's later sessions. An Epiphany 1963 letter from John XXIII to the bishops launched the "second preparation." He stressed their duty "to propose, discuss and prepare new texts." This was his way of telling some curial officials that the texts they prepared before the council opened no longer had status; but the pope's letter did not end that debate. All 70 of the texts drafted before the council opened were eventually discarded.

The first eight months of 1963 therefore saw aggressive efforts by curial officials to retain the old texts that they had prepared, and complex but often uncoordinated work by other bishops and theologians who were trying to promote various new texts. None of these was drafted by a Canadian. In early 1963, only the Canadian bishops and theologians already named to the council's work commissions were caught up in the secret battles to promote this or that text and prepare it for debate. However, as this work continued into 1964, a team of theologians organized by Roy at Quebec became increasingly involved.

Work began during this period on what would become the *Pastoral Constitution on the Church in the Modern World*. During the first session between October and December 1962, no one saw clearly how the council should express the concerns of many bishops about world problems. Possible initiatives were discussed in the informal group of bishops that became known as "the Church of the Poor." Similarly, at meetings of representatives of bishops' conferences where Baudoux was prominent as president of the CCC, there were discussions about how to open the council's horizon to the modern world's problems. However, the path to follow began to emerge only during the intersession when "a new preparation of the council" began. The work was influenced by what Suenens and Montini proposed as the first session ended in December 1962. They said that the council should speak of the church's internal life (*ad intra*) and of its external relations (*ad extra*). During the intersession, the document on the nature of the church, discussed briefly at the end of the first session, took its own direction, eventually to be promulgated as the *Dogmatic Constitution on the Church*. It deals with the church *ad intra*. Meanwhile work began on a text specifically devoted to the church in the modern world, *ad extra*. As this topic made its way, from early 1963 to the last day of the council in December 1965, there would be growing Canadian involvement in the development of the text, as we shall see later.[18]

The seven cardinals of the central committee directed the agenda of the 1963 intersession. When they met in January, they listed 17 texts for continuing council work. A text on the church in the world was last on the list, so for months it was referred to only as "Schema 17." The texts on liturgy and the media, studied in the first session, were being prepared by their respective commissions for final voting during the coming session. All other texts, however, either were still being drafted or were the subjects of hot debates. This applied especially to three topics from the first session, on revelation, unity, and the nature of the church. The theology commission was at the centre of these debates, and so were its three Canadian members: Léger, Pelletier and Roy.

On 21 February, the full theology commission met for the first time in two and a half months. Besides taking up other major issues, it reviewed work on the revelation text that the council had sent in December to a mixed commission of members from the theology commission and the secretariat for unity. In the following days, Léger was involved in both the continuing agenda of the theology commission and renewed debates in the mixed revelation commission.

The mixed commission discussed the revelation text during four meetings from 23 February to 4 March. The work began with renewed debate over whether scripture and tradition could be considered as "two sources of revelation." Bea, head of the unity secretariat, was supported 28 to 8 when he proposed that the council did not need to settle a scripture and tradition question "that did not seem ripe" for settlement. At the next meeting on 28 February, Ottaviani, head of the theology commission, challenged that vote on the grounds that he was absent when it was taken. He also questioned Bea's fidelity to Catholic teaching on the matter. Léger is credited with an intervention that "calmed the turmoil of the majority," although he included a threat to appeal against Ottaviani to the central commission. At a third meeting on 1 March, Léger's formula to eliminate reference to the "two sources" was proposed for a vote by Bea and supported 30 to 7. The mixed commission's final meeting on 4 March ended further debate about revelation until the third session in 1964, when a new text would surface for study by the whole council.[19]

While the mixed commission was debating the revelation text, the full theology commission was also at work. On 5 March it took up the text on the nature of the church. The text on this subject that had been heavily criticized at the end of the first session had to be rewritten to prepare it for renewed debate during the second session. Meanwhile, regarding the church in the world, there soon was a growing list of new drafts on the new topic, some of them proposed by individual scholars and others sponsored by groups of bishops. The commission decided on a division of labour for work on the new topic. Pelletier was named a member of a mixed group formed by the theology and lay apostolate commissions. Its first attempts to draft chapters on anthropology and marriage were marked by very strong tensions. Two different ideas about how to proceed were once again in conflict. Some wanted to retain large parts of texts prepared before the council. Others wanted a completely new text. Franciscan Ermenegildo Lio, asked to write chapters on anthropology and marriage, tried to synthesize in them the corresponding preparatory texts. The bishops opposed this and asked Danielou and Labourdette for a new draft of the two chapters. Pelletier attended the 8 March meeting but he was not at meetings the following week. However he prepared and sent brief comments on the texts. He asked for clarifications and simplifications, and in some cases he seemed to espouse positions in opposition to the majority of the mixed commission. As an example, he found inappropriate a phrase saying parents had the right and duty to decide how many children to have.

The first full meeting of the mixed commission responsible for the text was held only in May. At that time, the commission divided into five sub-commissions to work on separate chapters. Pelletier, involved meantime in drafting the text on mixed marriages, was left off these sub-commissions. However Léger and Roy, also members of the theology commission, were named to sub-commissions working on the new text – Roy to the sub-commission on the person in society, and Léger to that on culture. At this stage, Roy's sub-commission was also responsible for the chapter on economic and social life. A major concern was to insert a declaration on rights and duties, following the model offered in *Pacem in Terris,* John XXIII's 11 April 1963 social encyclical. These subjects did not come to the fore in the council until the third session in 1964.

Léger also was named to a seven-member sub-commission that discussed the choice to be made among five texts on the church in the world. There was one by Bishop P. Parente from a curia viewpoint, a French text, one in German, Philips' text presenting work done under Suenens, and a long text from Chile. Only that of Philips had been circulated widely during the first session. Some accounts say that Léger, under the influence of his peritus, Pierre Lafortune, initially preferred the French text, but later he joined the majority group supporting the text by Philips.[20] Léger's main preoccupation was the chapter on marriage. On this topic, some strong tensions were already building, which broke out at the plenary commission meetings. In particular, two themes were discussed. One was the problem of the doctrine on the ends of marriage, according to which procreation was the first and constitutive end, and love a secondary end. The second question was the doctrine on birth control, then much discussed because arguments about the Ogino-Knauss "rhythm method" were being joined by arguments over drugs that could suspend human ovulation. A number of Catholic moralists were studying the possibility of approving the drugs on the basis of traditionally accepted moral criteria.

Léger, very concerned by the pastoral repercussions that problems of conjugal morality had in modern society, maintained that the council could not avoid this question and must stimulate a renewal of traditional teaching. He asked Belgian theologian Charles Moeller for some observations that he might use as basis for a strong intervention on this point at a plenary session of the commission. He said the traditional language of the doctrine of two ends should be abandoned. He argued "love cannot be called only a 'condition' for procreation. It is not a condition but the central reality which includes procreation...."[21] During the process of succeeding drafting steps, Léger took no further part in the work of sub-commissions. However, he made strong interventions on the topic during the council's third and fourth sessions.

Léger thus often opposed the positions of Roman theologians, Ottaviani foremost among them. They held out against the idea of considering love as constitutive of the conjugal bond in order not to open the way to any legitimation of divorce. As for birth control,

Léger affirmed that natural physical integrity could not be the only basis for deciding the morality of the conjugal act. His statement was met with various reactions in the commission, in particular from Ottaviani and Browne who, on several points, questioned how Léger's thought conformed to recent papal teaching. But other members agreed with Léger, especially members of the lay apostolate commission, alert to the pastoral needs of the people. In any event, this discussion was the first of the clashes that would recur during the long process of drafting the text, and Léger stoutly defended his ideas to the end. For that meeting early in 1963, they tried to find a compromise solution in the text which however left the question open to further developments. Paul VI later removed birth control from the council agenda, and Léger and others had to discuss marriage in more general terms.

Catholic Information Services

The quality of services at the council press office was the subject of the 2 February 1963 Réunion internationale des informateurs religieuses (RIIR) in Switzerland. To prepare for this meeting, representatives of the CCC Information Service and other similar church-sponsored news agencies were asked to write evaluations of the Vatican press office at the end of the first session. Canadian views were presented through reports written by Réjean Plamondon and me. He stressed the names of French journalists who had quit trying to report on the first session and gone home, frustrated by the Vatican secrecy rule. For my part, after listing some needs in the press office such as reference books and some typewriters with international keyboards and not just European models, I supported Plamondon's view that secrecy had cost the church a great opportunity for presenting itself to the world. I argued:

> First, the positive opportunity to use every aspect of the council for teaching about the church through the world press. With enough journalistic imagination, every single development can be presented in a positive way that leads to greater understanding. If, on the one hand, the "difficult" aspects of the council are meant to be kept "secret," the result is doubt, suspicion, ill will

and lack of interest on the part of the press. It seems certain that the explanations given by the unofficial U.S. panel about such things as the pope overriding a council vote [on revelation] contributed in large measure to the press understanding the proper role of the pope in the council as its president. Without it, there is no knowing how tendentious the reports might have been. But why couldn't this sort of thing have been done regularly and officially in the press office? This leads to questions about the whole policy of secrecy. If the explanations about divisions of opinion being normal and healthy are valid, then there is little point in trying to hide those divisions. The explanations are that the various opinions show the true diversity in unity, and so on. They prove, it is said, that the church is not a monolithic monster which suppresses all individuals into cruel conformity. If these explanations are valid, then why hide this "great truth" about the church? The non-Catholic observers, we are told, have been reassured by these divisions of opinion and the way they are resolved. They wish more people could see with them the true nature of the church. Catholic newspapermen, who envy the observers, wish the same thing. Surely there would be some way of picking "pools" of experienced reporters from each language group, to open up much more of the council – indeed, all of it. To argue against secrecy by saying it isn't kept in fact is not a strong point, but it deserves mention. But the real point is that secrecy results in a certain loss to the church, so that it hides its reality at a time when the world most needs to see it.[22]

We saw some influence of the Geneva press meeting when, at the July meeting of the council's co-ordinating committee in Rome, ways of improving press relations were discussed, leading to the establishment of a press committee, headed by Bishop M. O'Connor, to improve the efficiency of the council press office.

Council lobbying

An example of lobbying by and of the bishops, to promote or oppose a point of view, can be seen in an exchange between Gregory Baum and Archbishop Philip Pocock, starting with a 30 May 1963 letter from Baum to Pocock. At the time, the secretariat for Christian unity, where Baum was a consultor, was concerned about the survival of a text promoting better Christian-Jewish relations. Baum wrote:

> It would be useful to Cardinal Bea if you sent a letter to the Vatican secretary of state, and a copy to Cardinal Bea himself, on a possible declaration on the Jews. Here is a little draft: "I understand that the secretariat for promoting Christian unity has been commissioned to prepare a statement on the Catholic attitude towards the Jews. I consider it of great importance that the council, which intends to be a council for all men, makes a clear statement on our relation to the house of Jacob, condemning hatred and discrimination against Jews and asserting authoritatively that the Jews are neither 'a deicide people' nor 'an accursed people.' The crucifixion of our Lord is a crime in which, according to the Catechism of the Council of Trent, all men are involved through their grave sins. While we should be outspoken in this matter, we should also make it clear that our statement has nothing to do with politics. We should avoid words that could be interpreted as referring to any present political community.[23]

Pocock's files show that his response carried over into the next year, including a 24 January 1964 letter to Cardinal Cicognani, Vatican secretary of state and chair of the council's powerful central committee. Pocock said he was writing in his own name and on behalf of Toronto's auxiliary bishops, Francis V. Allen and Francis A. Marrocco, about what was then the ecumenism text's fourth chapter, dealing with Catholic attitudes towards non-Christians and especially towards Jewish people. "We wish to express our profound belief that the statement on the attitude of the church towards Jews should not be dropped from the agenda of the third session of the council. Although it would no doubt be prudent to extend the chapter to include other major non-Christian groups, we are convinced that the omission of reference to the Jews during the third session of the council would be interpreted as a victory for anti-semitism."[24] On the same date Pocock also sent Cicognani a text about religious freedom. Pocock wrote: "The enclosed intervention in support of the Schema "De Ecumenismo," Chapter V, although prepared during the last month of Session II of the council, was never delivered. Since it was approved by 38 Canadian bishops, I thought it opportune to send it to Your Eminence, so that our convictions concerning the importance of the chapter on religious freedom might be made known."[25]

An example of the many turns taken by council events is a 26 May 1964 letter from Baum to Pocock:

> I have just heard from the Secretariat for Unity that the chapter on the Jews has *not* been handed over to the new secretariat on world religions. However, superior powers have made considerable changes in the chapter and at the moment the document is out of the hands of Cardinal Bea's office. It seems that Pope Paul has not yet given his approval of the corrected text. It may be better if you do not write to Rome on this matter at the moment. There may be other developments in the near future. You will permit me to approach you again as soon as I get more news from Cardinal Bea's office.[26]

Canadian special advisors

During April and May of 1963, the bishops were sent a first set of texts for study in preparation for the council's second session. They dealt with seminaries, Catholic schools, priests, the lay apostolate, bishops and dioceses, pastoral practice for the care of souls, religious, the eastern churches, revelation, the church, and ecumenism. Bishops were asked to send comments during July. At the end of July, texts were sent on the sacrament of marriage, and two more chapters on the church. Then, after meetings of the central commission at the end of August, the agenda for the second session was set. Discussions would take up four chapters on the church and texts on the Blessed Virgin, bishops, the lay apostolate, and ecumenism.

To help them with this work, and prompted by their experiences during the first council session, the Canadian bishops decided early in 1963 to organize a team of special advisors. The CCC named Bishops A. Carter of Sault Ste. Marie and Charbonneau of Hull to organize and direct the group, who included specialists in theology, scripture, church history, canon law and related subjects. They met in Ottawa in July and September to discuss texts that would be debated during the council's second session. One account of their July meeting in Ottawa is a 10 July letter from Baum to Pocock:

The meeting of the team of theologians appointed by the Canadian bishops was useful, enjoyable, and has produced many fruits. We came from all parts of Canada, from different schools and seminaries, and yet the friendship and general unanimity was remarkable. We worked hard and enjoyed it. We were told by Bishops A. Carter and Charbonneau that this team might be called again, even after the council, and we all feel that this would greatly encourage theological life in Canada, stimulate research in practical areas, and make the ideas of council and hierarchy more readily available in the various Canadian cities. We have divided into smaller groups, each one studying a few of the conciliar documents and then presenting a report to the plenary meeting. The plenary meeting discussed these reports and in general expressed its approval. Then each group was responsible for writing up its report for the bishops. I believe that you will soon receive the copies from Ottawa. We hope that they will be of some use to you and the other bishops of Canada. The reason why I write you these details, I imagine, is that I was really delighted with the meeting and its spirit. Though we had to hurry up and work from morning to late in the evening, it was a spiritual experience for all of us.[27]

When these specialists met for a second time in Ottawa in September, Baudoux as CCC president joined them, along with A. Carter and Charbonneau. Baudoux remarked that the bishops went to the first council session with an understanding of the needs of the Canadian church, and were preparing to return for a second session with a better understanding of the needs of the entire church. "The bishops were conscious of the gravity of the problems involved here, because these are basic questions concerning the church," he explained. "This is why they brought together these specialists, in order that the bishops may be in contact with the thinking of priests and people of Canada."[28]

This Canadian group continued work in Rome later in 1963. Only some members of the original team were able to come to Rome, where they have been joined by a number of Canadian priests already working in Rome.[29] Listed for the team in Rome were Lucien Foucreault of St. Jean, Quebec; Bernard Morisset of Quebec City; Antoine Hacault of St. Boniface; Gregory Baum; Marcel Bélanger, vice rector of the University of Ottawa; Léo

Laberge of Ottawa, who was also serving as a secretary of the council's theological commission; Jacques Gervais of Ottawa; Michael Hrynchyshyn of the Ukrainian archdiocese of Winnipeg; Jean-Marie Tillard of Ottawa; and Rev. Bernard Lambert of the Dominicans' Montmorency House near Quebec City. Other members of the team were Jesuits Roderick A. Mackenzie, a Canadian scriptural specialist who came from Toronto during the summer of 1963 to become rector of the Pontifical Biblical Institute, and Bernard Lonergan, a Canadian who was a professor at the Gregorian University.

The team was to be available for consultations and discussions on questions on the documents being discussed in the council. Tillard probably was the most visible member of the team, day by day in Rome. Baum's work was mainly done within the unity secretariat, and Lambert's role in drafting a chapter of the text on the church in the world would not be widely known until long after the council. Tillard, however, was active around the Canadian council secretariat, as a lecturer and drafter of interventions for Canadian bishops.[30]

Catholic-Protestant dialogue

While some Canadian bishops traveled to meetings in Rome in the spring and summer of 1963, others continued to implement the first fruits of Vatican II at home. In March, Edward Garvey, a Basilian priest, was named chair of a committee of priests and laymen set up to foster Christian unity within the Catholic archdiocese of Vancouver. "It is wonderful to see in our times what a change has taken place in the Christian world, now thoroughly convinced that Christian unity is possible," Archbishop Duke said in a Lenten pastoral letter.[31] On the other side of the country, J.M. O'Neill, bishop of Harbour Grace, Newfoundland, said in a pastoral letter for Lent that the next council session "may be expected to result in decisions which will have far-reaching effects on the lives of all Catholics, in fact on the lives of all Christians." He foresaw "a renewed fervor, a greater participation in the liturgy by the laity, and a better understanding of the teachings and practice of the church."[32] About the same time in Toronto, F.H. Littell, a Methodist professor of church history from Chicago, told clerics and laymen at a second annual dinner sponsored by a committee of Catholic laymen in co-operation with the Canadian Council of Christians and Jews, that "the most wonderful thing regarding the times in which we live is the double dialogue of Protestants and Catholics, Christians and Jews."[33] Meanwhile, in North Bay, Bishop Alexander Carter marked a religious "first" when he addressed 160 members of the men's club in Trinity United Church.

Media interest in the council continued to be high. CFRB radio in Toronto presented two special programs on Catholic–Protestant dialogue 28 April and 5 May.[34] Also in May, Vancouver Catholic and Anglican clergy attend a three-day symposium on Christian unity. First of its kind in the city, it was jointly sponsored by the alumni of the Anglican Theological College and the newly formed Catholic diocesan committee for Christian unity. They discussed three major topics – the pope, the mass and the Blessed Virgin.[35] Alex Carter, bishop of Sault Ste. Marie, summed up the 1963 springtime mood of Canadian Catholics when he remarked "it seems evident from events that there has been a kind of prophetic impulsion of the Spirit to adapt the church to the exigencies of a new world.... A new style of Christian is emerging for a new kind of world." [36] However, when he spoke the shock of John XXIII's death was still to come, and the uncertainties of three more sessions of hard work at the council.

Even if the bishops were worried about John XXIII's health in December 1962 when he closed the first session, they did not realize he would never meet them again. He died 3 June 1963. Legally, the council ended that day; but Paul VI, elected on 21 June, announced immediately that it would continue. For preparations for the second session, then, the transition from John XXIII to Paul VI was an interruption that was not particularly disruptive. Originally, during the first session, it had been thought the meetings would resume in May 1963. Next, a break in the work was planned from 8 December 1962 to 8 September 1963, with John XXIII hoping the council could end by Christmas 1963. Paul VI set the opening of the second session for 29 September.

One of the improvements in the council press office for the second session was the appointment of knowledgeable priests to brief journalists after each day's working session. Edward Heston, an American Holy Cross priest, briefed those working in English. Heston was always willing to discuss much more than the prepared notes in his hand. In a letter home during the 1964 session, I wrote:

> Fr. Heston, head of the English language section [of the press office], came up with an interesting point yesterday chatting with us. During the summer he had occasion to compare the English text of Pope Paul's talk at the close of the session with the Italian of same. He found the English "so bad as to be actually unfaithful in parts." The problem, he says, is that the original is Italian, translated into Latin for an "official" text, with the Latin then used for English and other modern-language versions. This means a risk of vagueness, imprecision and so on. He said *Pacem in Terris* was done in English from Italian; hence its strength. But Paul's first encyclical was "Englished" from Latin out of the original Italian. According to Fr. Heston, the "return to the fold" idea in the English, so annoying to the other brethren, appears only once in the Italian. Seems it crept more into the Latin and then the English. A technical problem, if you like, and hardly to be settled in a personal letter, but it is part of our life here, so you might as well know about it too. Another reason [a nudge aimed at our children] for trying to be a linguist.

4

The Second Session: 1963

The high drama of the first session of Vatican II was about faith. During the second, it would be about authority and power. The council's opening debate about the liturgy, about how the church worships, had been intense enough, but for all the bishops the high point of the 1962 session centred on the faith issues raised by the text about revelation, the second major topic. What is the source of Christian faith? How do people today understand the ancient written accounts that make up holy scripture? How do the scriptures relate to Christian traditions developed over the centuries? How do the experiences of the apostles with the living Jesus relate to Christian experiences today? Such faith questions were still around when the 1963 session opened under Paul VI. The text on revelation would come back for more debate. However, during the second session the main questions were about authority and power in the church. How does the church understand itself, and how does it organize its life and work in the light of that understanding? Who can claim membership, and how does the church relate to non-members? What is its mission, and how does it pursue that mission? How should decisions about church life be made, and who has the final word? With branches all over the world, how should the centre relate to far-flung parts at the periphery? In Christ's mind when he left them, where did Peter stand with the other apostles – a question with far-reaching contemporary significance for all who believe the pope represents Peter and the bishops other apostles?

Questions such as these were on the minds of the 77 Canadian bishops scattered in 18 different residences in Rome as the second session opened on 29 September 1963. They were starting work with a two-room office in the Canadian College. For the second session, it was headed by Raymond Limoges, the French general secretary from the bishops' CCC secretariat in Ottawa. He replaced the cohort of priests pressed into part-time service when the office was hastily improvised as the first session opened. At mid-point in the second session, Limoges was joined by John Carley, his English counterpart, so both general secretaries from Ottawa would be in Rome for the CCC annual plenary meeting to be held later in two afternoon sessions. Carley would then remain until the session's end. The board of the CCC met at the Canadian College during the first week of October under chairman Baudoux to plan their annual meeting.

Secrecy "always and everywhere"

The council began its second session with study of the nature of the church. This was followed, early in November, by texts dealing with the mission and work of bishops. These topics clearly dealt with various aspects of authority in the church. They were followed, from 18 November until the council closed on 2 December, by debates about ecumenism. An important new feature of the new session was a new information policy. Priests authorized to be present for the daily debates came out at noon, at the end of each day's plenary meeting, to give oral briefings to media people, grouped according to the major languages. American Edward Heston did this for those who worked in English. He identified each speaker in order and gave a short summary of what he said. These notes later were printed and became that day's official council press release. Although not intended for the bishops, the releases were avidly sought by many of them as an informal "Hansard." The bishops received no minutes or other daily record of proceedings, so the press releases helped them check their understanding of what had been said in sometimes hard-to-grasp Latin. For the press corps, the new system was a great advance from first-session releases which at first did not identify speakers and said only that "some speakers tended to this view, and others to that...." Despite the new press briefings, the official policy of secrecy "always and everywhere" was reasserted, especially for the work in commissions. Felici, the council general secretary, frequently warned bishops, and especially the authorized theologians, to avoid giving interviews.

The positions taken by Léger and other Canadians during the second session cannot be understood if the council's political realities are ignored. Felici as general secretary and some other council officials often chastised journalists for using political language, but after the first session's debates and votes on liturgy and revelation it was undeniable that the bishops divided as a clear and constant majority and minority, whatever one called each group. Some Vatican officials, bishops and theologians, were leaders of like-minded bishops from many countries who made up the minority. In the words of an Italian writer at the time, the general aim of this group was "to prevent any lessening of papal prerogatives; to avoid a reform of the curia itself by the council; to check the increase of the bishops' powers; to resist meddling of the laity; to moderate and apply gradually reforms of any kind."[1] A later historian added that

> a complementary aspect of their program was an extreme 'papalism' that found expression in an intransigent defense of what they called the rights or intangible privileges of the Holy See, which in many cases were simply the rights and privileges of the curia. Thus, in the discussion of the liturgical schema, they rejected anything that might be interpreted as the council telling the Holy See what to do. For this reason, the greatest of errors, in their view, was the claim of episcopal collegiality, which they saw as an attack on the authority of the curia. During the debate on the schema on the church, (Cardinal) Browne maintained that if collegiality gave the bishops the right to share in the government of the church, the pope would be obliged to respect it and therefore would no longer have a real primacy over the entire church.[2]

Nature of church

The second session opened with study of the new text on the church that worried Cardinal Browne. An earlier draft had been heavily criticized as the first session ended in December 1962. Two major developments occurred during the intersession period. One was John XXIII's death and Paul VI's succession during June 1963. The other was the intense work in council commissions during the spring and summer to prepare new texts. By the time the first session ended, it was clear that the majority of the bishops wanted to set aside all 70 of the texts that had been prepared before the council opened. The drafters of the new text on the church that opened the second session had worked with knowledge of what elements had been criticized in the old text. They also received a number of suggested new versions from which to choose ideas. The text that opened the second session was therefore entirely new in content and format. It had four chapters, dealing with the mystery of the church, its hierarchic constitution, the people of God and the laity, and the call to holiness in the church. (There are eight chapters in the final version.)

Hermaniuk (1 October) was the first Canadian to speak as debate resumed. He gave a Ukrainian Catholic view of the church. He said he liked the new draft, its scriptural content, frequent use of eastern traditions, the stress on the collegiality of bishops and its ecumenical spirit. However, it was silent about the actual authority of the college of bishops over the universal church. The two-fold authority – that of the pope alone, and that of all the bishops with the pope – should be expressed in a kind of "apostolic college," he urged. Hermaniuk was returning to a suggestion he had made, without getting much support, at a meeting of the preparatory theology commission in March 1962. He stressed the importance of having the college of bishops fully involved with the pope in leading the church. In the church there is universal authority with a double aspect, he argued. That authority is given to all the apostles with Peter (Mt. 28, 18-20), and to Peter alone (Mt. 16, 18-19) – the same power, given in a double way and therefore to be exercised in a double way. He was convinced that this reality should be given a definite institutional form. He proposed that this would best be done if a representative group of bishops met regularly with and under the pope as a permanent body to discuss and decide on policies and programs. Its members would be the patriarchs, the cardinals who head dioceses and other diocesan archbishops and bishops, to be selected by some future norms, and perhaps elected by national conferences of bishops. This new body would have two secretariats, for the eastern and western churches.

The offices of the Vatican curia would have an executive role, and no longer one of decision-making. The new body would emphasize, he said, that the universal jurisdiction of bishops as successors to the apostles is not limited to an infrequent ecumenical council. During the rest of the council, a number of other eastern-rite bishops and others made similar proposals for a new structure to give bishops from dioceses scattered around the world some direct share in decision-making at the centre. One outcome of this debate can be seen in the council's *Dogmatic Constitution on the Church*. It says the pope "has full, supreme and universal power over the whole church." It adds "together with their head, the Supreme Pontiff, and never apart from him, they (the bishops) have supreme and full authority over the universal church" (*Lumen Gentium*, 22). However, the council itself did not indicate how this double reality of authority would be expressed in institutional form. (The synod of bishops, announced by Paul VI as the fourth session began in 1965, is to some extent the kind of institution Hermaniuk and others had in mind. However, the synod can only advise the pope and has no authority to make decisions. Its agenda, procedures and results are controlled by the pope and Vatican offices behind a veil of secrecy. It is called the synod of bishops but is really a papal synod.)

Referring to the possibility of diversity within the church, Hermaniuk proposed that the text should state clearly that union of Christians in the Holy Spirit did not destroy other unions, such as families, cities and nations. The church is not a kind of super state aiming to absorb all natural unions, he said. Touching on an aspect of eastern concern about excessive "latinization" of church affairs, he said he preferred terms like "pastor of the universal church" or "supreme pontiff" instead of "Roman pontiff" where the text referred to the pope. In a long interview at that time, Hermaniuk told me that a new body like the one he proposed would involve vast changes in canon law and in the practical working of the church. However, he was certain it would neither diminish the authority of the pope as head of the church nor involve the risk of fragmenting church unity. The "apostolic council" would represent in a practical way the responsibilities of all the bishops under the supervision of the pope. The collegial power of the entire episcopate would be real, exercised concretely. It would be seen and understood by people as an actual, present reality, not a kind of formula on paper. Such a body would express what Hermaniuk considered to be the true nature of the church's universal authority as recorded in scripture. Hermaniuk cited the ecumenical councils of Nicea, Constantinople and Calcedon to recall that the early church organized and presented this universal power in the form of five patriarchates. First among them was the patriarchate of Rome, with the pope as its head; and, after Rome, Constantinople, Alexandria, Antioch and Jerusalem. All five represented the complete episcopate, and through them the college of all the bishops participated in the administration of the church. This particular pattern of authority was eroded by quarrels, climaxing with the great east-west schism of the middle of the eleventh century.

After that separation, the patriarchate of Rome, being alone, and being the true church, developed a marvellous missionary action that converted practically all Europe and much of the rest of the world to the Catholic church. Power became concentrated in this one patriarch. For Hermaniuk, Vatican II, the most ecumenical of councils, was trying to find once more the church's universal unity and how to apply it in the situation of today. He said: "We try to come back to this first and biblical formula, having a double aspect for the universal power of the church – the power of Peter as head of the apostles, and the power of the apostles with Peter but always under the supreme authority of Peter." The church's present way of doing things was, he thought, a carryover, admirable in itself, from the days when the church was concentrated in Catholic Europe, which was more or less a social and political unit. Then, general universal laws could readily be applied, and they still might be applicable in some areas. "But not any more in Japan, China, the Ukraine, Poland, Africa, Russia, where the church says we want something else because we need something else. And we need it in the name of the gospel," he argued. In recent years there had been a tremendous evolution of the church's practical aspects, Hermaniuk noted. "If we really want the church to be present – not present abstractly but by the reality of its life in life everywhere – I think the works of the church should come from everywhere, from all parts of the world.... In such a case, the laws and practices of the church would be less static. There would be a code of canon law, but it would be interpreted in the light of the church's varying needs in the different countries."

As a twentieth century member of the ancient eastern church, Hermaniuk lived with the inherent realization that some day the universal unity of the church would have to be restored. Because it started that way, it should be again that way, but there was the question of how to do it. As I quoted him at that time: "Our Lord said to all the apostles, go and preach to all the nations, and so every bishop, as successor of the apostles, is not only bishop of his own diocese but must go and preach to all nations. How, I used to ask myself, how can I think of this duty of mine in the world?" Through the experience of being a member of the Canadian conference of bishops, he saw how he and every other Canadian bishop could share concern for the whole of the church in one country. If, then, the bishops of the world first joined in national or regional conferences, and each of these in turn sent a representative to an apostolic council to join the Pope in decision-making for the whole church, the church's universal unity would have concrete expression and her universal mission would have direct, practical impact. All would still be under the supervision and final authority of the pope, who could act independently of any council decisions he did not favour. In reaching his own decision, however, the pope would have the advantage of knowing how all the assembled bishops understood the situation and what they thought should be done. And just as Peter's authority was not diminished by Paul's disagreement with him on the matter of admitting Gentiles into the church, so, in Hermaniuk's opinion, there would be no danger for the church in the variety of views that would be brought to such an apostolic council. Rather, these would be a tremendous help for the church.[3]

On 4 October, three days after Hermaniuk had spoken, Baudoux made his second council speech. He regretted that the text on the church was silent about relations with non-Catholic churches and communities. It gave the impression that the council was interested in other Christians only as individuals. The Catholic church sees herself as the only true church. However, there are other Christian communities that preach the gospel of Christ, announce the kingdom of God, have baptism and other sacraments, and are sources of holiness and salvation, he said. The Catholic church therefore should recognize "openly and with joy" that God works in this way in the separated churches. On another point, Baudoux observed that if the Catholic church is truly holy in herself, she should not be afraid to admit the faults of church members arising from their earthly situations. "We must be ready," he said, "to acknowledge that many sad events in the history of the church have been due to the failings of its members." This, he added, is a condition for understanding certain historical facts, which unhappily have been the cause of schisms, divisions and decreases in faith. God knows how to use these calamities to chastise or purify his people, he stressed. This positive aspect of divisions among Christians should be clearly recognized so that all Christians could understand better that the ills afflicting the church are usually the fruit of infidelity.

When Léger entered the debate on 7 October, two main positions had emerged regarding bishops and their relation to the pope. Just as a deep and sharp division emerged during the first session over revelation, two sides were forming in the second session over the question of authority in the church. A majority clearly wanted the text to say that all bishops as a "college" share authority with the pope, in a way the council should define. Their view was summed up by the term "collegiality." Once again, however, some officials of Vatican offices led a determined opposition. They saw clearly that any organizational change to give bishops collectively a greater role in making decisions would also change how the Vatican bureaucracy operated. So long as the pope alone was seen as the only authority, Vatican officials serving him could claim, as they did, to share in his authority in dealing with individual bishops and all church affairs. But where would they stand if all the bishops were given a defined share in papal authority?

The two main positions in the collegiality debate had their roots in Vatican I nearly a century earlier. For some, Vatican I had clearly defined papal primacy, and any Vatican II emphasis on the authority of bishops might weaken or contradict that teaching. Others held that the interrupted Vatican I had been unable to take up and complete the second half of the question, the role of bishops, and that Vatican II must now do that. In support of the second view, Léger said there should be no fear about expressing in a new way the traditional teaching about bishops. He recalled that Paul VI in his opening address a few days earlier said that the mystery of the church was such that it always allowed for new investigations of its nature. The church's teaching on papal primacy would be enhanced, not weakened, by recognition of the real character of bishops. The more bishops acted collegially, the more the papacy would be seen as a necessary guardian and centre of unity. It would be opportune, Léger added, to affirm that the episcopal college was built up by episcopal consecration. Noting that the text did a good job of presenting the bishop's mission as primarily one of service, Léger urged that a "spirit of humble service and evangelical poverty" should be more evident in a bishop's daily relations with church members and with the world. Certain insignia, ornaments and titles had perhaps seemed necessary when some bishops were also temporal princes, but a contemporary study should be made and rules laid down about titles or other customs that had become obstacles to pastoral ministry. "We should emphasize the presence of Christ in the church and the special dignity of bishops as mirrors, signs and living sacraments of Christ," Léger said. The council text, he thought, did not show clearly enough the links between the bishop and Christ.

By this time, after some 10 days of speeches favouring one side or the other in the collegiality debate, the four moderators who directed daily proceedings decided to get a reading on how to proceed. The moderators – Agagianian, Doepfner, Lercaro and Suenens – had been chosen by the new pope as his legates to give the council a more focused leadership than it had during the first session. In consultation with Paul VI, the moderators therefore decided on a new procedure. They hoped it would help the commission responsible for redrafting the text to sort out the sharply divided opinions. The moderators announced that five "trend" votes would be taken. They would deal with the idea of collegiality, whether bishops as successors of the apostles formed a college, whether that college was of divine origin, how it related to the primacy of the pope, and whether the diaconate should be restored as a permanent order in the church. Central to the fifth question was the issue of ordaining married men to be permanent deacons. These would not be final votes to end the debate, the moderators stressed, but would indicate trends and help the drafters to make decisions about the many oral and written suggestions being made.

The announcement that these "straw" votes would be taken was followed by one of the most controversial developments of the entire council. The complexity of the council's leadership provides some explanation for what happened. It was noted at the time that, besides the pope who had ultimate authority, "the council had four bodies of authority ... to which [dissatisfied bishops] could appeal – the four moderators, the twelve-man presidency, the ten-man coordinating committee and the six-man secretariat. Which body took precedence? The rules of the council did not make this clear."[4] After the four moderators decided that the trend votes would be taken, they directed that ballots be prepared. There was intense debate behind the scenes about the ballots, lest the wording should tip the vote in favour of one side. The moderators announced on 15 October that the ballots would be distributed the next day for a vote on 17 October, but opponents to the very idea of trend votes continued their efforts. Acting apparently on his own great authority, Cardinal Cicognani, head of the council's coordinating committee and Vatican number two man as secretary of state, ordered the ballots to be destroyed the evening of 15 October.

The next day, the bishops were simply informed that the trend votes had been delayed. Debate on the text about the church continued. One question on the floor was whether the council should issue a separate statement about Mary, or whether the description of her role should be handled as one chapter in the document on the church, the current agenda topic. As this debate continued during the following days, most bishops had only media reports to inform them about the behind-the-scenes maneuvering over the trend votes, so tension mounted. Until Paul VI's personal archives for the council period are released, there will be some doubt about just how the crisis was resolved. The next major public event in the procession of events was the adjournment of debate on 28 October so the bishops could participate in a public mass to mark the fourth anniversary of John XXIII's election. Paul VI chose Suenens, one of the four moderators, to give the homily honouring John XXIII. In eloquent French, better understood by all than the usual Latin of council debates, Suenens recalled and praised John XXIII's vision for church renewal through the council. His homily was interrupted by applause three times and there was more hand clapping when he concluded and was embraced by the pope. The next day, when council work resumed, a narrow vote of 1114 to 1074 directed that the statement on the Blessed Virgin should be a chapter in the document on the church. Then, on 30 October, the five trend votes finally were taken. The results overwhelmingly guided the drafters to favour and develop the concept that the bishops as a college share authority with the pope. Only the idea of ordaining married men to be permanent deacons received a substantial, but not fatal, negative vote. Collegiality and the diaconate therefore moved forward, for more debate later, and eventual final votes.

Praying with the bishops

The first ballots for the trend votes were secretly destroyed the evening of 15 October, but that day began with a great personal privilege for some of us in the council media corps. For the first time in the second session some journalists were admitted at the beginning of the daily assembly to be present at the mass and opening ceremony. Réjean Plamondon and I obtained tickets for the CCC Information Service. I wrote at the time:

> *A religious experience could scarcely have more emotional overtones, more personal impact for a Catholic layman. St. Peter's that morning had the quiet calm of a parish church, in marked contrast to the jostling and uproar of great ceremonial occasions. The only sound half an hour before mass began at nine o'clock was the muffled scuffle of heels on marble, as fathers of the council, observers, and authorized officials entered singly or in quiet groups. Shoes on marble paving: shoes with silver buckles; stout black oxfords; worn*

shoes, too, indicating unspoken privation. For many, the first minutes were spent in prayer, kneeling before the tabernacle in the chapel in the left transept of the basilica. As some departed others arrived, the crowd before the blessed sacrament never numbering fewer than about 100, until a bell announced that mass would soon begin. For many, the path from chapel to their seats led by way of the papal altar, where they knelt again to pray above the tomb of St. Peter. Above, too, the new tomb of John XXIII, surrounded by flowers in the crypt below the basilica. Beside the chapel, a number of confessionals, Roman style, with the confessor in each seated behind the door of the enclosed centre section and the penitents shadowy figures kneeling at slide openings on either side. The penitents that morning, at times lined up like well-behaved altar boys, were fathers of the council from around the globe, availing themselves of the gifts of this sacrament of mercy, of which all mankind has need.

Bishops of the Latin rite in purple choir robes; eastern-rite bishops in black, red-bordered robes with black pot hats and short black veils hanging down their backs; bishops of the Franciscan order, in grey episcopal robes; priests who are council experts, in simple black soutanes: steadily they filed in. Some walked slowly alone, praying the hours of divine office from their breviaries; others carried council documents with the air of men off to the office. One of the busiest among them, Cardinal Suenens of Malines-Brussels, moderator of the assembly that day, moved about, speaking now to one, now to another.

About twenty minutes before nine, a low murmur of voices became audible, as the crowd increased on the long floor between the rows of benches, a mass of purple to the eye. A bell sounded, and a wave of colour surged up each row of seats, as council fathers climbed to their places from the centre aisle where they had been chatting. Another bell, and the Auxiliary Bishop of Toledo, Spain, entered in simple procession to celebrate the mass. That morning, mass was in the Mazarabic rite, better known as the ancient Spanish, or Hispano-Visigothic liturgy, developed and perfected during the sixth and seventh centuries. The great Spanish prelates of that period were the authors of most of the texts, marked by sentiment and emotion, in Latin, with chant and music of a tonal quality quite distinct from the more familiar Gregorian modes of the Latin rite. On the feast of the Spanish mystic, St. Teresa of Avila, mass in the rite that was the common liturgical practice of Christians in Spain until the end of the eleventh century. After that it was suppressed in the desire for uniformity following upon the reforms of Pope Gregory VII, and only after four centuries re-established on an exclusively local basis in the Corpus Christi chapel of the cathedral of Toledo. Now it was in St. Peter's.

Showing the diversity that is possible in unity, it was a "different" mass. For students of the Pontifical Spanish College in Rome who had sung at the mass, for a number of the 13 lay auditors admitted daily to the council session, and for 11 of the Catholics among the 100 press representatives admitted for that morning alone, the tremendous opportunity to participate fully by approaching the altar to receive communion as 2,200 fathers of the council knelt in prayerful concentration around it. The mass ended, the altar was stripped, two clerics placed on it the "throne" for the book of the gospels, which was carried in solemn procession to the altar by the bishop of Zamora in Spain, while the choir sang. Then, in powerful unison, the fathers of the council recited the council prayer, Ad Sumus; the secretary-general of the council, Archbishop Pericles Felici, called out, "Exeunt Omnes"; and "all unauthorized persons" obeyed the command to leave, not without backward glances intended to prolong the wonder."[5]

All called to holiness

The day that the trend votes were taken (30 October), Léger again entered the debate about the nature of the church. The specific topic was the way members of the church are called to holiness. The way monks lived had long been held up as the model for all Christians seeking holiness. To be sure, untold benefits came to the church from monastic life, but the ideal for monks did not suit ordinary priests or the laity. Holiness seemed unattainable by laity because their lives are so different from those of monks and religious. Léger regretted that marriage was the only aspect of lay life specifically mentioned. Holiness for laity, he said, had to be shown to all ages, including those not yet married and those who never would marry. And holiness should be shown to extend to all sectors of lay life – daily work, politics, cultural activities, leisure and recreation. When speaking to Christians about holiness, let it be with the full spirituality of Christ's sermon on the mount, Léger urged. Thus, holiness for laity would no longer be thought to be tied to the so-called evangelic counsels, poverty, chastity and obedience, as these are practised in religious life. Faith and hope also had to be mentioned, and justice, humility, gentleness, mercy. To develop a spirituality truly adapted to laity, more lay people would have to participate in the intellectual life of the church, he added. Research into such matters, particularly "the theology of terrestrial realities," would make great progress if lay people were invited to teach in faculties of religious science and in seminaries. The life of a religious and other types of consecrated life are of great interest to the church, Léger added, and the theology that is basic to such a life should be clearly set out. He suggested that a return to sources is the heart and centre of all theological renewal. To renew the theology of consecrated life, scripture and tradition must be studied better. As for many expressions used habitually for those who take the three vows – "those who live in the state of perfection," "those called to the evangelic counsels," "those who are pledged to the imitation of Christ" – such terms appear irreconcilable with the very important affirmation in the text. It said that all are called to perfection, to holiness and to the imitation of Christ by their baptismal consecration and profession of faith.

Bishops visit graves

While Canadians at home were observing the 1963 remembrance day, three former Canadian army chaplains, then taking part in the council, traveled out of Rome to offer mass for the dead at a soldiers' cemetery near Cortona, Italy. There are 1,700 Canadian graves at the Moro River cemetery that was visited by Archbishop Roy of

Quebec, Archbishop O'Neill of Regina, and Auxiliary Bishop Wilhelm of Calgary. All three had connections as chaplains with the troops who died 20 years earlier in the December 1943 fighting at the Moro River, and whose bodies were later moved from temporary field graves to a cemetery on a promontory overlooking the Adriatic Sea. The chapel at the cemetery was dedicated in 1950 by Cardinal McGuigan of Toronto. The then Archbishop Léger had attended that ceremony, one week after his own ordination as bishop.

Canadian council observers

During the second session, two Canadians joined the ranks of the official non-Catholic observers, and participated in the last three council sessions. Eugene Fairweather, as a leading Toronto Anglican theologian, not only attended the council but also had a long post-council involvement as a member of the Anglican-Roman Catholic International Commission (ARCIC). Richard H. Davidson came to Vatican II as a prominent Toronto United Church pastor and continued that work after the council. According to one writer, "During the first session (1962) the number of non-Catholic observers reached 54 (among them eight guests); at the second (1963), the number rose to 68 (including nine guests); at the third (1964) to 82 (with 13 guests); and the fourth (1965) to 106 (of whom 16 were guests. Altogether there were present at Vatican II, for one or more sessions, 192 non-Catholic observers or guests."[6] One guest during the second session was Charles R. Plaskett, then minister at St. Andrew's church in Chatham, Ontario. Promotion of church unity and Christian fellowship cannot be left to the church hierarchies but must become the concern of local priests and ministers and people, he said in an interview summing up his visit.

Plaskett headed for home saying he was confirmed in his mission of promoting Christian understanding. He came to the council in a personal capacity, on short leave from his parish, but said he intended to make a first-hand report in Toronto to James R. Mutchmore, moderator of the United Church of Canada. He was also scheduled for a number of speaking engagements before

Presbyterian and Catholic groups in western Ontario in coming weeks. Plaskett was in the council for two days as a special guest of the secretariat for promoting Christian unity. He said he had been very impressed by the friendliness of Vatican authorities, and by their willingness to "do as much as they could to make my visit a significant one." Working with Msgr. John Ewen, pastor of Blessed Sacrament in Chatham, he had been able to arrange through Bishop Cody of London and the Apostolic Delegate to Canada, Sebastiano Baggio, to see the council at work. He was impressed by the freedom and frankness of the discussions, and by the freedom with which official non-Catholic observers gave their views to the council at special meetings, one of which he attended. At the time, when there was some concern around the council about a procedural delay, Plaskett said he was impressed to hear an American Methodist observer explaining that he thought the delays necessary because the council needed time to mature.[7]

Anglican greetings

At about the time of Plaskett's visit, Canadian bishops at the council received greetings and assurances of prayers from Anglicans in Canada. A resolution passed 11 October in Banff at a meeting of the executive council of the general synod of the Anglican Church of Canada offered greetings and good wishes. The motion added "the assurance of our prayers that God will use this council for the increase of brotherhood and unity among Christendom. We further assure the Roman Catholic bishops of Canada of our pleasure at the dialogue now in progress in many parts of Canada between Roman Catholics and Anglicans, and look forward to an increase in understanding and mutual trust between our churches; and pray for the union of all who love and serve our Lord and Saviour." Notice of the resolution was contained in a letter to Baudoux as chair of the CCC board, from the general secretary of the Anglican synod, Archdeacon Edward H. Maddocks of Toronto. The letter was delivered in person to Baudoux in Rome by G. W. B Wheeler, a Toronto Anglican pastor, who came to Rome as special events editor of the *Canadian Churchman,* the Anglican national paper.[8]

Text on bishops

Discussion of collegiality and related concepts in the text on the church was followed by study of practical aspects of the pastoral duties of bishops. Particular topics included reforms in how curia offices deal with dioceses, a retirement age for bishops (leading to the present norm of retirement at age 75), the authority of national conferences of bishops, and the size of dioceses. On 5 November, the first day this text was discussed, Baudoux called for a radical revision. The practical decree, he insisted, had to reflect faithfully all that had been agreed about the doctrine of collegiality during debate on the text on the nature of the church. It had been agreed that episcopal consecration incorporated a bishop into the "college." The text on bishops, Baudoux said, in effect down graded bishops in the way it spoke of "a grant" of faculties or powers to them. Hermaniuk took up the same topic the following day. He too called for the text to be amended and perfected. It should declare that bishops have their authority from God, even though at times that authority may be circumscribed for the common good of the church. He also repeated his proposal for an "apostolic college" of bishops to share responsibility with the pope.

The general superior of the Oblates of Mary Immaculate, Léo Deschatelets, a Canadian, spoke on 7 November to stress the importance of having a separate chapter on church members who are "striving for perfection." This included more than those in religious orders, so he proposed the special chapter should be entitled "Concerning those who profess the evangelical counsels," and not just "On Religious." From what others had said, he saw some questions, difficulties and doubts regarding the different states of striving for perfection, even in religious life. The council had to reply fully to these questions. This required more than a few articles, as in the text being discussed. The issues raised had to do with the origin and nature of the evangelical counsels and precepts, the nature of the religious life and of the states of striving for perfection.

The council wanted to give a more precise and complete definition of a life lived according to the evangelical counsels. Many in the church expected it to do so. "It is urgent to do this at a time when we wish to further holiness within the church, when laity are more and more seeking holiness, when the holiness of bishops and priests needs to be elucidated," he argued. He mentioned also "the several thousands of missionaries entrusted to my care." This topic, he stressed, truly has its place in a dogmatic constitution on the church. One of the church's "finest ornaments" is the crowd of those who consecrate their entire lives to live out the evangelical counsels in the various states of acquiring perfection. The states of perfection are not merely accidentally linked to the church but quite intimately so. They "flow from the very gospel itself, respond to the universal church's purpose and to the vocation of the faithful to procure God's glory and one's own sanctification. They are like a seed divinely planted which, over the centuries, has developed into a large tree with all kinds of branches." Their root origin is found in the example and words of Christ. Thus, there had to be a specific chapter on the states of perfection. While all the faithful are called to one and substantially the same holiness, those in a given state of perfection tend to holiness as a special profession, according to a special discipline by which they live the evangelical counsels: thereby they live in a special "state" or "condition." If treated in a separate chapter, "the states of perfection and the religious life" will not be eclipsed by the universal call to holiness, he said. "It will also be more plain that they have no monopoly or privilege in terms of striving for holiness, so that the chapter on the universal call to holiness will become even stronger." He concluded by suggesting how the entire text on the church could be structured if a separate chapter were given to the states of perfection.[9]

A week later, on 14 November, in the continuing debate about the pastoral work of bishops, Coderre spoke in the name of 45 Canadians about what they considered "a major defect" in the text. It said nothing about the eastern church although it was intended to deal concretely with church government. The tendency to consider only the Latin viewpoint not only continued but also grew worse, he said. Too often the eastern churches were made to appear as some sort of appendage that the Latin church accepted with charity and even by way of exception. In truth, they are of the very heart of the church. Coderre also said the text should note that the pastoral duties of bishops arose from episcopal consecration. It should fully set out the true nature of the patriarchates. And, in dealing with bishops' conferences, it should show clearly what these bodies would become, after having examined eastern traditions and the very important fact that everything found in the apostolic patriarchates relates to the very mystery of the church.

Final votes on liturgy

The text that became the *Constitution on the Sacred Liturgy* was debated and approved in general during the council's first session. Suggested amendments were incorporated by drafters between sessions. As the work wound down, it was clear that switching from Latin to local languages had not been the hottest issue, as it seemed at first. Vatican officials were even more stubborn and inventive in their efforts to retain control over liturgical matters and so limit the right of local bishops or their national conferences to made decisions. Voting to approve a final text began on 8 October 1963, and was completed 22 November. During the same period, a final vote was completed on the decree on the media of communication. Both these texts, the first fruits of Vatican II, were solemnly proclaimed by Paul VI during the 4 December closing of the second session. Bishop Martin of Nicolet, as a member of the council commission for liturgy, was the Canadian most involved in the process of finalizing the liturgy text. The initial stage of this work involved rewriting the text by studying the amendments suggested during the debate and incorporating those found to be acceptable. Changes then had to be reported back to the full assembly for approval. Martin was assigned to lead this work for the text's all-important introduction and first nine "general principles for restoration and promotion of the sacred liturgy," as well as for fourth chapter on the divine office. An interesting example of the kind of decisions made can be seen in the opening lines of the final text. An early draft said the council aimed to foster whatever can promote "union with separated brothers." The final text speaks instead of "union among all who believe in Christ." During the council, Martin did not speak in the debates, but he was frequently at the microphone during the first two sessions, presenting and explaining how the commission was handling amendments to the text.

"Trimmings on the mass"

Vatican II defined the celebration of the eucharist as "a sacred action surpassing all others." Before the council, however, after this "unsurpassed" prayer was concluded by the dismissal and final blessing, there were still other prayers that had been added, first by Leo XIII and then Pius XI. After blessing the congregation, the celebrant turned back to the altar to read verses 1 to 14 of the beginning of the gospel according to John. This was followed by prayers in the vernacular that were added by Leo XIII " for the general needs of the church," and were recited "for the conversion of Russia" after Pius XI so directed in 1930. Kneeling on the altar step, the priest led the people in three Hail Marys and the Marian prayer Hail, Holy Queen. A prayer followed to God, Mary, Joseph, Peter and Paul and all the saints "for the conversion of sinners, and for the liberty and exaltation of our holy mother the church." Then, "Holy Michael, Archangel" was asked to "defend us in the day of battle; be our safeguard against the wickedness and snares of the devil…(and) by the power of God thrust down to hell Satan, and all the wicked spirits who wander through the world seeking the ruin of souls." Then, "Most sacred Heart of Jesus, Have mercy on us" was repeated three times. With that, the mass did end – except, as noted in the missal at the time, "in some places it is customary to make an additional commemoration of the dead by reciting after mass psalm 129 and the prayer Fidelium." In their pre-council suggestions to John XXIII, a number of Canadian bishops asked that these prayers be discontinued, and this was done as part of the general liturgical renewal after the council.

Implementing renewal

Martin was among the first group of bishops named by Paul VI early in 1964 to the post-council *consilium* for implementing liturgical renewal in the light of the council's decisions. At the end of the council, Emmett Carter, then bishop in London, Ontario, also was named to the *consilium*. Martin, and later Carter, therefore experienced at first hand the bureaucratic battle between the new *consilium* and the existing Vatican office for liturgical questions.

The struggle was over which body would control how the council's liturgical directives would be interpreted and implemented. With negative results for the rights of local bishops, the *consilium* gradually lost out, even though it was Paul VI's creation. To pursue the story of how all this came about is, however, beyond the scope of this account of Canadian participation in the council. What remains to be sketched is how the Canadian bishops began to bring home the results of the council's decisions about the liturgy. Paul VI established the *consilium* in January 1964 and the new body issued an initial instruction the next September. Even before that date the Canadian bishops had decided on the first liturgical changes for Latin-rite parishes. In February 1964, the bishops approved French or English instead of Latin for the scripture readings at mass. More changes were voted in April and October. The *consilium* confirmed the CCC's April changes two months later, and those of October within six weeks. The Canadian bishops therefore were able to initiate some changes on 1 January 1965, and major changes for the first Sunday of Lent, 7 March 1965. This, however, was 15 months after the council had voted for changes. Expectation of these reforms were so high, theologian Gilles Routhier has noted, that there was disappointment – "a first brake on reception" of council decisions – when Canadian bishops had to "call for patience" while liturgical instruments such as mass books were prepared and approved.[10]

Two outside events

Paul VI's 14 November visit to the Canadian College in Rome was a non-council event that made history for Canadian council participants. It was the first time in its 75 years of operation that a pope had visited the residence for Canadian priests doing advanced studies in Roman universities. He was greeted by all the bishops attending the council, as well as by the student priests. Also in mid-November, the Canadian bishops sent a message "of respectful and prayerful greetings" to Governor General Vanier for all Canadians from the CCC annual meeting in Rome. At the council, they said, they had been studying "those eternal verities which hold out for all of us a hope and a consolation which far transcend the limited vista of this short and sometimes agonized earthly existence. Above all we have been striving, in the presence of observers of practically every faith and every clime, to discover the profound significance of the mind of modern man, so that we may direct to him that light and guidance which we humbly and firmly believe to be entrusted to the church and to be our sacred responsibility."They said they wanted their message "to be extended, not only to our beloved Catholic people, but to every one of our fellow Canadian citizens."Vanier responded to this message signed by Flahiff as CCC chairman to say he had "conveyed it to the government and people of Canada." [11]

Ecumenism again

On 18 November the council returned to the topic of church unity. During the first session, a text on this topic prepared by the commission for eastern churches was accepted in principle and sent back to be combined with two other draft texts. The new version had five chapters: principles of ecumenism; practical aspects of work towards unity; separated Christians, Orthodox and post-Reformation; Jews; religious liberty. Léger argued on 19 November that while a statement on Catholic attitudes towards Jews was badly needed, it should be a separate document, not just a chapter in an ecumenism text. He also warned against trying, in the second part of the third chapter, to describe all the Christians separated from Catholicism since the sixteenth century. The "authentic treasures of truth and spiritual life" of separated Christians needed to be understood and honoured, he agreed; but they represented such a variety, and had such different backgrounds, that any summary description would be unsatisfactory, and should be avoided in a council text. The risks of over-simplification were too grave.

He reflected on the profound nature of the ecumenical movement. It could not be interpreted as a simple impulse of sentimental generosity that soon would dissipate. The new disposition of hearts was truly inspired by the Gospel, and proceeded from the Holy Spirit. Although it would be difficult to work free from under the weight of history, no one should be frightened by this. The text helped to open the way, Léger said.

The next day (20 November), Baudoux welcomed the text, but added that the way it related to the mission of the church should be clarified. He insisted that dialogue was not merely a human initiative but was a genuinely supernatural conversation under the guidance of the Holy Spirit. It had nothing in common with doctrinal relativism. The chief means of promoting understanding were mutual pardon, friendship and trust. The draft text, he added, gave rise to great hopes for the future. It recognized the real though imperfect communion of Catholics with separated brethren because of their incorporation into Christ through baptism and their profession of Christ's name. No betrayal of traditional Catholic theology was involved. As CCC chairman he cited a letter the Canadian bishops had received from the general synod of the Anglican church in Canada, and called it a sign that "Christians not of our faith are expecting great things of the council."

In his 25 November remarks on the principles of a Catholic approach to ecumenism, Léger made two suggestions about promoting unity in the area of doctrine. One was a call for "a more accurate presentation of the mark of unity" of the church. The other concerned better means for settling doctrinal differences. Many Catholics and non-Catholics think the Catholic church favors too monolithic a unity, he noted, "and frequently we have somewhat neglected certain legitimate demands of freedom and diversity within the bounds of unity." Now, bishops from mission areas wanted "a strong statement saying that unity in the church of Christ can never stand in the way of legitimate liberty and diversity." The council should explain, Léger stressed, how, in the unity intended by Christ, "perfect obedience is compatible with supreme freedom, true unity with great diversity." He recalled that Paul VI himself praised this diversity in his opening address of the 1963 session. Regarding better means for settling doctrinal differences, his second suggestion, Léger thought the council should go farther than saying that love and truth should never suffer harm. Humility should be stressed equally. "In my opinion, these differences will not be resolved unless the separated brothers and we Catholics study the revelation of Christ together in humility," Léger affirmed. Especially now, the church needed intellectual humility. The statement that the Catholic church possesses the full truth revealed by Christ "can be correctly understood if the proper distinctions are made. However, I am afraid that for many such a statement covers over our radical inability, while on this earth, to understand the truth revealed by Christ completely and exhaustively."

The apostle Paul spoke of "the unfathomable riches of Christ" (Ephesians 3:8). Augustine advised Christians to "seek in order to find, and find so that you may continue to seek." Paul VI had just remarked in his talk to non-Catholic observers at the council that "this saying of Augustine applies to all of us, Catholics and non-Catholics alike: the true Christian finds no place for immobilism." In Léger's view, this approach pointed the right way to a solution of doctrinal difficulties. "And I would suggest," he concluded, "that theological investigation be described in such a fashion that it will not only constantly spur on our separated brothers, but Catholics as well, to a deeper and more accurate expression of the revelation of Christ."

During this ecumenism debate, Flahiff submitted written comments which were later published (and sometimes mistakenly identified as a council speech). Flahiff had specialized in church history before being named archbishop of Winnipeg. He wrote, for the attention of those amending the council text, that there should be more emphasis on the historical aspect of the very fact that there is an "unhappy division" among Christians. Schisms among Christians should be described dynamically. "We all know," he said, "that schisms among Christians have very unhappy consequences, which weaken the missionary drive of the church and set up many obstacles to the spread of the gospel. But since God, the Lord of all the events of history, has allowed schisms, we must search out their positive meaning. For we fully believe that the history of salvation which begins in Israel and reaches its peak in Jesus Christ, still continues in the pilgrim church." What, then, is the significance of divisions in the history of the church? Divisions are the result of sin, Flahiff stressed. Therefore, "these terrible schisms" should always remind the church that it is not yet as holy as it should be, nor obedient enough to its call to be truly universal. He called attention to "another still more positive aspect of our divisions." He was fully convinced, he said, that the ecumenical movement is the work of the Holy Spirit through which, out of the effort to overcome divisions, "all churches profit immensely, are challenged to renewal, find new ways of acting in love, and come to a deeper understanding of the gospel." In this movement, for the first time in history all the churches and ecclesiastical communities "witness together to Jesus Christ the Saviour, thus giving new vigour to the proclamation of the gospel in the world." He thought this historical and dynamic aspect of ecumenism should be explained in the text. It would then be more evident that what was said about ecumenism was not a final judgment but only "the beginning of an action or development whose author is the spirit of God himself."

Three eastern-rite Canadians also spoke during the second session's closing days. Bishop Vladimir Malanchuk (28 November), who was provincial of Ukrainian Redemptorists in Winnipeg before being named in 1960 to head the eparchy for Ukrainians living in France, said he wanted the ecumenism text to mention that there were also non-religious causes of church separations and divisions in the past. Politics, race, excessive patriotism, mutual ignorance and distrust, and the desire to be free from outside influences had played parts. He also wanted Paul VI's words about mutual pardon inserted in the text. With regard to Catholic-Orthodox relations, he added, it should be made clear that for the Orthodox the suppression of local particular churches could not be a condition of union. Hermaniuk (2 December) took up some of the same points. The text suffered from insufficient reference to the spiritual heritage of the eastern churches. He recommended that the secretariat for promoting Christian unity should have Catholic-Orthodox and Catholic-Protestant commissions. The traditional eastern form of synodal government should be fully recognized, and full account taken of the differences of the eastern and Latin codes of canon law. As for the ecumenical movement in general, he urged the Catholic church to find a way to participate actively in dialogue within the framework of the World Council of Churches. Roborecki (2 December) of Saskatoon also stressed that the age-old Orthodox traditions had to be respected. Synodal government was an important aspect of this. The primacy of the pope was no longer the chief obstacle to union. Rather, the mode of applying primacy had a tone of rigid centralization. The early church had not been marked by centralization and it was not needed now, he argued. Eastern Christians should be allowed to keep their traditions and should not be urged to change rites. Ecumenical activity among the Orthodox, he added, should be entrusted to those who know the east, its history and traditions. This work should not be left to westerners and members of the Latin rite of the church.

Canadian Catholic media at council

When the Canadian bishops agreed before Vatican II opened that two representatives of their CCC Information Service should go to Rome to help report on council events, it was decided to arrange with *Le Devoir* of Montreal to have Claude Ryan join me in Rome for the first session. (Réjean Plamondon, my French counterpart as editor of CCC information service, was in Rome for the second and third sessions, but missed the fourth because of illness.) When he came to Rome for the first session, Ryan had only recently begun the journalism career that would lead to the top post at *Le Devoir*. However, he had vast knowledge of church affairs in Quebec from his earlier years as general secretary of l'Action catholique. He also had experience in the church politics of Rome. In October 1959 he represented Canada in Rome at the first meeting of the board appointed by John XXIII to direct the permanent committee for international congresses of the lay apostolate. (Planning began at that meeting for a third world lay congress, following those of 1951 and 1957. It was held in October 1967 without memorable results.) Some people who had been involved in this earlier work were in Rome for the opening of the council. Ryan therefore had prior acquaintance with Belgian, Dutch, French and German church activists who were planning how to get the council story into the news media despite Vatican rules for strict secrecy.

These strategies were discussed enthusiastically at a meeting to which Ryan led me on my first evening in Rome. The Canadian bishops, represented by Ryan and me, had the distinction, with the Dutch and Germans, of being the first to open their own information "centre" in Rome.[12] That meeting also marked one of the starting points of what became the CCCC (Centrum

Coordinationis Communicationum de Concilio [Centre for coordinating council communications]). The CCCC expanded during the four sessions as a centre that was independent of the Vatican. It supplied documents, translations and some broadcasting resources, and also staged press conferences and lectures. It aimed to provide some coordination for the 13 council information or documentation centres that grew up, 10 related in some way to bishops' conferences, including the Canadian CCC, and three to religious orders. The official Vatican press office eventual cooperated but was never a CCCC member. The Canadian bishops had a leading role in launching the CCCC and aiding it with finances and personnel. As we have seen, J.M. Poitevin, a Canadian priest involved in media work in Rome with the international Catholic office for cinema, was named in 1960 a consultor of the council's preparatory secretariat on media questions (chapter one). He was later involved in the first 1963 formal discussions about the CCCC. After the first council session, the Canadian bishops agreed to help fund it. Yvon Desrosiers of the CCC social communication office in Montreal eventually joined the CCCC staff and took over as its secretary general for the third council session and until he returned to Montreal in June 1965 to continue his studies.[13]

From two print journalists during the first session, the media team sponsored by the Canadian bishops grew during the course of the council with the addition of radio and television specialists. Jean-Paul Belleville of CCC's Office des communications sociales in Montreal was joined for French language programs by Pierre Forest of the diocese of Hauterive (today Baie-Comeau). For English radio and television, Bonnie Brennan of the Toronto Catholic Information Centre was later joined by Edward Bader from the same centre. Besides writing for various Catholic and secular publications, Plamondon and I also helped with taped interviews and commentaries for radio and television. In general, these were for local stations. For Canada's national network, Radio Canada had a full-time French crew (Gerard Lemieux and Émile Legault) in Rome for the four sessions, and the English CBC network sent crews occasionally and for highlights. Starting in the second session, Plamondon helped Quebec bishops prepare tapes for local radio stations in their dioceses. These included

Charbonneau in Hull, Coderre in St. Jean, Frenette in St. Jerome and Caza in Valleyfield. For the last two sessions, Belleville and Forest took over most of this work and expanded it. Similarly, at the highpoint of their work in English, Brennan and Bader were sending radio tapes to 85 commercial radio stations across Canada. They tailored them by the regions, so listeners in the west, Ontario and the Atlantic area would hear bishops from their areas.

The tapes featured a newscast, a statement from a bishop and an interview with one of the "stars" of the council from other countries. These were played weekly during the third and fourth council sessions. They also did a half hour television program for the CTV network near the end of the council, with Irish journalist John Horgan as host. During the fourth session Brennan also taped a weekly 15-minute program in Ukrainian by Archbishop Hermaniuk that was used in Winnipeg and Toronto. Brennan recalls "it was the first time Radio Vatican staff were faced with a female producer. It was also the first time I was faced with working in another language. When Archbishop Hermaniuk wanted to change something I would have him go back to the last time he mentioned Cardinal Slipyi. Then I would edit from Slipyi to Slipyi. At least in radio I did not have to know how to spell his name. Small mercies. The CBC did their own programming. When they were in Rome I worked with them, helping to arrange interviews, etc."

Besides writing longer feature articles for English newspapers and periodicals in Canada, I sent short news items to Canadian Press (CP) about Canadian participants. Though a major news service for Canadian newspapers and broadcasters, CP decided not to assign reporters to the council, as the other major news services did, including Reuters, Associated Press (AP), United Press International (UPI), and Agence France Presse (AFP). When there was breaking news involving a Canadian at the council, I would write a short item, carry it to the Reuters office and send it to (CP). It would move by the Reuters telex line to London and then be resent to Canada, taking advantage of the Commonwealth "penny rate" then in effect for news items sent by transatlantic cable. Because of the six-hour time difference, an item sent in this way from Rome at noon would reach most Canadian news outlets early the morning of the same day.

I spent most forenoons writing in my hotel room, when all the bishops and theologians were in the council hall and inaccessible. Each day that Léger spoke, I would be informed by the hotel desk clerk that I had a message. It would be a French summary of Léger's speech. I never knew whether Lafortune or Naud, Léger's theologians, or someone else brought it. I would write a short English news item for Canadian press, and take it with me to the oral press briefing held shortly after the bishops came out of the hall at noon. I would verify that Léger had indeed spoken, amend my story if necessary, and walk it to the Reuters office for transmission to Canada, to reach morning readers and listeners. A few hours later, at a daily panel sponsored by the US bishops, council specialists would stretch secrecy rules as far as they could to answer journalists' questions and still keep their council passes. To handle the complexity of the debates and the swirl of rumours, a number of us banded together. We worked for English media in Australia, Canada, England, Ireland and the USA that did not compete for the same public. Early afternoons we would decide which bishop or theologian might be particularly helpful that day. If over an evening meal he would talk freely, we would guarantee anonymity and a free meal! We heard many brave and helpful words, and kept ours!

Some days, though, working for the bishops and helping any Canadian journalist who called, meant that I could keep no daily routine. My letters home reflected this.

> Letter 13 November 1963: *I've been trying to get some writing done this morning, have to go soon to the noon press briefing, to interview a Canadian missionary in New Guinea at five, and to talk to some CBC people coming in tonight.*

> Letter 16 November 1963: *Spent part of the morning helping Archbishop O'Neill find some pictures that might make up a special page in the* (Regina) Leader-Post. *He really is a tremendous man when you get to know him; one of the true Liberals.*

And sometimes I was sent "on a wild goose chase."

> Letter 21 November 1963: *Tuesday night just before midnight I got a call from the* Toronto Star, *wanting me to interview Cardinal Léger on that story in* La Presse *of Montreal that he*

had asked to be relieved of his duties. Next morning I was at the Canadian college before 7.30. Saw, but didn't talk to the Cardinal, because he wasn't talking to anyone, after no fewer than eight phone calls from Canada the previous evening. So I didn't get the 750-word interview for which they were paying so handsomely, but I did file them 200, for which they wired back thanks. But that was Wednesday morning gone. (Incidentally, he isn't resigning, though he did say he had asked to do so as (according to those 'close to him') an "expression of missionary zeal." As Pilate said, what is the truth? (However, immediately after the second session, Léger did visit Africa, "to learn," he said, about that vast continent.[14] That visit was a forecast, though we could not know it then, of his 1968 resignation as archbishop of Montreal to work among lepers in Africa.)

A synodal conclusion

The question of collegiality provided the main drama of the second session. It was the central issue for the famous "straw votes" of 30 October, and also was a constant background for the later discussion of the pastoral office of bishops. Divisions of opinion about such questions as the role of conferences of bishops arose mainly from the continuing disagreement about how local bishops share responsibility with the pope. This question also served to focus attention on the formula Paul VI used when he proclaimed the liturgy and media texts during the 4 December ceremony to close the second session. In it he made clear that he was acting along with the fathers ("*una cum...Patribus*"), and that the decisions, which he was confirming, had been made in a conciliar and thus synodal manner. He said: "In the name of the Most Holy and undivided Trinity, of the Father and the Son and the Holy Spirit. The fathers have expressed their agreement with the decrees just read out in the presence of this legitimately assembled Sacred and Ecumenical Second Vatican Council. And We, in virtue of the apostolic authority given to us by Christ, and in union with the reverend fathers, approve, establish, and ordain them in the Holy Spirit, and We order that what the Council has so ordained be published for the glory of God."[15]

The conclusion of the council's work on the liturgy text led to one of my personal council highlights. My 27 November 1963 letter home began with mention of how we in Rome had experienced the assassination of President Kennedy earlier that week. On a happier note, I referred to my growing friendship with the Minnesota liturgy expert, Benedictine Godfrey Diekmann, who lodged and worked in a little hotel next to mine; and I told Mae what I had just been doing with Godfrey. He said his morning mass in a church around the corner from our hotels, and I often joined him as "altar boy." One morning soon after the liturgy constitution was approved, he asked me to help him later that afternoon with a bit of work he had to do. When I arrived in his room, I learned the job was to proofread the mimeograph stencils of the English translation that he, U.S. canonist Fred McManus and English Jesuit Clifford Howell had just done of the council's new liturgy document. Every so often, Godfrey would interrupt our proofreading to digress into a story about the history or importance of this or that phrase in the text. With his encyclopaedic knowledge, in his clipped, rapid-fire style, he would refer to a bit of scripture, to a fourth-century text, or to a recent argument by a bishop or theologian during the council's work. So far as I know, after Godfrey and I had marked a few typing errors, those stencils produced the English text of the liturgy constitution officially handed to the world's journalists the morning of 29 November. My only regret after that unforgettable afternoon is that he did not tell me in advance why he wanted my help. I still wish I could have recorded all he said, as his first spontaneous commentary on the historic text.

Some members of the Vatican II English-language press corps taking notes during a briefing by Fr. Edward Heston. Standing: At Heston's right, light coat, checking watch, George Armstrong of the *Manchester Guardian*. Behind Heston in light trench coat, John Organ of *Reuters*. To Organ's left, side view, Desmond Fisher of the *Catholic Herald*, London. Michael Novak of *Harper's*. Donald Campion SJ, editor of *America*. Last on right, Bernard Daly, CCC Information Service. Seated at table in front of Fr. Heston, left to right: Sean MacRaemoinn, Dublin, Irish radio and television; right, facing Heston, with dark-rimmed glasses, Milton Bracker, *New York Times*. Others unidentified.

John XXIII speaking at an audience for media representatives in the Sistine Chapel on 13 October 1962 as Vatican II began.

Facing John XXIII at an audience for journalists, in first row standing, Bernard Daly is sixth from right.

During the afternoon of each council workday, a panel of council experts, sponsored by the U.S. bishops, met journalists for an hour-long question-and-answer session. Seated along the wall, left to right: Elmer von Feldt (suit with tie), panel chair, U.S. Catholic News representative. Leaning forward with notes, Jesuit Gustave Weigel SJ, ecumenist. Francis Connell, Redemptorist moral theologian. Jesuit John Long, ecumenist. Jesuit Francis McCool, scripture specialist. John Sheerin, Paulist editor (at table). Bernard Haering, Redemptorist moral theologian. George Higgins, social doctrine. Fred McManus, canon law. Robert Trisco, church history. Eugene Maly, scripture specialist. (And two unidentified U.S. bishops.)

Cardinal James McGuigan of Toronto, reading Breviary, is seated, front left, beside Cardinal P.G. Agagianian, as Vatican II participants gather in St. Peter's Basilica for the start of a council workday.

In the council press office, journalists take notes as Cardinal Augustin Bea SJ, head of the Vatican Secretariat for Christian Unity, outlines the ecumenical importance of Vatican II.

Late in October 1964, the International Union of the Catholic Press held a small convention in Rome. Bernard Daly, above, reported on the situation of Catholic English-language weekly newspapers in Canada. Chairman of the session, seated, was Raimondo Manzini, then editor of *l'Osservatore Romano*, the Vatican's Italian daily newspaper, who was also named a lay auditor of the council.

In conjunction with the October 1964 convention in Rome of the International Union of the Catholic Press, Paul VI celebrated Mass for convention participants in a small Vatican chapel. Bernard Daly is kneeling, front row.

Paul VI kneels in prayer at a solemn ceremony in St. Peter's Basilica during a Vatican II session.

5

The Third Session: 1964

The third Vatican II session, in the fall of 1964, was the busiest of all four. The bishops studied 11 texts; and Paul VI joined in promulgating final versions of three others. The pace of work led many bishops to think until near its end that the third session might be the council's last one. In contrast, the first session debated five texts, while the second studied only three and promulgated two from the first session: liturgy and the media. Several texts studied during the third session renewed debate over how decision-making should be shared between the pope and diocesan bishops, but the drama of the session came with other issues. Heading that list were questions about marriage and birth control, and the fate of texts on Jews and on religious freedom.

Expanded commissions

Near the end of the second session, after a second round of elections and papal appointments, Baudoux and Hermaniuk joined the list of Canadian bishops who were members of council working commissions. When it came time for the CCC to suggest Canadian names for the new choices for the second round, it was agreed that Baudoux would stand for the commission on eastern churches and Hermaniuk for the Christian unity secretariat. That would add Baudoux's Latin presence for the study of eastern questions, and Hermaniuk's eastern experience for unity issues.[1] In any event, the voting produced that result. Hermaniuk's work in the unity secretariat will not be fully documented until his personal council notes in Ukrainian are studied. Baudoux's work in the eastern church commission is more easily reported. He involved himself actively early in 1964 after attending just one commission meeting before the end of the second session.

His files record some of the ideas he advanced in the commission. Its proposal for a separate text on eastern churches was the second last text debated at the end of the council's first session. That text was sent back to the commission, to be combined in a single document with the decree on ecumenism composed by the unity secretariat and with the chapter on ecumenism in the draft constitution on the church. As the eastern commission began its 1964 work, Baudoux's was one new face at the table. His papers for that period include a copy of the letter Maximos IV sent to John XXIII in October 1959. The Melchite patriarch asked that the traditional patriarchs should have a place in all council events ahead of the cardinals. He argued that by "ancient and unanimous tradition, the Sovereign Pontiff of Rome is *immediately* followed in the church hierarchy by those who hold the four other apostolic patriarchates, Constantinople, Alexandria, Antioch, Jerusalem." When this did not happen for the opening of Vatican II, he publicly absented himself from the procession and that day's other formalities. However, Maximos IV later was active in council debates, and he was named a cardinal (with Roy of Quebec and others) by Paul VI before the fourth session.

Baudoux's early 1964 submission to the eastern church commission, written between 3 February and 3 March, recalled "observations that I sent in 1960, 1962 and 1963." His interest in eastern questions therefore was not new. Indeed, he said "my points are basically the fruit of my long and never-interrupted contacts with the Ukrainians of Canada, amidst whom I lived as a pastor for 18 years, and of conversations with many eastern bishops of other rites who have extended their friendship to me since the beginning of the council." He went on to urge that the project for a separate text about the eastern churches should be abandoned because it would be "no benefit, unnecessary, useless and unfeasible." The existence of a constitution on the eastern churches, Baudoux argued, "results in putting them outside the norm, which is diversity in unity." He preferred that the council's basic constitution on the church "would deal with what is common to the eastern churches and what we customarily call the western church, and with how they differ." A single text, "a seamless garment," would help both eastern and western Christians to know, "without studying specialized works, that the church is diverse in its unity, as Christ wished it to be."The main task of the eastern commission, Baudoux added, should be to study where eastern concerns should be inserted in all council texts. He called it "striking, if not stunning" that at that stage, in all council texts,"nothing but Latin situations, measures and solutions are envisaged, without even a reference to situations, measures and solutions that concern the easterns." It was true, Baudoux added,"that, by a mysterious arrangement of providence, the eastern churches have only a minimal place quantitatively in the body of churches. That is doubly unhappy for them when the massive west thinks about and guides the destinies of the universal church in such a way that the eastern tradition can only with great difficulty develop fully in fidelity to its roots." He had, therefore, "an urgent request" for eastern church leaders. They "must understand, consult and agree with one another." There was no need, he added,"to list the areas in which there have been and still are clashes, misinformation, standoffs."The work of the commission had suffered from this. Baudoux concluded: "It is surely not a question of the various eastern churches planning to unite against the west – even though we may have merited that more than once. But it seems to me that the weakness of the eastern churches comes often and more from their division than from 'domination' by the Latins."[2]

The session begins

The third session began with an expanded Canadian office for the council. The rooms at the Canadian College, hard to reach in rush hour traffic, were abandoned in favour of two rooms rented in a building in front of St. Peter's. The staff was also enlarged. Both general secretaries, Limoges (who would be succeeded by Charles Mathieu at mid-session) and Carley, came to Rome with their Ottawa secretaries, Marie Clusiau and Nora Smith. Except for staff changes, this would be the set-up until the council ended. The relocation made it easier for the Canadian bishops to get various services from their office, and the larger space allowed small groups to organize afternoon and early evening meetings and lectures.

Another new Canadian face around the council was that of Charles De Koninck. A few weeks before the session opened, Roy made council history when he announced in Quebec City that he had chosen a layman to accompany him as *peritus* (expert) during the third session.[3] De Koninck, dean of the faculty of philosophy at Laval University, came to the precedent-setting post at the council with doctorates in philosophy and theology. De Koninck's appointment was a signal that Roy had been quietly putting together a team at Quebec City for a major contribution to the work on the text on the church in the modern world.

Roy's consultative committee

We noted earlier (Chapter 3) that between the first and second council sessions Léger, Pelletier and Roy were involved in commission work on the text about the church in the world. For that work, Roy was a member of the sub-commission on the person and society. A text prepared by the mixed commission in the spring of 1963 failed to win support. Suenens with a small group of experts at Malines produced a text that, in the end, also failed to advance. The commission then started a new project by consulting bishops and theologians on their expectations for the text.

In the spring of 1964, there were two meetings, in Paris and Rome, of the sub-committee to which Roy belonged. About that time, Roy also organized a group at Quebec to work on the problems in the text. The Quebec Dominican theologian Bernard Lambert coordinated this work.[4] The observations and proposals they wrote in April 1964 were amplified later. They disliked the commission's new draft because it was too western, depended on a limited view of the church, and had a dualistic notion of reality. It seemed to speak of a Christendom where the church had a central position from which it talked to everyone. They proposed an allegory to illustrate a different approach. They pictured a church with doors and windows closed and Christians singing hymns inside.

Someone suggested opening the doors and windows so outsiders could hear better. Those outside could hear better but still could not understand, even after the songs were modernized in the language of the people. So someone said, let's go out into the street. Still, they do not reach everyone because they tended to stick together. They started to become "the salt of the earth and the light of the world" only when they mixed with everyone. "What we want to do, surely, is to take the hand of modern man and lead him to the Lord," the Lambert group wrote. "Therefore the council text must translate this *leading* of modern man to God." This approach, Turbanti has noted, "dealt with themes and positions typical of Canadian Catholic Action at that time, characterized by great freedom and openness in meeting others." What was needed, the Lambert group believed, involved "restarting evangelization" by looking at what Christians believed in common with other people. The things to be researched were more at the level of common feelings than at the theological level of distinctions between the natural and the supernatural. They pictured the church working with the world in seeking a common plan for human existence. In relation to the world, the church would stand in solidarity with all humans, stand apart from sinful worldly structures, and recapitulate all things in Christ. To describe the Christian presence in the world, they found ideas like mission or dialogue somewhat partial. Instead, they developed the idea of *presence* – "not facing the world, but in it … not side-by-side, or opposed, or outside, but inside like the body's soul." With such ideas in mind, the Quebec groups developed a new draft plan for a council text on the church in the world. Their draft did not arrive in Rome in time to be taken into account by those writing the council text, but it remained the foundation for later work in the commission by Roy and Lambert. Their involvement in this undertaking reached its high point, as we will see later, during the fourth session's final work on the text on the church in the world. For his part, De Koninck worked especially on what the text might say about marriage and birth control, as we will see.

About the church

The third session opened 14 September with four days of renewed discussion about the text on the church. Its seventh chapter, on the theology of "last things," affirmed the unity of the people of God in time and the mystical body of Christ in eternity. Hermaniuk joined the opening day's debate. The true significance of the chapter, he said, was the way it described the church's sense of expectancy, its manner of waiting for life after death and union with Christ. This sense of vigilance of the faithful should be stressed more, he said. It should be related to their sacramental union with Christ in the eucharist. Concern about the last days was a matter of individual vigilance, he agreed. But there was also the element of communitarian vigilance in the eucharist. Salvation, which entails perfection, is not just a concern of each church member individually. It is also the goal of the entire church as a body, and the eucharist is the most perfect form of communitarian vigilance for the people of God.

The final chapter of the text on the church dealt with the place of the Blessed Virgin in Catholic teaching. During the first two sessions there had been an intense effort on the part of some council members to have a separate document about Mary. They failed to win over the majority, who preferred that the topic should be a chapter in the document about the church. This debate was settled during the second session by a close vote that ruled out a separate text. Roy, as a member of the theology commission, had the task of reporting on revisions made to the text during the intersession. Léger (16 September) was the only Canadian to speak during the third session about the redrafted chapter on Mary in the text on the church. He was pleased that it looked to the scriptures for inspiration in its effort to describe Mary's great dignity and her role in the plan of salvation. At the same time, it happily situated her within the mystery of Christ and of his church. He went on to propose amendments, based on his agreement with those who had spoken earlier of the need for some renewal in teaching about Mary and in devotions to her. The style of speaking about Mary needed renewal, he said. Clear and precise words should be used to describe her role. Preaching about her frequently was marked by ill-considered use of superlatives and a lack of concern for the exact meaning of words and phrases. Exaggerations do not help people today to pray to Mary and understand her dignity, he argued. Rather, such a style was an obstacle to piety for many. Sober language was more effective, and the chapter itself should be written in such a style. Mary's place in the work of redemption was particularly hard to conceive and express. There were only a few scriptural texts that could be used as a basis for teaching about her role, and they did not describe it in detail. In popular preaching and devotions she was given many titles, but these were not proposed as strictly doctrinal. The council, however, was writing a doctrinal text, so great care was needed. A council text was a solemn act of the church's teaching authority. It must express itself clearly and precisely, in accord with scripture and tradition. The origin and meaning of every title used for her should be studied carefully. It would be best if the term "mediatrix" were not used, he said. It was hard to interpret and received different explanations by various authors. It appeared late in the history of church documents and was rarely used by itself alone. Moreover, it seemed to contradict the scriptural reference to Christ as the sole mediator, and so could hinder a correct understanding by Catholics and also impede ecumenical dialogue. Regarding renewal of Marian devotions, Léger found that the draft text was accurate enough but too theoretical. He recalled that Cardinal Newman had observed that devotions to Mary often are not sufficiently directed to God and Christ. Therefore the text should recall to pastors and people that they should see to it that their devotion to Mary was directed and subordinated to worship of God and Christ.

Pastoral work of bishops

After brief debate on the document on the church, the council again took up the decree on the pastoral office of bishops. Léger (21 September) was the only Canadian speaker. The council must lead to pastoral action, he said, and this called for a new approach in the ways bishops taught and governed. As compared with a generation ago, people were more interested in technical things. They had new attitudes towards religion and authority. They objected to paternalism by bishops or priests. Bishops, he argued, should use social research methods, and be personally present to people. The language used, he warned, often was archaic, abstract, artificial and cut off from life and modern reality—"which might be one reason why we are like voices crying in the wilderness." Care had to be taken to teach "the whole mystery of Christ," and not just lists of things to be done or avoided. Essentials had to be stressed over secondary aspects of religion, such as particular devotions. Doctrines held with certainty by the church had to be distinguished from theological opinions. He concluded with a point he had made earlier: The dress and titles of church leaders should be studied for possible reform.

Religious liberty debate

Léger took the floor again (23 September) when study of the text on religious liberty began. The topic originally was just a chapter in a document on ecumenism. It returned in the third session as a separate text. Opponents argued that such a declaration would have the unfortunate effect of granting rights to error, or at least favouring subjectivism and religious indifference. Also it would undermine the Catholic church in traditionally Catholic countries. In contrast, supporting the text, Léger stressed that by proclaiming that persons and groups have a right to religious liberty, the council would respond to several needs. It would help dissipate doubts regarding Catholic teaching about religious freedom. It would respond to the expectations of all those actually suffering persecution, injustice or prejudice because of religious faith. It would satisfy a requirement for dialogue with separated Christians and non-Christians. He thought the text made all the necessary distinctions, but suggested that it should describe religious freedom in a way that dealt with the rights not only of Catholics and non-Catholics but also those who did not believe in Christ. The intent, he said, was to declare the true freedom of everyone in matters of religion. This should be written so that everyone could understand it. To win the assent of everyone of good will, it should be added that religious freedom rested on the fact that such freedom is the highest and most sacred requirement of the use of human reason.

If written in this way, Léger argued, the text would help everyone see that the person and human reason are under attack in any action that frustrates a person's religious aspirations.

Jewish and other religions

On 28 September, Léger and Pocock spoke about the statement on Jews. Originally just a chapter in a document on ecumenism, it now was a separate document that had been broadened to include references to Moslems, Buddhists, Hindus and other non-Christian religions. This declaration, Léger said, was a necessary act for a renewed church that wishes to turn toward the non-Christian world and enter a fraternal dialogue with it. It was also needed to enlighten those Catholics who did not know that many non-Christians seek God in all sincerity. Because of confused ideas on matters of doctrine, he explained, it was not rare for Catholics to hold prejudices that were in no way in accord with the Catholic faith. The text recalled the Jewish origins of Christ, Mary and the apostles. To avoid any possibility that this might be called just a coincidence of birth, Léger wanted the text to specify that this had been willed by God. According to Our Lord, "salvation comes from the Jews" (John 4:22), and the gospel was intended "not to abolish, but to fulfill" the old law (Matthew 5:17). Hatred and persecution of Jews should be deplored and condemned not only because all injustice should be reproved, but also because the Jews, as St. Paul said, are "by election, cherished because of their fathers; for the gifts and call of God are irrevocable" (Romans 11:28-29). The text did well, he added, to refer to the church's desire that Jews might "approach" the Christian faith, rather than to speak of their "conversion."

Pocock said he wanted to join those who had asked for clear rejection of the charge that Jews are "God-killers." The council should condemn past and present religious persecution and racial discrimination against Jews. He defended the text against the objection that it painted a more positive picture of Jews than the scriptures did. The prophets of Israel, he agreed, often used harsh words about people being hard-hearted and stiff-necked, and the New Testament echoed these accusations. But Jesus, Stephen and

Paul belonged to the Jewish people, and their harsh words were exhortations meant to convert the people to whom they belonged, whom they loved, and with whom they identified. Also, in John's gospel, "the Jews" often refers to organized enemies of Jesus and not the whole Jewish people. In trying to define the relationships of Jews to the church, the text should turn to scriptural passages that announce the fulfillment of the old covenant in the new, and proclaim the mystery of God's mercy present in the people of His first love. Pocock's council files show that media reports of his remarks quickly won him plaudits from Toronto, including this 30 September telegram from a prominent Jewish member of the Ontario legislature: TODAYS NEWSPAPER REPORTS PROMPT ME TO EXTEND HEARTIEST COMMENDATION OF YOUR PRESENTATION ON THE SCHEMA UNDER DISCUSSION BY THE COUNCIL WHICH HAS IMPORTANT IMPLICATIONS IN BOTH THE CHRISTIAN AND HEBREW WORLD COMMUNITIES STOP GOD BLESS YOU. ALLAN GROSSMAN[5]

In addition to Léger and Pocock who spoke on the topic, the Canadian most involved in work on the Jewish statement was Gregory Baum as a consultor in the unity secretariat that was responsible for the text. Baum's 1956 doctoral thesis at the University of Fribourg studied papal teaching about Christian unity. Published in 1958,[6] it led to his appointment to Bea's unity secretariat when it was formed in 1960. While still at Fribourg, Baum, "from a family of Protestant culture and Jewish origin," also wrote a book on *The Jews and the Gospel*, published later.[7] At the first meeting of the unity secretariat, 14-15 November 1960, Baum heard from Bea that John XXIII wanted the unity secretariat to add a document on Christian-Jewish relations to the work it planned to do on Christian unity (and also, eventually, on religious liberty). Baum indicated his interest, and was asked to write an outline of a short text on Jews for the secretariat's 6-9 February 1961 meeting. He suggested three themes that later were central in the council debate and help define the final council text. He proposed that because the church and the New Testament are rooted in the history of Israel and the old testament, the church must reflect on its relations with the Israeli people to understand its own being and vocation. It must refute those popular fictions that consider Jews to be rejected and cursed by God as punishment for crucifying Jesus and failing, for the most part, to believe in him. And, because God's promises are forever, the Jews remain a chosen people who, accepting Christ at the end of time, will be reconciled with Christ's church. For Baum, these propositions flow in particular from chapters 9 and 10 of Paul's letter to the Romans, which were given "an original and daring interpretation" by the council's teaching about the Jews.[8]

A domestic interlude

> *Two Canadian bishops provided a little Canadian domestic drama in Rome the morning of 29 September, the second day of the long-awaited debate on the text about Jews and other non-Christians. Roy at the time was both archbishop of Quebec and bishop for the Canadian armed forces. In the latter capacity, his auxiliary bishop was Norman Gallagher, later first bishop of Thunder Bay, ON. That morning they absented themselves from the opening council Mass to preside at a wedding. By the time they left the party to walk to nearby St. Peter's for the beginning of debates and voting, they had thrilled a young Canadian couple, strangers to both of them, "with organ music, champagne, wedding cake at the breakfast in Hotel Columbus. The bride & groom had hoped for the 'bare essentials'– they were overwhelmed!" [Mae Daly letter 29 September 1964 to Daly children]*
>
> *Events leading to that morning began when Lawrence McMann of Owen Sound and Patricia Anne Morris of nearby Barry planned "a quiet little wedding" in Rome in the fall of 1964. McMann, a corporal with the Royal Canadian Ordinance Corps, had been on duty with the United Nations Emergency Force in the Gaza Strip. He and Patricia began about a year earlier to make plans for a wedding in Rome. She would come from Canada and he from Gaza at the beginning of an extended leave, prior to a new posting in Camp Gagetown, NB. The drama of a wedding in Rome would compensate for the absence of friends and acquaintances, they thought. The necessary paper work was begun by Capt. L. J. M. Marsolais, padre in Gaza. It included forms to be sent to the*

military chaplaincy in Canada, where they reached Gallagher's desk. Also, letters were sent to Romuald Bissonette, rector of the Canadian College in Rome, about local arrangements. After the young couple arrived in Rome by their separate ways, they went to the Canadian College to meet Bissonette. That Saturday morning the Canadian bishops were meeting there, so Bissonette introduced the couple to Gallagher and Roy, who promised to help with arrangements. Because they were English-speaking, Roy thought his anglophone auxiliary should preside at their wedding. Gallagher, in turn, suggested they would be more honoured to have their marriage blessed by the archbishop of Quebec, primate of Canada and bishop for the armed forces.

Roy found that he could not resist this argument. He busied himself the last few days before the wedding in a personal effort to round up a little Canadian wedding party, in particular inviting guests from among the Canadian news team in Rome for the council. He recruited Group Captain W.A. Hockney, Canadian Air, Navy and Military Attaché in Rome, to give the bride away. Mae Daly of Ottawa, just arrived in Rome for a short visit as guest on a Canadian Pacific Airways courtesy flight, suddenly found herself a bride's maid for the first time ever. I was the other official witness. Fr. Jean-Paul Belleville, of the Montreal national Catholic office for broadcasting, was assigned to be the official photographer. That morning the usual eight o'clock church-goers in Santa Anna, just inside Vatican City, discovered themselves in the midst of a wedding mass conducted largely in English. Roy anticipated the liturgical changes then being planned for Canada, following the council vote the year before. In English, Gallagher read the Epistle and Roy the Gospel, turning at the altar to face the little congregation. It was almost certainly the first time in that church, and perhaps in all Rome, that the texts were read in a vernacular language and not in Latin. The ceremony completed and all forms signed, the little party walked to the Hotel Columbus for a breakfast arranged by Roy, complete with a special cake and a toast to the bride. Then the newly-weds drove off for a day of sight-seeing in a car with a driver put at their disposal by the archbishop, while Roy and Gallagher hurried off to nearby St. Peter's to take part in some *crucial council votes, and the rest of the party tried to get their day back to normal.*

Canadian lay auditor

One of Paul VI's early decisions about the council concerned the participation of some lay Catholics as "auditors." They would have some of the privileges of non-Catholic "observers." They had a place in the hall for the daily debates, and were assigned to various working commissions with the right to speak but not vote. The first list may have been drawn up by Paul VI himself. All men at first, leaders in various national and international Catholic organizations, they were admitted to the council for the first time on 2 October 1963, during the second session's study of the nature of the church. Later, women were added to the list, and a Mexican couple representing the Christian Family Movement. There was speculation about whether a Canadian lay auditor would be named. The wondering ended when Stephen Roman, best known to most Canadians as a Toronto-based uranium mining magnate, was named during the third session. This prompted Pocock to protest to Sergio Pignedoli, newly named apostolic delegate to Canada. Pocock wrote that

> my conversations with our English-speaking bishops and with His Eminence Cardinal Léger confirm my statement to Your Excellency that this appointment has embarrassed the Canadian church. Mr. Roman is a good Catholic of extraordinary wealth who has been generous to the church. He has had no education of a formal nature beyond the age of 16 or 17 when he arrived in Canada. He has taken no part in Catholic Action at any level. He is unknown except in financial circles. The fact that he has been chosen over Canadian Catholics who have devoted much of their lives to Catholic Action and to Catholic endeavours of every kind, men of national and even international reputation, has damaged the image of the church and will cause criticism on the part of Catholics and non-Catholics in Canada. May I respectfully ask Your Excellency to request the Holy See to take some effective action to repair the damage that has been done. This could be accomplished, I believe, by the immediate

appointment of an English-speaking Catholic who would be favorably known nationally and internationally. It could also be stated that Mr. Roman was chosen as a representative or member of the Byzantine rite.[9]

Pocock added a "humble request" that the Holy See be asked "to pursue useful consultation with the Apostolic Delegation and the Episcopal Conference in matters of importance so that unfortunate incidents of this kind will not take place in the future." A day later Bishop G. Emmett Carter of London, Ontario, wrote to Pignedoli to "present for your consideration the name of Mr. John Francis Leddy, Ph.D., LLd, D.Lit., etc., in connection with a possible appointment as auditor of the council." Leddy had recently been named as the first lay president of the University of Windsor in Carter's diocese.[10] However, despite these and perhaps other efforts, Roman was the only Canadian named as auditor. His appointment, it is now known, was successfully recommended by Toronto's Ukrainian Bishop Borecky with support from Sebastiano Baggio, then a curia official recently replaced by Pignedoli as apostolic delegate to Canada.[11] While at the council, Roman supported the futile efforts to have communism formally condemned. In later years, he was the major contributor to the building of the Byzantine Catholic Slovak cathedral north of Toronto, which John Paul II formally dedicated during his 1984 visit to Canada. Roman died soon after, before the building was completed.

Revelation study again

After a two-day discussion of the text on Jews and other religions, the council again took up questions about revelation. Léger and Flahiff were the two Canadian speakers. This topic had created a stalemate during the first session that was broken only by John XXIII's direct intervention. Now a completely new text was on the floor. Léger (1 October) spoke in favour of the new text, which he said was in accord with the spirit of the modern biblical movement. He suggested some ways it could be improved. He wanted the transcendence of the revelation handed down by the apostles to be distinguished clearly from the traditions and teachings of the post-apostolic church. The apostles were "the witnesses to the resurrection" and their preaching itself built up the deposit of revelation. It was not so with the preaching of today's bishops, their successors. It did no little harm to ecumenical dialogue and to the progress of the science of theology, he said, that some in the church sometimes "insist in an indiscreet way on the infallibility of the teaching authority in the church, neglecting to make the necessary distinctions." Léger stressed that the word "tradition" should be used carefully. He said the text itself skipped from one usage of the word to another. He asked that this defect be cleared up. An improved text, he said, would do much to foster the spirit of Christian unity.

Flahiff (2 October) approached the same point from a slightly different angle. While he is listed as that day's final speaker, his remarks required only a minute or two at the microphone, and take up only seven lines in the official record of council speeches. He said the text pleased him in general, and that he agreed with what Cardinals Léger, Meyer of Chicago and Landazuri-Ricketts of Lima had already said about it. However, he had "a few comments" to add about the second chapter on tradition, and submitted these in a written text he did not read. They are recorded among the council's written interventions. He wrote that he was concerned that the text seemed to identify tradition with the entire life of the church. There had been times, he noted, when certain truths clearly found in scripture and tradition had not been fully understood and assimilated in the life of the church. At other times, certain teachings and practices had been prominent though they did not correspond to divine tradition. There could be no loftier task for the human mind, Flahiff said, than to ask it to fathom the true meaning of scripture and to ascertain what is authentically Christian in all the things that make up the life of the church at any given moment. He agreed with those who had noted earlier that the church is not automatically preserved in the purity and integrity of its doctrine, but must constantly examine its life in the light of the bible, guided by tradition and the church's teaching authority. About the time he submitted his written text, Flahiff wrote a letter about the debate to his fellow Basilians in Toronto. He said: " ...(W)hat strikes me personally most forcefully in the new text is the emphasis on the *personal* element in revelation. It may always have been obvious to some others, but I had not adverted sufficiently to the fact that Christ himself *is* God revealed and that this is the fundamental notion of revelation, with the result that the latter is to be conceived less as a book or as a series of clearly formulated truths than as a person who still speaks and acts and with whom we have present contact through faith."[12]

Place of laity in church

In the Catholic church's nearly 2,000-year history, Vatican II was the first general council to discuss the nature, dignity, spirituality, mission and responsibility of lay members of the church. Important passages about the laity are to be found in such major Vatican II texts as its *Dogmatic Constitution on the Church, Constitution on the Sacred Liturgy,* and *Pastoral Constitution on the Church in the Modern World*. Besides references in some other texts,[13] the council also produced a decree devoted specifically to the apostolate of lay people. When the third session began on 7 October to study this text, four Canadian bishops joined the discussion. As we think of them now, they were young bishops. Alexander Carter of Sault Ste. Marie, seven years a bishop at the time, was the eldest at 55 years. William Power of Antigonish was 49, Paul-Émile Charbonneau of Hull, 42, and Remi De Roo of Victoria, 40.

Carter had served as a consultant in the preparatory commission for the lay apostolate. However, when the council began with elections for its working commissions, Carter was not elected although his name was in the Canadian list of nominees. The commission for the combined topics of the lay apostolate and social communications was therefore the only one without a Canadian member. The text prepared before the council by the lay apostolate commission did not get on the council floor. Like all other pre-council drafts except for the one on the liturgy, it was judged during the first session to be unsuited for discussion and was sent back for rewriting. The lay apostolate text eventually discussed during the 1964 session was a third draft. When Carter spoke about it (9 October), he did so with direct knowledge of the debates and maneuvers concerning this topic during the months before the council opened. Besides, although not a member of the council commission, he kept in touch with its work. His was also the voice of an energetic bishop who was working hard to enliven the lay apostolate in his own diocese. He had come to that task well acquainted with Quebec's then-vibrant Catholic Action movement as a priest in Montreal; he had also been a close collaborator of Montreal's legendary Archbishop Joseph Charbonneau before the latter's enforced resignation. Carter's council intervention, he recalled later,[14] came out of personal experience and conviction.

Carter told the assembly that he thought the draft text should be rewritten once again. It was too clerical. It lacked organic unity and links with the doctrine on the laity already approved by the council. Thirdly, it would not respond to the expectations of lay people around the world. "Our schema (draft text) was conceived in sin – the sin of clericalism," Carter said. During work of the pre-council commission, its president and many of its members "were conscious of the fact that it was absurd the commission on the laity should be composed solely of clerics ... but nothing was done about this. However, when several men and women were invited to make a contribution (late in 1963) the great part of the commission's work was already done. They were introduced too late and their contribution remained minimal – a case of 'too little and too late,' as we say in English." Regarding what the text said, Carter remarked "we clerics are preachers by reason of our office. Notwithstanding the attempt to eliminate language that seemed clerical, the style still comes through with the tone of pious pleading. What is lacking is a contemporary language that is intelligible to the laity." He cited a passage dealing with family life that "shows no awareness of the concrete circumstances in which families are living. It is abstract and philosophical, sounding like a sermon plan prepared by some diocesan office to be preached on the feast of the Holy Family." He noted that as a result of a decision taken towards the end of the 1963 session, a second draft had been greatly reduced. In fact, in his view, it had been gutted, not just compressed, so that the third version being discussed was "something of a compendium of ideas which, so to speak, hang in the air." The concept of the lay apostolate should flow from the doctrinal premises already outlined in the council's *Constitution of the Church*, "but our text proceeds as if the council had never elaborated that doctrine on the laity." He noted a passage that spoke of the lay apostolate as having greater urgency "not only because of the shortage of clerics but even more because certain areas of human life have been alienated from every religious and ethical order."

This way of speaking, Carter said, "seems to be negative and far inferior" to what the text on the church said about the life of the laity being engaged in the work of salvation and the apostolate. "The eyes of the laity are turned toward the council – a council which has already been styled the council of the laity. But in this text we clerics are addressing ourselves, not the laity. No dialogue exists, nor is the foundation for serene and sincere dialogue posited. Certainly, there are in the text useful and well-founded observations. What is said ... about the responsibility of the laity for restoring the temporal order is praiseworthy. But alas! The image that emerges from the text is that of the organizational man, the one who of necessity belongs to some Catholic Action group." He noted that the text distinguished between the general and special apostolate, but scarcely envisaged an authentic apostolate outside some association. The church needed associations, but the vocation of the apostolate of the laity should draw on a wider constituency. Regarding Catholic Action as such, it would be better to make some propositions and leave to the conferences of bishops the task of completing a directory with specifics on the apostolate. "Then," Carter said, " the council would offer in a dignified and fruitful way what is so well expounded in the treatise on the church about the laity and the people of God." He concluded with praise for "all those lay people who desire and expect from the council inspiration and an invitation to the full Christian life; all those perceptive Christians who, either in associations or on their own initiative, struggle to establish the reign of Christ, and including all those heroic lay persons who often at the risk of their lives, and lamentably sometimes against the wishes of ecclesiastical authorities or with their opposition, strive for the right of all to freedom and a decent human life through social legislation."

Charbonneau, De Roo and Power lived at the same residence during the council. They wrote their interventions as three parts of one thesis. They drew from recent pastoral service as newly named bishops but, more importantly, from their formation and experiences as priest chaplains of Catholic Action lay movements – Charbonneau and Power, respectively, in Quebec's French and English sectors, and De Roo in the bilingual milieu of Manitoba. De Roo set out the theological vision that was basic to all three. Charbonneau outlined practical implications for the church that stemmed from that vision. Power sketched the kind of formation laity needed to enter intelligently into that vision and grow ever more active in showing their love of God, of fellow humans and of all creation. Each of the three, in turn, noted that the draft text had some positive elements but should be rewritten so that, in De Roo's words, the council would respond to the wish of laity for "a dynamic invitation to follow a vocation rooted in an authentic biblical theology of the people of God." In this they seemed to echo Carter's theme and conclusion. However, De Roo, Charbonneau and Power were talking about specialized Catholic Action and its specific program for preparing Catholic laity to be social leaders. Carter had in mind a much more general lay apostolate.

"The time has indeed come," De Roo began (7 October), "for the church in council to tell the world what she thinks about the laity who are the vast majority of church members and upon whom depends the future progress of the whole world." He noted Paul's letter to the Colossians (1, 16–17) says that all things both in heaven and on earth were created in Christ and through Christ, who exists before creation itself. It must be concluded, De Roo argued, that God's creative plan was not set aside by his plan for the redemption of the world. Rather, creation and redemption are united as one in Christ. Moreover, since the church is the body of Christ, "we must find in the church as well, and united as one, the two (creative and redemptive) aspects of God's divine plan for the universe." Every Christian therefore has a twofold vocation, De Roo stressed. All human beings have a basic original vocation "to work for the completion of creation and the perfection of the universe. Their very creation as intelligent beings, with a mission to transmit life, is the source of their human dignity and of their responsibilities in the fields of labour, economics, education, science, technology, and so on." This vocation, De Roo added, "is elevated to the rank of an apostolate because of the laity's adhesion through faith to the people of God and their call through baptism and confirmation to cooperate with Christ in the restoration of all things according to the divine plan of redemption."

These two aspects, natural and supernatural, are inseparable "in the concrete, existential vocation of all Christians," for in the Christian vocation all things are assumed by Christ and directed to the glory of God. The lay apostolate is likewise twofold: to proclaim God's kingdom and to transform the universe. First, "the whole of God's people is responsible for the spreading of the word of God and the advent of God's kingdom. On the part of the laity, this will entail various degrees of collaboration with the hierarchy." Second, "where the transformation of the temporal universe for God's glory is concerned, the role of the laity is of the greatest importance. Any apostolate which does not have as a consequence the spiritual transformation of the universe operates in a vacuum and labours in vain. The temporal order of creation or the 'profane' world must be restored to its sacred meaning and achieve its divine purpose." This second aspect, De Roo emphasized, "is a basic and unique aspect of the apostolate of the laity. This is the authentic *lay apostolate, which the laity alone can perform as lay people.*" Therefore, he concluded, every layman and laywoman must assume responsibility for the welfare both of the temporal and spiritual orders; and these two are inseparably united in the one concrete and existential vocation of all Christians.

Charbonneau (7 October), like Carter, criticized the draft for presenting the lay apostolate simply as a response to the shortage of priests or a remedy for the religious crisis humanity was undergoing. The laity's role is not to do what priests cannot do at the moment but would do if they could. Instead, there is a specific lay mission that is radically irreplaceable, rooted in their baptism and their own place as adults within the people of God. They experience and live the *entire* apostolic vocation of the people of God as such, although in a way that is specifically theirs, distinct from that of the hierarchy. It is not enough, he added, just to tell the laity once more that they need supernatural union with Christ, prayer, participation in the eucharist, or even the witness of a holy life. They already know all that. The text should especially insist on their baptismal obligation to bring the church to life in the structures of the world. "Just as Christ incarnated himself in the world, in a real and concrete incarnation, so the church must incarnate itself in it: *No redemption of the world without an incarnation in its structures.* The church must be in the world, not just as one structure among others but as the one that, from within and actively, takes on all the sufferings, hopes and struggles of humanity in its growth towards justice, peace, happiness." For this reason, Charbonneau said, formation for the lay apostolate could not be dealt with only abstractly. It needed two basic aspects. One is an authentic theological life, focused on the mystery of Christ's paschal charity with its realism as explained in the scriptures by John and Paul. The second aspect of lay formation, he added, "is *real* contact with life. It is by *sharing concretely* in the conditions of life of those around, and especially of those one wishes to lead to Christ, that an apostle discovers the real way to present the gospel, with the Holy Spirit inspiring, guiding and strengthening from within that situation. The gospel must be presented not as a doctrine from outside life but as a reply to people's basic search for a world of peace, happiness, justice, fraternity – which is in fact the unique kingdom of God." Charbonneau went on to criticize the draft text for being "gravely deficient" in its treatment of the Catholic Action movement. He thought it urgent to show clearly the specific role of Catholic Action among the other forms of the laity's baptismal apostolate.

Specialized or mandated Catholic Action did not itself monopolize all of the lay apostolate in a given community. Nevertheless, it played an irreplaceable role within the entire apostolate. Catholic Action established the main structures around which the church got involved in the human situation in order to lead it to Christ. Also, because of its close relations with the hierarchy which mandated it, Catholic Action enabled the apostolate to be a sign of the presence of the church as such, in communion with the bishop. Charbonneau's final point dealt with the kind of clergy-lay relations implied by his other ideas. The text should show clearly "the need for the clergy not only to dialogue with lay apostles but especially – and for me there is a big difference – to work in close collaboration with them." Therefore, "it is extremely important to form seminarians to respect the laity and definitively to wipe out clericalism, the apostolic error that is the source of so much harm."

Power (12 October) outlined principles on which lay formation should be based. He was sharing "the fruit of consultation with lay persons who in their daily lives are working at the development of the world and the building of the reign of Christ." Because the vocation to the apostolate is an integral part of the Christian vocation, "it is necessary that all lay people be given an apostolic formation that makes them conscious of their responsibilities in the saving mission of the church as well as disposing them to assume the apostolic role proper to themselves, according to the call of the Lord." Reinforcing what Charbonneau and De Roo said, Power added "in God's plan of things, the work of creation is harmoniously coordinated to the work of redemption accomplished by Christ and put forth for our times by the church." The apostolic formation of the laity therefore must take account of "the secular character proper and peculiar to the laity," and it must lead them to involve themselves profoundly and actively in the reality of the temporal order. In this way the laity learn to live their lives as persons and as Christians, in an autonomous and responsible way, even if traditional Catholic institutions are lacking. Thus lay people learn to become "at once the witness and the living instrument of the mission of the church." As well, they learn to "make the church present and fruitful in the heart of the temporal reality." To bring all this about, Power continued, five elements were needed for the complete apostolic formation of the laity. Their human gifts should be developed. They should be really involved in the world. They should enter into the real mystery of Christ. They should learn through group action. Their formation should have some direct contact and relationship with the hierarchy. Lay apostles, Power explained, "must develop those human qualities generally acknowledged as necessary to a mature adult. These include an acute sense of justice, civic spirit, a sympathetic openness to the world's values, a constant concern for all that is human, excellence in his or her own field, and a sense of service, initiative and responsibility." Experience showed, he added, that "a true apostolic formation of lay people does not come about without their personal involvement in the actual reality of their daily lives."

Power reflected his own experience as a chaplain for Catholic Action groups following the "see-judge-act" method for involving their members in social actions. When lay apostles are grouped in teams, Power said, "the sense of solidarity gives a greater meaning to the work of salvation as well as that of the natural order." Obviously, each member of the laity may make his or her contribution by an individual apostolate. However, grouping is required for the most efficient work of the apostolate as well as for the apostolic formation of the laity. Grouping is required by "the very way of salvation given by God to the church and to us through the church, as well as the law of historical evolution by which people tend more and more to associate with others." He added that if this type of authentic formation is to be acquired, "then it is necessary that there be priests who by their human qualities and spiritual depth can work with the laity for their formation in the church's mission."

What impact did these four Canadian interventions have on the final Vatican II *Decree on the Apostolate of Lay People*? Careful reading shows that some of the points they stressed were taken into account while others were ignored. Their main point – that there is a specific lay role and mission, which is not just to fill in when priests are scarce or absent – is clear in Vatican II teaching. However, the decree most clearly fails to take up the views of De Roo, Charbonneau and Power in what it says about specialized Catholic Action. Carter's text shows that he did not entirely agree with his three countrymen on this matter. The final council text, in turn, shows that the bishops as a whole remained divided to the end on the Catholic Action approach to lay formation. At that time, for thousands in Canada's francophone sector of the church, and for members of the Christian Family Movement, Young Christian Workers and Young Christian Students in English dioceses, the see-judge-act method of Catholic Action, as developed especially by Belgium's Joseph Cardijn, was a powerful and fruitful means for introducing laity to the apostolate and sustaining them in it. Charbonneau, De Roo and Power were among those who brought this conviction to the council. It was clear, though, that in some countries Catholic Action did not mean what it did in Canada. Other bishops, Carter among them, were also aware that members of some other lay associations – such as St. Vincent de Paul, Knights of Columbus, Catholic Women's League, Daughters of St. Anne – resisted the idea that Catholic Action as such should be accorded a favoured place in the church. The lay apostolate decree reflected this divergence of opinion when it noted (no. 19) that "great variety is to be found in apostolic associations" before it went on to speak (no. 20) about Catholic Action as such, in terms that did not fully satisfy such bishops as De Roo, Charbonneau and Power. While a detailed cause-and-effect analysis cannot be pursued here, it is important to note that the Vatican II ambiguity about Catholic Action flowed back into church life in Canada. Within a decade after the close of the council, the once-so-fruitful Catholic Action movements were declining in both French and English sectors of the church in Canada. Public attention in the church turned to a host of newcomers, including Opus Dei, Communion and Liberation, The New Catechumenate, and various charismatic endeavours. However, these have not succeeded in replacing Canadian Catholic Action's proven program for inspiring and training lay church members to involve themselves openly and creatively in temporal affairs and to work at shaping them according to God's will.

"Magno cum dolore"

While the four Canadian and other bishops were discussing the lay apostolate text in early October, Léger was involved in a tense behind-the-scenes drama over the fate of the texts on Jews and religious liberty, for which the unity secretariat was responsible. According to council rules, a text remained with the commission or secretariat that prepared it, unless reassigned by the four moderators or the pope, who alone had the right to make such a change. There was consternation in the unity secretariat during the 9 October weekend after Bea received two letters from Felici, the council general secretary, announcing that the texts on Jews and religious liberty had been reassigned. The letters said the Jewish text was to be turned over to a theology sub-commission for integration into the text on the church, and the religious liberty text was to be reworked by a new special mixed commission, named by Felici himself. Bea knew the moderators had not reassigned the texts. He learned from the pope that the idea had been discussed with him, but no decision had been made. Bea therefore rightly concluded that Felici's letters were part of the continuing minority effort to sidetrack the two texts. He mounted a counter offensive. At an 11 October Sunday evening emergency meeting, Léger was one of 14 cardinals (17 by some counts) who wrote a letter to Paul VI to ask that the council rules be upheld and the texts not reassigned. "With great sorrow (*magno cum dolore*)," the letter began, and informed the pope of their concerns. The affair ended with Felici's letters being set aside. The two texts remained with the unity secretariat, although Paul VI authorized a new mixed commission to make suggestions about the religious liberty statement.

Eastern churches

Baudoux was the only Canadian (26 October) to speak when the council moved on to discuss the draft decree on the Catholic eastern churches. Canadian representatives of these churches at the council, Ukrainians of the Byzantine rite, were Hermaniuk of Winnipeg, Savaryn of Edmonton, Roborecki of Saskatoon and Borecky of Toronto. Early in 1965, Michael Rusnak of Toronto was consecrated as Borecky's auxiliary, to serve as bishop for eastern-rite Slovaks in Canada. (Also at the council was Bishop Malanchuk, who was head of the Ukrainian Redemptorists in Winnipeg when named bishop for Ukrainian Catholics in France.) Baudoux spoke as a member of the council's commission for eastern churches that prepared the text. He urged its adoption. (It will be recalled that earlier in 1964 he had written to the commission itself that he opposed a separate text on the eastern church. He did not mention this in his council speech or explain why he had changed his mind.) It was proper, he said, to insist as the text did that an Orthodox Christian becoming Catholic should remain within the corresponding eastern Catholic church, instead of being received into the Latin rite. It was also important to restore and strengthen the patriarchates of the eastern churches, as the text aimed to do. (Both of these points were endorsed by the council in the final text of the *Decree on Eastern Catholic Churches*.) On the matter of changing rites, at issue in the debate was the desire of eastern bishops to safeguard their rites and traditions by blocking too-easy and too-frequent entry into the Latin rite. Strict laws on this matter would be in conflict, however, with the council's strong wish to endorse full freedom in all matters of religion. (The council's final position on this question was a general rule with the right of appeal to change rites.)

Church in the world

Baudoux's eastern church intervention came early the morning of October 20; and later that same day Léger entered the debate as the council began its historic discussion about the church in the modern world. Altogether, in the third and fourth sessions, there were 17 Canadian interventions on this subject, far more than on any other. Léger immediately put himself among those who approved the text. The text material offered an excellent base for fruitful discussion. It was well distributed, which was very important for good order in council work, and each chapter had a clear aim. It took up themes that people expected to hear from the council. None of these themes could be excluded from the council's doctrinal and pastoral responsibility. The bishops' pastoral experience would enable them to pose these questions clearly and to shed light on them. The text showed concerns arising from the realities of today's world and from listening to the voice of God through the signs of the times. In this regard it would be good if, during the discussion, the council could hear lay experts specialized in such questions as hunger in the world, the family, and peace. He was pleased the text spoke in a positive language, the only one that would be heard by today's people. The council should avoid "sterile condemnations" of the modern world. It should show positively that building up the world is a task to which Christians can make very special contributions. However, the doctrine in the text should be completed and made more precise on several points. He wanted it to speak more clearly about humanity's earthly and heavenly vocations. It should show that those vocations are linked, pointing out the demands of the gospel in temporal affairs, showing that being present to the world is an obligation for Christians. They contribute in this way to the church's interior renovation, an aim of the council. But he also had a concern in this regard. Temporal activities are important, but in Christian faith a person's supernatural vocation comes first. He wanted more clarity about the spiritual dimensions of human activities, about the gospel requirements for human relations.

The next day (21 October), Hermaniuk also commented on points to which Léger had referred. He saw in the text an "unfortunate" dualism between the natural and supernatural vocations. It should be demonstrated clearly, he insisted, that the latter demanded the perfection of the former. To assure the text some efficacy for the future apostolate in the church, the supernatural transcendence of the human vocation must be stressed, but not excluding – indeed assuming – engagement in the construction of the earthly city. Hermaniuk's main criticism of the text concerned the ambiguity of the concept "world" as used in it. The world could not be defined simply in theoretical terms. The text must also describe the different major and divisive perspectives of modern ideologies, in particular Christian and Marxist. The mission of the church in the world would take its meaning in this context, and one could understand that the Christian's supernatural vocation required engagement in building up the world. (No one paid particular attention at the time that the speaker immediately following Hermaniuk was Archbishop Wojtyla of Krakow, speaking in the name of all the bishops of Poland. The draft used the mentality and language of the church, he observed. The text, he said, should be directed to all people, Catholic and non-Catholic alike, so the problem of the language to be used for both must be considered further.)

Two days in the council

By the middle of the third session, many bishops were obtaining passes for visiting friends to enter the council hall to see it in operation. De Roo gathered the signatures of 20 Canadian bishops on two petitions asking for passes for Bonnie Brennan and me. They requested that we be admitted during the discussion of the church in the world, and stressed the importance "to the press and church in Canada that this loyal and loving servant" should be there. Ed Bader, who took the petitions to the general secretary's office, told of a monsignor reading the petitions and stammering, "…but a layman! …but all those signatures! … but a woman! … but all those signatures!" That was Friday afternoon, and Monday afternoon we received our green cards, marked "Rev. Sac. Bonnie Brennan" and "Rev. Sac. Bernard Daly." The morning of 20 October we entered with a wave from the guard at the door. My 21 October letter home recalled that a few weeks earlier, as part of a group of Canadian and US members of the Christian Family Movement, Mae and I had assisted at a mass opening a council session:

We sat yesterday in that box in which you saw Miss Monnet and the other auditors, and Msgr. O'Mara, Cardinal McGuigan's secretary, did some translating for us, although I did understand a bit. So the "Exeunt omnes [All strangers leave]" rang out not for me. After three on the oriental churches schema, they introduced schema 13 and then came the big guns. All cardinals: Liénart of France, Spellman, Ruffini, Lercaro, Léger, Doepfner, and Silva of Chile. Ottaviani and others were on the list, and we'll get them today. I was impressed with the orderliness of it all. The schedule is run very tightly. A lot of bishops move around, but my impression was that they listened even when standing about. I suppose it may be a bit different when some of the bishops get down to repeating their own favorite little formulas. But certainly the cardinals had a good audience, and I heard a bishop say that he hadn't left his seat all morning to the end. (My 22 October letter home told of the end of the adventure.)

Yesterday, our second day, a guard who asked no questions the first day challenged Bonnie. I saw it coming and had my chance to slip away and save my pass; but to what purpose? Both of us were identified as "Rev. Sac."– Reverendissimo Sacerdoti – and the guard didn't believe Bonnie looked like a priest. Bishop De Roo worked hard again, and tried to get the passes simply changed, but the word came back from Archbishop Krol (of Philadelphia, acting secretary for that day) that there had been "an oversight" at the office; that they weren't admitting press; and we could stay yesterday, our second round; but that the passes were withdrawn. I might have "swindled" a round or two, if I had abandoned Bonnie, but there seemed no point. This point was made: that the Canadian bishops wanted us in, and so applied. If they had simply called us "important lay people" it would have worked, probably. But they, honestly, labelled us as press, and we got in at all only because someone wrote that "Rev. Sac." It was fun. (The two days also made it clear for me that just getting into that sea of Latin was good for a colour story but meant little for real news. Effective, open press coverage of the council would have required special organization for that purpose.)

Quebec influences

Roy's 22 October intervention reflected the work of his Quebec consultative committee headed by Lambert. He was generally in support of the text, with suggestions for improvements. He wanted it more clearly addressed to everyone, not just Catholics or Christians. Its language must be that of "man to man," clearly intelligible to everyone. "This means avoiding pompous phrases," he specified. The text should begin from what is better and more easily known before going on to what is specific to Catholics. The dignity of the human person, basic justice and the nature of true progress were, he added, among the more easily known realities that should be starting points for the text. The text should be able to lead people to the Lord, taking them "by the hand," getting into dialogue with them, assuming their problems. It need not deal with complex theological questions far removed from common understanding. St. Paul spoke of the resurrection too early, and the Athenians did not hear him. The council text should begin with problems common to all, Catholics and non-Catholics. He mentioned hunger and poverty, injustice and violence as some of the modern world's most urgent problems. The council should express the desire of all people for development, unity and peace. In assuming these responsibilities, Christians could also respond to their own supernatural vocation.

On 26 October, three Canadians spoke about the text on the church in the world. By then the general discussion of the text had been completed. Léger and De Roo addressed points in its prologue and first chapter; and Bishop Hacault, making his first council intervention just seven weeks after being consecrated as auxiliary bishop in St. Boniface, spoke of the content of the second and third chapters. Léger said the first chapter on humanity's total vocation had its proper place at the beginning of the text. That should be its foundation; but the council should look for a better way of affirming the primacy of the supernatural character of this vocation. On this point, Léger was reiterating a concern he expressed a few days earlier when discussing the text in general. The chapter must present this vocation in all its aspects, he insisted. The primacy of the supernatural is affirmed in several places. It would be better that it be shown from the beginning. The text rightly spoke of the value of temporal ends, but care must be taken that the supernatural not appear thereby diminished. On the other hand, the human vocation has many aspects, and the complexity of the human condition must be brought out. In the introduction, it would seem that neglect of the world is the only temptation for Christians. People certainly need explanations about how their supernatural vocation may be accomplished through the tasks of living in the world. But there were other, sometimes more subtle, questions. For example, it must be shown that spiritual life involves other things than the accomplishment of temporal tasks. The meaning of religious and human duties should be shown. Another difficulty for people today is the problem of good and evil. The text said nothing about the meaning of suffering, and must be completed in this regard.

De Roo spoke the same day for a group of bishops regarding the first chapter. More than Léger, he strongly underlined the natural aspect of the human vocation and the need for Christians to be present in history, as leaven in the dough. He applied in this context the theological principles he had discussed during earlier study of the apostolate of the laity. He wanted the council to instruct Christians to avoid any split between the supernatural and natural missions that are part of their vocation. De Roo's theological argument was centred on the mystery of the incarnation. Christ became present in the world starting with the incarnation, entering the world fully as a human being, even if his presence was fully revealed only by the paschal events commemorated at Easter. In like manner, a Christian must therefore plunge into the world and get involved in it, like a vicar of Christ in the midst of the world, taking on all its challenges and cares, weaknesses and setbacks, De Roo urged. Christians achieve their total vocation, he concluded, "when in the spirit of Christ they engage themselves in the structures of the world, share in its struggles and commune with the inner dynamism of humanity. Indeed they fulfill the very mission of the church itself. This they must be taught. Of this they must be convinced." No one could effectively collaborate in developing the Christian community unless an active participant in building the human community, he added. "Here lies the deep and ultimate meaning of charity. For charity does not concern only a limited number of actions added on to our human vocation. Charity must order the whole life of the Christian." The spirit of Christ is "to perfect creation and to redeem it."

The same day, Hacault complained that the text "presents the church too much as a structure which is superimposed on the world and something of a stranger to it." His arguments and tone resembled those of De Roo. He spoke about the importance of the church's historic dimension. As a human institution, it was limited and could not solve all human problems. That was exactly why it was important for it to see itself as participant in the common destiny and to aid people along their way, perpetuating in history the mystery of the incarnation. It was the church's specific duty to discover God's voice acting in humanity. While the church in this world cannot be expected to solve all the problems that everyone has, the council must insist that constant efforts be made in this direction. Through closer contacts with all people, a more vital dialogue, and a more faithful awakening of the Holy Spirit, it would become easier for the church to compete its mission, which is to lead every person to God through Christ.

Two days later (28 October) Coderre spoke in the name of 40 Canadian bishops to urge that the text should throw a brighter light on the personality and role of women in the world. He noted in his personal journal "I spoke tenth, at 11:35 AM, coffee-break time. But I did my duty and so paid homage to my mother and sister and all other still greater women who have made our world more human."[15] The council, he stressed, should state that woman has her own God-given personality and therefore a specific and necessary task to perform in church and society. This had been obscured by the prevailing false idea that women are inferior. Coderre proposed that the text should say that women are necessary for completion of the divine plan for human perfection, for the perfection of the family and of society. Men should be urged to give women their proper place in the world. "Today we live in the midst of universal and profound evolution," Coderre argued. " Little by little, woman has become aware of her own dignity and her God-given place, which is not that of an inferior being. That is one of the signs of the times offered to the church in council. It is not sufficient for the church to acknowledge this evolution. Within itself, and also within the whole human community, the church must proclaim and promote this evolution to its culmination." To this end, the text should affirm more clearly "that woman has a unique and necessary role in the realization of God's plan," and "that without the real contribution of woman, human society and even the kingdom of God could not attain its perfection or fullness, and that mankind would be unfaithful to God's very plan for it."

The pill and all that

The next day (29 October), the council began to discuss what the text on the church in the world had to say about marriage. In the council's historical context, "marriage" became a code word for birth control. "The pill" had come on the market in Europe in 1962-63, after slightly earlier release in North America. Some Catholic moralists were discussing the pill as a new scientific fact that required new moral evaluation that might modify earlier papal condemnations of contraceptives. By 1964, everyone seemed to be talking about the pill and what the council might say about it and related matters. Almost nobody knew that, following a suggestion by Suenens, John XXIII secretly set up a commission on population, family and births that did not meet before the pope died. Under Paul VI, it held three secret meetings before the pope announced its existence on 23 June 1964, just four months before the council began to discuss related subject matter. Paul VI also ruled that birth control, being studied by his commission, was not on the council's agenda. This ban was well known inside the council but not by most other people, who still thought the bishops would talk about it. Work on the council text began in early 1963, as we have seen. There was never any thought that a text on the church in the world would not include something about marriage and family life. Its drafters, working well before the pope's ban on birth control as a council topic, focused on theological reflections about marriage. There was a large body of church teaching about marriage. Typically for the time when it was written, its starting point was not the facts of family life. Instead, theologians explored questions such as the purpose or end of marriage according to the creator's will, as revealed in the first chapters of the bible and related material in the gospels, and especially as understood in natural law terms. In this teaching, procreation was the primary end of marriage. The council text in effect opened broad questions about whether and how such existing teaching should be renewed. However, every word in the debate was scrutinized for hints about what each speaker thought about birth control, which was never mentioned.

Léger noted that many Catholic couples had problems and were not satisfied with the answers they received. "Pastors, confessors particularly, are assailed by doubts and uncertainties and, many times, no longer know what they can reply to the faithful," Léger noted. "Many theologians feel more and more strongly the need to examine more deeply in a new way the fundamental principles concerning marriage." Some people, he added, seem to fear any revision of the theology of marriage. Some argued that in so doing the church would be giving in to popular wishes. The aim of any such renewal, Léger insisted, was "to enhance the holiness of marriage by deeper insight into the plan of God." The church also should seek to learn what contribution recent biological, psychological and sociological discoveries could make to the solving of marital problems. He spoke of "a certain pessimistic and negative attitude regarding human love" which had veiled the importance and legitimacy of conjugal love in marriage. This negative attitude did not come from scripture or tradition, he insisted, but from "philosophies of past centuries." He was pleased that the text did not put procreation and love into opposition as "primary and secondary ends" of marriage.

However, it still failed "to present conjugal love and mutual help as an end of marriage" and did not deal in any way with the purpose of expressions of love in marriage. Conjugal love, he said, "is good and holy in itself and it should be accepted by Christians without fear.... In marriage the spouses consider each other not as mere procreators but as persons loved for their own sakes." It was not sufficient, he argued, to establish the doctrine that concerns marriage as a state. The problem of the purpose of the actions themselves had to be dealt with in its most general principles. "It must also be stated," he said, "that the intimate union of the spouses also finds a purpose in love. And this end is truly the end of the act itself, lawful in itself, even when it is not ordained to procreation.... (The text) should clearly present human conjugal love – I stress human love involving both soul and body – as a true end of marriage, as something good in itself, with its own characteristics and its own laws. The schema is too hesitant on this point." He found the text adequate in what it said about fecundity as a purpose of marriage. "It reminds us opportunely that procreation should be governed by prudence and generosity. It would be good, however, to consider this duty of procreation as linked not so much with each act as with the whole state of marriage. I would also like to see the special dignity of parenthood expressed more fully. Parenthood is indeed a participation in the highest act of creation: It contains something of the infinite, since it brings into being a person destined to see the Infinite Himself."

A full review and analysis of the ensuing debate is beyond the purpose of this book. In general, Suenens, Melkite Patriarch Maximos IV, Alfrink and others joined Léger in the search for new ways to express the church's teaching on marriage. Ruffini, Ottaviani, Browne and others insisted that the council text should enshrine the old natural law formulas and, especially, should specifically reaffirm previous papal teaching. What one Canadian bishop thought about the debate is recorded in letters by Flahiff at the time. He wrote to a Basilian colleague in Toronto:

> Today we reached the section on Marriage. Cardinals Léger and Suenens and Patriarch Maximos IX [should be IV] gave speeches to make Archbishop Pocock's letter of last June look relatively innocuous. They sounded more like the new book *Contraception*

and Holiness. No one of the three was proposing a teaching on the subject but they went a long way to expose the problems and to sympathize with the anguish of many couples and to urge a thorough re-investigation from every point of view. Cardinal Suenens used the expression: "One Galileo case is enough!" ... I am sure that the vast majority will seek a careful reassessment of the church's teaching on the whole matter not only of family planning but of the ends of marriage, which may have been viewed too mechanically... without sufficient consideration of the *total* view of the purpose.[16]

Later, in a "Dear Family" letter Flahiff added:

There is no question of altering basic truths and principles; however, it is quite possible that we have been trying to apply these to situations about which insufficient knowledge existed, with the result that not the truths or principles but the applications of them were faulty. It is also possible that in putting the truths into human language, we have used expressions or placed emphases that involuntarily have been misleading. Certainly there is grave need of more information.[17]

The third session debate did not settle the matter. When it came up again during the fourth session, Léger and Roy, as we will see later, were at the centre of negotiations for the compromise solution that was finally accepted.

Contributions by laity

Outside the council hall, and especially through documents circulated in Rome at that time, Canadian lay women and men were more directly involved in the debate about marriage than about any other council topic. Two texts were particularly prominent during the third session. One came from an international group of 148 lay Catholics, including some from Montreal and elsewhere in Canada. The other was the work of Roy's council team, led in this case by De Koninck. Those who signed the international text included Hélène and Jacques Baillargeon of Montreal, authors of the book *La Régulation des Naissances,* which described the SERENA approach to birth regulation developed by Rita and Gilles Breault of Montreal, who also signed. Others, from the University of

Montreal, were sociologist Colette Carisse, demographer Jacques Henripin and philosopher Bertrand Rioux. Laurent Potvin, a professor in the University of Ottawa school of medicine, and his wife, Colette, also signed. When their text was sent to the pope and council members and made public in October 1964, it was not known that the Potvins would be one of three married couples later named to Paul VI's birth control commission for its fourth meeting in March 1965.

The lay group wrote that they were responding to Paul VI's plea in his recent encyclical for dialogue within the church. The presence of the church in the world clearly required addressing problems of family life in general and birth regulation in particular. Millions of well-intentioned Christian couples had great difficulty, within the framework of existing directives, in reconciling procreation, education of children, and mutual love. As well, a large part of the world's population had mounting demographic problems. As death rates dropped "thanks to human intelligence,... the human race has reached a point where its fertility is seen to be quite excessive," their statement said. "Appropriate measures" to meet these issues "must clearly show the maximum respect for the human values involved," but at the same time they must be effective. Regarding the church's customary natural law approach to such matters, the group urged "extreme prudence...both in our attempts to formulate that law and in the precise meaning we derive from it." Acceptable surgery and organ transplants were cases of "interference" with nature. Advances in the understanding of physiology, they added, made it "clear that even on the physiological level the sexual act and procreation are a good deal less closely linked than has long been supposed. It is now recognized that the majority of sexual acts are not fertile, and therefore it is no longer possible to consider fertility the direct end or meaning of each individual act: what is known and experienced as impossible cannot be considered an end."

Traditional natural law concepts about marriage, they suggested, were both related to and challenged by new demographic realities and new medical scientific findings about human sexuality in general and human fertility in particular. In a broader understanding of procreation related to the total welfare of children, the importance of love and unity between the parents had to be more fully integrated. "These facts indicate that a certain concept of the natural law, of man's rights over his body, and of the finality attributed to the sexual act, appear to have become at least debatable," the brief said. They concluded: "We would like therefore to ask that the teaching church lay less emphasis on certain formulations of her doctrine which are largely the products of their historical context. We would further ask that a way be opened for the new scientific and philosophical discoveries in this field to be integrated with the theology and living thought of the church. We are convinced that a place must be found for a concept of natural law which does not exclude man's effective responsibilities with regard to procreation. It would also seem essential not to exclude a view of sexual morality in which the objective morality of the sexual act, within the context of married love, would depend, not on a certain character of direct fecundity in each particular act, but on the orientation of the whole of married life toward a generous fecundity." Many bishops read this text but there is no record of what they thought of it.

The De Koninck texts

The argument about birth control that De Koninck presented and explained to council groups in evening lectures in the fall of 1964 was quite different from that of the international lay group. A specialist in Thomistic philosophy at Laval University, De Koninck made headlines as a lay *peritus* (expert) accredited by Roy for the third council session. De Koninck's sudden death in Rome early in 1965 meant that he had only a few months of direct involvement in council work. Few outside Roy's immediate circle knew that towards the end of 1963, Roy had asked De Koninck, a member of Roy's consultative committee at Quebec led by Lambert, to coordinate a group of experts from several Laval faculties to do an in-depth study of birth control. In September 1964, the studies encouraged by Roy and co-authored by De Koninck and Msgr Maurice Dionne of Laval were distributed widely around the council.[18] Two De Koninck-Dionne texts circulated around the council at that time. Both were made public in Rome by the Centre for Coordinating Council Communications (CCCC). (At that time, the CCCC was headed by Yvon Desrosiers of Montreal.) One published on 6 November 1964 was in question and answer form. A note said it was the transcription of a discussion by Lambert's group in Quebec. The second, published by the CCCC on 16 November, was densely argued in Thomistic language that served almost as a disguise for its topic: "Is infecundity also for the good of the child?" For my personal benefit, De Koninck also prepared an English "paraphrase and explanation" of their official Latin version. It reads today like a curious cultural artifact. It said in part:

> The problem is whether infecundity can be for the good of the offspring. Now we observe from experience that there are normal periods of infecundity, and that these are good for the offspring. Suppose a wife could conceive again during pregnancy; this would be monstrous. Or suppose she could conceive every day of the year; that's ridiculous. Or suppose a woman could have a child when she's 75 years old? So you have periods of infecundity that are plainly for the good of the offspring and of the mother – and, of the mother *as* mother of the child. So if a woman as mother is for the good of the child, it simply follows that a woman ought to have periods of infecundity, and this already happens naturally. So nature must intend this. You have the same thing during the period of lactation. Now the main cause of the infecundity is nature itself. Just as in the case of healing nature is always the main cause. If we consider in nature the intention that is directed towards the offspring, then the offspring so considered (and that's why it is so important to view the offspring in its primary principle) is what is most essential to matrimony. And it is from this end that the whole order of ends of wedlock between themselves, and the order of whatever is for the sake of the ends, becomes plain. In this way we see the proper purpose of infecundity, and the principal agent, nature. Although nature is always the principal agent of health or healing, nature is not always sufficient to achieve this, but needs an extrinsic means, such as medicine. In this case, the doctor is the minister of nature. (I give a quote from St. Thomas in which he insists upon this: that the doctor, although he is the principal cause of applying the medicine, or in surgery of removing the limb, or of restoring something to the body, the principal agent in healing is nature, in that nature wants a gangrenous leg to be removed but she can't do it, just as she cannot distinguish between a foreign graft

that would be harmful and one that is helpful. Her defence mechanism is not sufficiently discerning.) So when a doctor amputates a leg, he is working according to the intention of nature. Nature cannot, for example, perform a graft, say the grafting of a cornea. But the doctor can, and in doing so he is merely co-operating with nature, doing what nature would if she could. But nature remains the principal agent, and that's the whole point that St. Thomas insists on so much here – in Question 11, Art. 1, *On Truth*. So it is plain from all this that the doctor is no more than an instrumental cause of health. This is what he adds as doctor when he is "in the office of nature." He can likewise be the instrumental cause of infecundity. When he does this, knowing that it is for the good of the offspring, he's not acting contrary to nature, but rather helping nature, as Dr. John Rock says, inasmuch as without the instrumental co-operation of the doctor, the principal end or purpose of nature, and accordingly of wedlock, could not be achieved.

The end of De Koninck's text was devoted to comments on papal teaching, in particular Pius XII's 12 September 1958 talk to the International Congress of Hematology. De Koninck suggested the pope's affirmations, apparently opposed to any justification of contraceptive means, could be interpreted in several ways and opened the way to new moral principles. Pius XII, he noted, "distinguished between infecundity directly induced, and that which is indirectly induced. The first is forbidden; the second is permitted. If we look more carefully into what he said, it is plain that what he had in mind was the principal agent." For De Koninck, it was "plain that the doctrine of Pius XII and Pius XI is a certain one. But we understand it only in a confused and imperfect way, as happens most frequently, even in the study of scripture. Furthermore, we must always distinguish between transition from confused knowledge to distinct knowledge, and transition from error to truth. These are two utterly different types of change." De Koninck's text concluded with some questions:

> The question for Pius XII was about direct or indirect sterilization. But what does it mean for a person to be the cause of direct sterilization? It is plain that Pius XII intended the principal cause. He did not touch upon the instrumental cause, that is, a person considered as a minister of nature. It was simply

not explicit in what he said. Why was he not asked about this? Who knows?

Similar themes and arguments were advanced in a third De Koninck-Dionne article at the beginning of 1965.[19] At that time, as Turbanti records, De Koninck had been invited to participate, as Roy's expert on the topic, at the mixed commission's work session planned for February at Ariccia in the suburbs of Rome. After the 1964 council debate and in view of another council session, the mixed commission had decided to do more work and drafting on the text. A new drafting committee was formed, headed by Pierre Haubtmann, professor at the Catholic Institute of Paris and a member of the secretariat of the French bishops' conference. He would replace Redemptorist Bernard Haering as the text's main drafter. De Koninck was the only Canadian participant at the Ariccia session. At it, the guidelines were set out for the new draft that, after successive corrections, became the definitive version of the council document on the church in the world. De Koninck worked in the sub-commission responsible for the chapter on marriage. After a general study of the chapter, it discussed the more urgent problems raised during debate in the council, especially birth control. The sub-commission was cautious because the pontifical commission was working on the same subject. Haering probably served as the link between the two bodies, as a member of both. It was decided to formulate precise questions to submit, if possible, directly to the pope. This was De Koninck's last work. Arriving in Italy already sick, he died in Rome at the end of this session, on Saturday, 13 February. Who knows if the papers by De Koninck and Dionne were of any help to the bishops at the council? And, because secrecy still shrouds the files of Paul VI's birth control commission and later work on his 1968 encyclical *Humanae Vitae*, who knows if their argument was taken up again by anyone involved in that process?

Missionary activities

When Léger spoke in the council on 6 November, it was to open discussion of the text on missionary activity. The situation was dramatic. That was the only morning during the council when the Pope came in for a working session. Paul VI was not only present but gave an opening statement, stressing the importance of missionary activity in the church. The text to be discussed could be improved, he said, but was generally satisfactory and he hoped it would be passed eventually. Then he blessed the council in its work and left the hall. Opening the debate, Léger was in the position of welcoming but also calling for some major changes in the text the pope had just highly recommended. Léger noted that from the beginning of the council all bishops, not just those from mission lands, had hoped that new impetus might be given to the missionary apostolate of the church. The council had encouraged hope of such new impetus. It had recognized the need for true diversity in the church. It made this diversity possible by recognizing needed freedom in liturgical matters for national episcopacies. Such liberty was nowhere more clearly needed, he said, than in mission lands. History taught that without such liberty it was impossible to adapt the gospel message to the various needs of each region. The text should speak with more vigour and at greater length about this. The restoration of the permanent diaconate was another reason for hope about the missionary apostolate, Léger said. Churches that were young or lacked vocations might receive precious assistance when their wishes in this matter were realized. New hope for the missionary effort also arose, Léger suggested, from the beginning of dialogue with non-Christians. He was disappointed that the text dealt with relations with non-Christian cultures, but said almost nothing about relations with other religions. He also welcomed the fact that the text tried to increase co-operation by religious orders among themselves and with bishops. Fragmentation of missionary forces was a great obstacle to progress. The bishops at the council had vigorously affirmed that the first task of collegiality was the evangelization of all peoples and mutual assistance among all the churches. But for this doctrine to be effective, the church needed to create structures through which bishops, under the pope, could discharge their common responsibilities. He noted that the text referred to a "central council of evangelization." It should be considered precisely as an institution through which bishops could truly exercise their common responsibility to evangelize. He called for clarification of the relationship of such a council to the Vatican congregation for the propagation of the faith, already in existence. He suggested the new council should be within the congregation, and its top element, the superior council of the congregation. That would create a vital link among the bishops and between the centre of the church and its various parts.

Renewal of religious orders

Germain-Marie Lalande, a Montreal priest who was general superior of the Holy Cross Fathers, spoke 12 November for 140 council members, including 43 heads of religious orders, when he criticized as "insufficient" a proposed text on renewal of religious life. He called it a weak response to what members of religious orders of men and women were expecting from the council. The text's suggestions for renewal seemed to him to be too juridical to result in anything but exterior changes in the lives of religious. The suggestions lacked pastoral vigour, and were not sufficiently rooted in the concrete problems of the church, religious life, or the world. The general shortage of religious vocations was, he agreed, a complex problem with many causes, but perhaps it was explained by the fact that today's young people felt that religious orders no longer satisfied their aspirations. They perhaps appeared to the young as too tradition-bound and disincarnated; or perhaps they did not correspond to the ideas young people had about religious life – its evangelical character. The text should put more emphasis on the links between the general renewal the council had stirred within the church and the particular witness that religious orders should give in today's world. He wished that a new text might be written. There should at least be a new introduction, along biblical, theological, pastoral and sociological lines. This would provide the basis for a profound interior renewal of religious life, and would justify the exterior and juridical reforms set out in the text being debated. It should be shown how, in today's world, poverty, chastity and obedience, as well as life in common, can and must be a witness against materialism, a thirst for riches, the search for physical pleasures, and the tendency to make gods of liberty and unbridled individualism. The text also should show how religious life can be a sign of universal charity. It should teach, he concluded, that religious orders should have "a sense of the church," universally and locally. This would create a deeper interior life. Such a sense should also foster the co-ordination of the activity of each religious community with the life of the church universal and local, while remaining true to the proper goal of each congregation according to the spirit of its founder and the will of the church.

The formation of priests

Léger made the last two Canadian interventions of the third session. On 14 November he spoke about the seminary programs for the formation of priests, and on 18 November about Christian education in general. The decree about seminaries began with the principle that the conference of bishops in each nation should prepare a program for seminaries of their country or region. This approach was in line with the teaching developed earlier by the council about the collegial responsibility of bishops. The bishops were generally pleased with the text. Seminary formation should help students become "priests of our times," apostles who could evangelize the world according to the most profound intentions of the council, Léger said. The text, he thought, took into account the variety of conditions and needs of each region, and proposed in a very timely way that from their student days priests should be concerned with the needs of the world and learn how to understand them. He welcomed the stress on philosophy in seminary studies. He had questions, however, about the way the draft recommended the "perennial philosophy." If this referred to scholastic philosophy, it was ambiguous. Historians of philosophy had shown there were several scholastic philosophies. "Besides," he added, "this request to teach one philosophy, 'the perennial philosophy,' does not seem to agree with the nature of philosophy.

By its nature, as St. Thomas noted, philosophical research does not start from authority but from looking at what is real. The aim of philosophy is not to say what authors have written but to speak of what things are. Moreover, it was contrary to the nature of philosophy, and not the role of the council, to impose just one system of thought. Especially, a system of western philosophy should not be imposed on non-western seminaries. Regarding the teaching of theology, he was pleased that the text did not insist excessively on the teaching of St. Thomas Aquinas. The value of his work could not be minimized, but "unfortunate the man with only one book; unfortunate the church with one teacher." He proposed that the text should say "the Catholic church proposes St. Thomas as teacher and model for all students of theology." In this way, rather than imposing St. Thomas' system and teaching, the council should propose St. Thomas himself, in his scientific and spiritual stance, "as the prototype researcher and creator in theological studies, who knew how to put the science of his time to the service of the gospel." In turn, regarding the teaching of theology, the text did well to stress holy scripture as the soul of theology. However, Léger wanted more said about dialogue with the world so seminarians would not live in ignorance of the real problems, the thoughts and even the language of the real world. "It is important to note," Léger said, "that for several decades a great number of theologians have had no dialogue except with the philosophers of the Middle Ages. This attitude has been detrimental for the church, which must enter into dialogue with the contemporary world. He wanted the text to suggest concrete remedies for this problem, such as "the presence and constant consultation of some lay experts in seminaries, courses in which church teaching would be compared with current secular thought, and pastoral experience for professors and students."

The teaching of moral theology in seminaries suffers from several faults, Léger concluded. "It is too preoccupied with casuistry, legalism, juridicism and moralism. If I dare say so, it does not seem to be mainly and fully Christian. Since these faults have deep roots in history and in our own minds, we cannot root them out if this text does not say a serious word of caution about them. I therefore propose that in one paragraph we should deal explicitly with the teaching of moral theology. It must affirm the need for a moral theology that is intimately linked with dogmatic theology, well grounded in scripture, and integrated in Christ's plan for salvation. If our text speaks in this way about moral science we can certainly hope that, through our priests, the renewal of Christian behaviour could reach to all the faithful. The council of Trent renewed the education of priests of its time. Following Vatican II, may this text, after amendment, be the source of a new evangelic dynamism that will transform our seminaries."

Léger on Christian education

Speaking in the name of many Canadian bishops on 18 November, Léger recommended that the short draft text about Christian education be sent back for substantial improvement for the council's fourth session. "We should not approve too hastily what will be the *Magna Carta* of Christian education." He thought it unwise in the last days of the third session to deal hastily with a text that had some excellent recommendations but lacked inspiration and failed to deal adequately with some major problems. One of these, he specified, was the need for co-operation and co-ordination among Catholic universities. Modern states, he noted, recognized the importance of co-ordinating research in various fields. Similarly, the church should plan its research in the sacred sciences. The Vatican congregation dealing with schools and studies should have as its main task the advancement of common planning. It should be proposing to the world's Catholic universities the most urgent problems in need of research. He aligned himself with other bishops who had stressed the need for healthy freedom in scientific research. Those drafting the text should pay special attention to the question of freedom of research in the sacred sciences. If this were not perfectly assured, irreparable harm for the church could follow. In a world where everything was changing so rapidly, especially in scientific matters, the number of new and difficult problems for the church grew every day. The church, he insisted, could not hope for a solution to such problems if scholars were not able to pursue their studies with all necessary freedom. It was clear, Léger added, that new tendencies and discoveries in the sacred sciences had to be judged by competent church authorities, "in order to separate, so to speak, the chaff from the wheat."

This role of the teaching authority was a unique element, extremely useful and even necessary for scientific progress in the church. However, if the presence of the magisterium was to bear full fruit, it was evidently necessary that this teaching authority should not act hastily or without trust. On the contrary, it should encourage and promote research. Encouragement of research by those in authority stimulated dialogue among theologians and the teaching authority, prevented misunderstandings, and made reprimands unnecessary or at least less unwelcome. It had been noted by everyone, he said, how useful to the council had been the encouragement given by church authorities to those who worked on liturgical, scriptural and ecumenical subjects. He recalled in particular Pope Pius XII's encouragement of scriptural scholars in his 1943 encyclical, *Divino Afflante Spiritu*. In a similar way, carefully but clearly, the text on education should proclaim the freedom of research in all the sacred sciences.

How the mood of the council had changed over the first three sessions was noted by Emmett Carter, then bishop of London, in an article at that time for *The Catholic Register* in Toronto. "In the first session," he wrote, "when cardinals disagreed there was a gasp through the whole assembly and there was an initial attempt to keep this situation from the press. In the past week or so, Cardinal Léger has risen immediately after Cardinal Ruffini on two occasions. On both of them he has taken a position so clearly opposed to his predecessor at the rostrum that some wondered if he hadn't known ahead of time the text of Cardinal Ruffini's interventions! Now, in sharp contrast to two years ago, nobody was in the least surprised. Moreover, we heard words of praise, admiration, yes, and of affection, for the 'old warrior of Sicily,' a traditionalist to his heels, but a 'bonnie fighter' and a man whose devotion to the church we might all emulate to our advantage."

Mixed feelings at the end

The early October incident that prompted the "*magno cum dolore*" letter to Paul VI focused attention on the work of the unity secretariat during the session's final weeks. Three texts, on ecumenism, religious liberty, and relations with Jews and other non-Christians, were involved. What was happening to them behind the scenes, in commission debates about which even most bishops were not kept informed? Voting on 12 and 14 November, the council approved the last amendments to the ecumenism text. What, then, was delaying a final vote on the text as a whole, so it could be promulgated along with texts on the church and on eastern churches during the 21 November closing ceremony? More worrisome still, what was happening to texts on religious liberty and non-Christians that were discussed at the end of September? A council majority, led by bishops of the United States and Canada, wanted to be sure before the session ended that these two texts received confirming votes. Finally, on 17 November, the revised text on religious liberty was distributed in the hall, and a vote was announced for Thursday, 19 November.

The previous day, the text on Jews and other non-Christians also appeared, to be voted on 20 November, the last workday. On Thursday, closing debate about the text on Christian education was proceeding normally at mid-morning until, unexpectedly, Cardinal Tisserant, the day's president, announced there would be no vote on religious liberty because "many fathers" had requested more time to study the text. Immediately, commotion spread throughout the hall. An observer wrote "one would have to go back to one of the early church councils, that of Trent, for example, when an enraged bishop pulled another's beard, to find a precedent for the scene of consternation, outrage, and disarray that took place on this memorable morning."[20] U.S. bishops rushed about to gather more than 400 signatures on a handwritten Latin letter to Paul VI: "With reverence but urgently, very urgently, most urgently [*insanter, instantius, instantissime*], we request that a vote on the declaration on religious liberty be taken before the end of this session of the council, lest the confidence of the world, both Christian and non-Christian, be lost."[21] Order eventually resumed, and at the end of the morning, Cardinals Meyer of Chicago and Ritter of St. Louis were joined by Léger to take the petition to the pope. He told them that since the requested delay was within council rules, he would not impose a vote, but gave his word, repeated two days later in his closing speech, that religious liberty would be the first topic of the 1965 fourth and final council session.

Further to calm troubled spirits, the text on non-Christians received an affirming vote on 20 November, and the ecumenism text won final approval. The *Decree on Ecumenism* was promulgated by Paul VI the next day, along with the *Dogmatic Constitution on the Church* and the *Decree on Catholic Eastern Churches*.

One evening during the second session I was to have dinner with Bishop Klein of Saskatoon, our former hometown. When I arrived at his hotel, he was meeting a bishop I did not know. There was nothing unusual about that, but after the other bishop left Klein was obviously still preoccupied by their encounter. "You'll never guess what I just did!" he exclaimed. "I just promised to send that guy three of our best priests!" Klein had agreed to send priests abroad, even though he came to the council hoping to find ways to get more priests for Saskatoon! "That guy," Klein explained, was Adelmo Machado, archbishop of Maceió, Brazil. Early in the council, Dom Adelmo approached several Canadian bishops and told them he was short of priests in his corner of northeast Brazil. One of them jokingly pointed to Klein and said, "Ask him; he has lots of priests" – an opinion Klein did not share at all. From then on, as Klein told the story, the Brazilian seemed to follow him everywhere. He'd go into a session and Dom Adelmo was close at his heels. He'd go for coffee and the archbishop was at his side. He would get on a bus and the Brazilian was on it. Dom Adelmo talked constantly about a parish with no priest to look after 60,000 people, twice as many as all the Catholics in the Saskatoon diocese with its 30 priests. The evening I went to meet Klein he finally gave in to the Brazilian's pleas. Klein went back to Saskatoon, asked for volunteers, and during 1964 the Saskatoon diocese sent a team of three priests – Bernie Dunn, Don Macgillivray and Bob Ogle – and two registered nurses — Cecile Poilievre and Ida Raiche — to Uniao dos Palmares in Maceio diocese. Klein and Dom Adelmo would meet other times during the council, but only one such occasion is recorded. By 1965 the Saskatoon team was well under way in Uniao. One day in the council hall, Klein led Dom Adelmo to the area in front of the statue of St. Peter. Klein reported that the Saskatoon team wanted an airplane. "He made me extend my right hand toward the statue," Dom Adelmo later recalled, "and said I must respond yes or no to his question: Does the Saskatoon team need an airplane? I began, 'Well…' but he insisted, 'No well, or anything else; just yes or no.' So I said, no." Some months prior to this incident, Ogle, enthusiastic about flying, had initiated the aircraft project and, confident of a positive outcome, launched a campaign to raise funds. After the episcopal anti-aircraft intervention, the Saskatoon team settled for a Volkswagen "bug."

6

The Fourth and Final Session: 1965

No dramatic debate defined the fourth and final session of Vatican II in the fall of 1965. Paul VI's 4 October address to the UN headquarters in New York was perhaps the most fitting public symbol for the period, during which the *Pastoral Constitution on the Church in the Modern World* was among the eleven texts promulgated. No longer "the prisoner of the Vatican," the pope went to New York to urge political leaders that there should be "no more war." The war then spreading destruction in Vietnam provided a grim context for his appeal.

How does Christ's church live and work in such a world, to help build it according to God's will? Nine Canadian speeches were made about this question, the major topic for debate during the final session. That brought to 17 the number of Canadian interventions about the church in the world, the topic that attracted by far the most Canadian comment at Vatican II.

Compared with earlier debates in the council hall, the final plenary assemblies were relatively calm, but the bishops were kept very busy with voting on final versions of the texts. The frantic activity of lobbying and arguing took place mainly at smaller meetings of the commissions responsible for preparing the eleven texts for final votes. Having lost the debates in the plenary sessions, the curia-led minority redoubled efforts to shape the final texts by influencing the revisions. Their main tactic was to submit written requests for hundreds of changes during the final editing process. This work was officially secret, known to the public in part through leaks to a few European newspapers. Pope Paul was heavily involved, through appeals made to him from all sides, and through notes he sent to the drafters on points that particularly interested him. His interventions indicate that he had two main concerns. He wanted council work to move ahead to a fitting conclusion and not get bogged down on points already rejected by majority votes. At the same time he wanted the final texts to achieve a balance that would rally as much support as possible from the minority side. That meant finding compromises on a number of issues. Paul VI's personal papers from those days are not yet public, but the main events are well documented from other sources. A council insider wrote soon after the session that "the final three weeks were as filled with maneuvering and surprises as any period in the council's six years."[1] The details of this convoluted process do not belong in an account of Canadian participation at Vatican II, but the involvement of Léger, Roy and Quebec theologian Bernard Lambert in finalizing the text on the church in the modern world was a highlight of the council's final weeks.

Church in world main topic

Just before the fourth session began, Paul VI issued a constitution for the synod of bishops. Its text was read at the opening of the first workday. Until the fine points were examined, the synod was heralded as the instrument of collegiality that many bishops had requested. In fact, over time the Synod of Bishops turned out to be tightly controlled by Vatican officials in the name of the pope. A structure through which the local bishops as a college truly share with the pope in church governance is still to be developed.

A five-day debate on religious liberty opened the fourth session, as the pope had promised when the third session ran out of time without reaching this item. No Canadians spoke on the religious liberty text during this final debate. Then, on 22 September general remarks began about the mission of the church in the modern world. Archbishop Jordan of Edmonton was the first Canadian to welcome the text. He began on a note that would prove ironic.

The council text mentioned "the need for constant and trusting dialogue between the clergy and laity in the church." Referring to the Social Life Conferences, Jordan said "we are fortunate in Canada in having a forum which makes possible this type of continuous communication between the bishops, priests and laity concerning these matters which deal with the problems of a social nature in our modern society." The May 1965 Montreal social life conference of which he spoke was the last one to be organized.

Jordan's main remarks were a summary of the conclusions of the Montreal conference, making good his promise to the 500 participants there. He said he was heartened to see how the text made the church, the people of God, one with the joys and hopes, the anguish and sorrows, of all peoples. "The spirit of optimism and confidence in humanity aroused by Pope John is carefully safeguarded, and thus this document is fittingly addressed to all in positive language they will understand and appreciate." He welcomed the fact that "the myth unfortunately cherished by many Christians that the church and its ministers possess ready-made answers to the world's problems is systematically exploded in this document, and the church is portrayed rather in the posture of a humble inquirer, striving honestly, not without the help of all people, to tap the sources of divine and human knowledge in its search for truth." The text had some gaps, however. It tended to overlook "the vital relationship that must exist between the Christian community at work and play and the Christian community at worship." It also was very weak concerning leisure activities. The creative value of these activities must be stressed. Also, although considerable attention was paid to the needs of the poor and the dispossessed there was no mention of the sick, the infirm, those suffering from various kinds of disease. He wanted explicit mention of the creative role of architects, engineers, and the builders of the physical environment. He concluded by calling for "an expression of our willingness to co-ordinate the activities of the church's foreign missionaries with those services being rendered to the poor peoples of the world by other churches, by the agencies and governments of individual donor countries, as well as by specialized agencies of the United Nations."

Hermaniuk, who followed Jordan the same day, also welcomed the improvements made in the text since the third session. However, he found that it still followed the scholastic method "too slavishly" when discussing such questions as human activity in the world, progress, and culture. The next day (23 September), Baudoux took a similar line. He praised the positive drafting on problems of the modern world and the perspective of openness to dialogue with everyone. In his view, however, the text's language needed to be corrected and the arguments used revised, the better to meet the council's intentions.

Concern about communism

After Baudoux spoke, the discussion moved from general remarks to specific parts of the text. Article 19 of the first chapter dealt with atheism, and became the focus of a concerted effort by those who wanted a specific condemnation of world communism. Rusnak of Toronto (28 September) made his only council intervention on this point. He was then auxiliary to Ukrainian Bishop Borecky and responsible for Slovac eastern-rite Catholics (and later would head their separate diocese, centred in Toronto). Rusnak was one of a number of bishops who called for a strong, direct condemnation of communism. Others took the view that specific or negative orientations should be avoided.

Truth and charity, Rusnak said, demanded that the council speak out about the perils of the atheism "which stems from a politico-economic system that touches eastern Catholics very closely." The situation in Czechoslovakia was deplorable. He urged that the council add a special declaration on communism. It should be in line with the message to all humanity issued during the first session in 1962. "There should be no fear," he said, "that speaking out will cause reprisals behind the iron curtain. Experience shows that communists will react only to forceful public opinion." Rusnak said, "It is easy to see in Czechoslovakia what atheism has done to the church. It denies God and the reality of all spiritual things. It has no respect for the dignity of man, works out its own theories of knowledge, and establishes its own principles of social life and political government." It would be worse than saying nothing at all if the council text said only a few things about this problem. Giving specific examples, he said that in one night all the religious community in Czechoslovakia were suppressed, their members arrested and taken to concentration camps. Priests were taken out of their parishes and not replaced. Out of 15 seminaries functioning some years ago, only two remained. "These acts are eloquent proofs of the real nature of atheistic communism." At commissions meetings and other events outside the council hall, one of those supporting Rusnak was a leading member of his Toronto congregation, Stephen Roman, who, as noted earlier, was named the previous year as the Canadian lay "auditor" for Vatican II. As the final results of the council show, the majority rejected this effort.

When Léger spoke the next day (29 September), the council had moved on to final study of the chapter on marriage, the topic Léger and others had addressed sensationally during the third session. Léger again focused on the issues that had concerned him earlier, referring to the doctrine on marriage and how that doctrine was expressed. The text was improved "in what it has to say about the importance and lawfulness of conjugal love." Its main weakness was that it did not give a proper explanation of the aim of marriage. It was not enough, he said, to affirm that the purpose of marriage was procreation and the education of children. "We should declare clearly that marriage is not merely a means of procreation, but likewise a community of life and love." The text could also be criticized for its order and style. "We must take care that our declaration does not turn out to be a diplomatic compromise between various schools of thought," he urged. Also, it should avoid referring too often to what people should do, giving the impression that the council was moralizing.

The formula, which defined marriage as an "institution ordered to the procreation and education of children," could perhaps express the meaning that marriage has for the *human race*, he said. "For the human race, indeed, marriage has only this meaning: that is how it conserves and propagates itself. But, since marriage unites persons, it is especially important to describe the importance marriage has for persons, obviously without neglecting its meaning for the human race." For humanity, Léger said, marriage is not just an institution ordered to the procreation of children. "It is also – it is especially – a community of life and of love." He proposed that it be said "clearly and openly that marriage is an intimate union of life and of love, and that the profound meaning of the child for love and conjugal life be carefully set out." Then it could be said how it is the will of God that couples beget children and thus become co-creators with God. This was evident from the words of Genesis and from the very nature of love and the conjugal union. "In this way, spouses will understand that their love is not closed on themselves and that they must be part of the grand plan of the creative providence of God." About the style of the text, Léger said everyone knows that the council must express itself clearly on the subject of marriage. "That is why, despite the great doctrinal difficulties the council has encountered in dealing with this question, I believe that it cannot promulgate a text whose intentions will be grasped only with difficulty by pastors themselves." He said he would propose in writing "some formulations which might help towards improving the text."

De Roo spoke (30 September) with the support of 33 other bishops when he outlined what he had been told by Canadian couples. He too called for a stronger statement about conjugal love. His vote on the text would be "yes, with amendments." The council should avoid preoccupation with the problems and pitfalls of marriage and family life, and insist instead on the positive vision of the riches of human love that marriage could attain through grace. While they appreciated the value of church teaching, married people knew "that conjugal union cannot really be understood unless it is realized that carnal union gives rise to a communion of the whole persons and lives of the partners," De Roo said. "The classical view of procreation as the end of marriage must be perfected, for procreation requires that parents be not only the authors of life, but also an unfailing source of love for the whole family." Christian marriage "is a vocation to seek perfection as a team," he stressed. "Married couples must never abstain from the daily practice and development of authentic conjugal love. The council will promote the redemption of all humanity by exalting the positive values of conjugal love."

The way world attention was focused on the church's study of family problems was a charismatic note of our times, De Roo said. It offered a unique opportunity for a positive promotion of conjugal sanctity, to the lasting benefit of the whole people of God. The whole Christian people must contribute to the solution of the grave problems that affect conjugal love. Married life is the vocation of the vast majority of Christians. The mind of the faithful (*sensus fidelium*) has a special function not only in matters of doctrine or belief but also in matters of Christian morals or practice. The Canadian couples he had consulted expected the council to recognize their proper gifts and the special characteristics of their vocation. "They want encouragement and help to move with enthusiasm towards deeper conjugal life in this age of church renewal." Christian spouses know that their conjugal union cannot be really understood "unless a central truth of prime importance is clearly recognized, that marital intimacy gives rise to a unique communion by the partners of their complete lives and persons." The classical doctrine, that marriage is intended for procreation, had to be perfected and completed, De Roo argued, to get away from the dualism frequently heard on this subject. "We ignore or distort reality if we consider merely one or the other gesture of conjugal love apart from the whole of daily family life. For the expressions of love proper to conjugal life fit into a total complex outside of which they lose their full and true meaning. Physical attraction alone fails to define married love; pleasure alone cannot describe its bounds."

He concluded that not for a moment would he think of minimizing the need for precise church legislation on this gravest of matters, "but this vital framework of laws must not inhibit the full development of Christian married love in all its dimensions. And we must promote and emphasize positively the unique redemptive values of Christian conjugal love." The council would promote the redemption of all humanity by speaking frankly of the positive values of conjugal love.

The next day (1 October) Hacault, making his second intervention, also called for a more detailed section on conjugal love. He noted there are many types of marriage: monogamy, polygamy, bigamy, concubinage. The council, he said, should not just condemn the forms that it considers inferior. Instead, it should show how they culminate in the Christian conception of marriage. The council text was "already worthy of approval in its present form." However, the pastoral and ecumenical perspective of the council called for better analysis of marriage in today's world. He noted that, regarding polygamy, the text dealt "only with the negative aspect of this social reality that is still very widespread in some regions. Couldn't we hope for a more positive formulation? Don't forget that the council wants to speak to all people of good will." Humanity in the course of history had known many forms of alliances between man and woman, including the practice of legal concubinage, bigamy and polygamy in general.

"The best of alliances," Hacault said, "is the one that sustains the human being in efforts to conquer the dangers of hedonism and selfishness, and which, as conjugal society, aims to lead man and woman to their human perfection. No one can deny that polygamy, for example, has some value, though sometimes a very relative one, and that it implies a union whose stability can lead to the establishment of a home. It is this positive aspect that is of interest to our current study." He therefore thought "that polygamy and other alliances of less value than marriage could be treated in a positive way. It is a question of showing in what way they are imperfect, and how they could be advanced to a more perfect stage, rather than to simply cast them aside with an anathema." Would it not be fitting, in the council text, to bring out first of all the positive, though relative, value of polygamy, and later the definite superiority of Christian marriage? "Thus we would show the value of the alliance of love according to the natural order, and the sacred character of Christian marriage would shine all the brighter. It is in this sense that I suggest that the council commission rework this chapter on marriage, in order to give a better presentation of the dynamism of Catholic teaching on the dignity of marriage."

The council was discussing what the text said about socio-economic life when Coderre spoke on 4 October. He was concerned that the chapter was already out of date. He asked that it be made more prophetic. "More than other areas, the socio-economic reality is fluid, constantly changing, always creating new forms," Coderre noted. "Therefore, if it wants to be pastoral, our text must look *forward* and not *backward,* already thinking about a future that is developing before our eyes, and trying to bring the light of the gospel to the world that is developing now, and, finally, giving people, the agents of these changes, the word of God capable of showing them the meaning and law of their mission." He noted "specialists in the social sciences and economics have studied this chapter carefully and have judged it severely. They especially criticize our text for addressing a type of economic society that is in the process of disappearing, for not taking account of issues in today's society and the currents of change already working deeply, and for ignoring institutional mechanisms now in place and already involved in the future.... We are in what the specialists call the post-industrial period, with all the characteristics of this unique stage in human evolution. In particular, progressively new institutions are being created to respond to the new situation. This is what our text should especially examine, for the immediate future of humanity will play out there from now on." The council should not talk in a purely abstract way about economic laws, the need for justice, fair distribution of goods, relations between rich and poor. It should not seem to be dealing with the situation that prevailed at the time of the industrial revolution. Instead, it should talk, for example, of the role of the state in social planning; the community organization of welfare; the policy of balancing work and leisure; the various para-government organizations for co-operation; the various social services responding to the post-industrial period. "If we want our text to be that of a council for today and tomorrow, and if we want the whole church to become aware of the *real* problems of the *real* world, this chapter needs to be profoundly changed. Otherwise, the church will not speak in a sufficiently competent way, and it will not show the world clearly enough the spirit of service called for by the gospel."

On 6 October, the day after the pope's return from New York, Léger completed Canadian comment on the text. In particular, he spoke of the morality of modern war, the duty of nations towards international society, conscientious objection, and collaboration of Christians with peoples of other religions in a search for peace. He noted the council was meeting in a time of uncertainty when humanity faced the risk of its own destruction. The war in Vietnam was raging. "The circumstances lead many people to hope that the council will use all the weight of its moral authority to eliminate war and affirm peace." The text, however, was "too ambiguous and even has some contradictions. ...The beginning supports those who want to condemn unconditionally both war and armaments, and it also supports – subtly, it is true – the thesis of those who would want war to be licit in certain circumstances."

He argued that in speaking of the morality of modern war or "total war" or of its arms, the council should not get into the technical discussion of the conditions for a just war. Nor should it try to condemn war in abstract terms. The council should first call to mind in a pertinent way the enormous and new risks and sufferings caused by modern wars. "Then it should say briefly, strongly and clearly only the following: That it is almost unthinkable that modern war could be an allowable and appropriate instrument for restoring a violated right." Regarding an efficacious international authority, Léger wanted the test to affirm in even stronger terms the duty of every person, and especially of politicians, to do everything in their power to strengthen and perfect this authority. A general kind of exhortation, even if strong, was not enough. "We still have to guard against the different ways of harming international society, either by inertia or by anachronistic state sovereignty, exaggerated nationalism, collective selfishness, or distrust of international society expressed by words or actions, or through neglecting to promote education of international awareness." He also wanted "a few minor changes" so that conscientious objection to bearing arms did not "seem like a sort of superfluous virtue that could be called Christian 'softness,' but rather true Christian charity itself or the spirit of peace according to the gospel." Finally, he stressed, in the search for peace Catholics must unite with believers in other religions. By such a common effort throughout the world, religious people would join those involved in political life in the search for peace.

Life and ministry of priests

The last four Canadians to speak at Vatican II discussed the life and ministry of priests. At times during the council, the complaint was heard that ordinary priests were being neglected among the topics studied. A text on the priesthood was among the 70 topics foreseen at the outset, but it did not come up until the third session. Further to emphasis the importance the council wished to attach to the priesthood, 40 pastors from around the world were invited to be present as their lives and work were discussed. The Canadians priests among them were Paul Dwyer of Oshawa, J.K. MacIsaac of Winnipeg, and Jean M. Thérrien and Jean Descorcy of Montreal.

Léger's 14 October remarks focused on the holiness of priests. There were good reasons, he said, why great care should be taken to distinguish the style of holiness proper to each state in life. People were increasingly aware of the inconveniences, and even the perils, of trying to live in a way appropriate to someone else. Priests felt the need for a spirituality that was truly theirs; they wanted the council to trace its main lines. The text gave only a feeble reply to this expectation. It should declare, he stressed, that holiness for a priest "is that union with Christ which he attains primarily by offering mass, preaching, hearing confessions, administering other sacraments, visiting the sick, helping the poor and doing the many other daily tasks of his state of life." He objected to a passage beginning with a warning about the dangers of ministry, as if pastoral duties might leave a priest too busy to look after his own holiness. These duties were the priest's way to holiness, he insisted. True, there were difficulties for priests in their work. But the text must show that Christ himself and his grace were to be found in the people with whom the priest came into contact each day, and in the realities of the lives of these people. The virtues of the Good Shepherd, Léger said, are proper to the priest because of the demands of his life. They included zeal, concern for the salvation of others, generous self-giving, care for the gospel, concern and love for all but especially the poor and sinners, patience and the humility to listen to people, availability, perseverance despite failures. It would be timely to speak about poverty, chastity and obedience, he agreed, but these virtues should not be presented for priests the same way as for members of religious communities. Prayer and eucharistic worship should be shown as "privileged activities" for priests, along with study of holy scripture and meditation on the word of God. "Care must be taken," Léger said, "to avoid presenting priestly holiness like a struggle between the interior life and the exterior life."

Cardinal Roy (16 October) stressed that for the sake of the priests involved in the changes in modern dioceses, the text needed to speak clearly about some of these new developments. It said excellent things about the fraternal union of priests in the diocesan "presbyterium," but in general it gave a too static picture of a diocese. For example, while the parish remained the centre of liturgical and charitable life, a parish could no longer be looked upon as a little town living unto itself. Now there were apostolic associations, such as Catholic Action movements, that reached out to people across parish boundaries. Some parishes were being grouped as zones or regions. Bishops were naming some priests not to parishes but to new functions such as diocesan directors of various services. Roy wanted the text to promote respect for priests who were not strictly parish clergy.

The speeches of 16 October, Roy's among them, marked the technical end of council debates. A standing vote closed discussion about priests, and the text was approved in general by 1,521 to 12 ballots. That total vote was about 700 lower than the usual daily attendance, perhaps a sign of fatigue and flagging interest. However, 2,399 were present for the final promulgation of texts and the formal close of Vatican II on 7 December. The last two Canadians to speak at Vatican II were De Roo and Charbonneau. On 25 October, when final comments were accepted from those speaking in the name of at least 70 bishops, they added final comments on the text about priests.

To understand the ministerial priesthood as a service for the welfare of the people of God, De Roo pointed out, one must begin with the idea of the priesthood of the entire church. At this stage of salvation history, the priesthood of the church was not simply to offer worship. It involved mission as well. Until the return of Christ, the people of God are sent on a mission to the world, to guide it to the Father. Hence it is missionary, dynamic. But to enable the entire people to fulfill its mission, God gave it the hierarchy, bishops and priests. The essential function of the hierarchy is "to lead this movement of the missionary church marching toward the Father." Seen in this light, and according to the scriptures, the priest-minister is essentially one who is sent, in the biblical sense. The priest was placed at the head of the people as a servant to lead, and not as one who dominates. De Roo urged that the council's description of the ministry of the priest should be inspired by the idea that he shares and prolongs the mission of Christ, the chief pastor. The priest's functions as minister of the word, servant of the eucharist, and leader and servant of the people find their unity in this mission. Such a description, he concluded, would dispel the fears of some priests that their functions might be presented too statically.

Charbonneau's main concern was the way the text dealt with priestly obedience. In stressing the authority of the bishop in all pastoral matters, it cast too much shadow on the personal initiative required of a priest precisely so the bishop's aims could be realized. The obedience of the ordinary priest, he argued, was not intended chiefly for the personal perfection of the priest himself. It was defined by the objective welfare of the church. It must not be confused with the obedience of a member of a religious order. The priest had to be obedient so that the gospel might be proclaimed faithfully and the life of the local church would conform to God's wishes. This obedience was essentially pastoral and ministerial. At his consecration, he added, the bishop received the grace and power to lead the people toward perfection. The priest was not simply the bishop's aide or consultant. At ordination, the priest also received real pastoral grace – a real share in the bishop's pastoral grace, but concretely distinct from it. The priest possessed his "gift" in communion with that of the bishop.

It followed, Charbonneau argued, that the obedience of the priest in concrete pastoral action is not simply passive submission to the will of the bishop, but above all active communion of his will with the bishop's. Two movements came together. From the bishop came not only directives but also the very spirit that would make the priest's action truly pastoral. From the priest came submission, but also responsible creativity. The priest must be on the alert for everything that would enable his particular people to live the gospel better. The welfare of the church itself forbade a priest to depend solely on a precise order or permission from his bishop. By his communion of responsibility with the bishop, and by his union of action with other priests, a priest was truly the bishop's collaborator, Charbonneau concluded, the last Canadian to speak in Vatican II debates.

Other concerns in writing

Through a written text, De Roo played a role in the restoration of hermits in Latin dioceses where the discipline had almost disappeared. As bishop of Victoria, De Roo supported a group of hermits led by a former abbot of Clairvaux in Belgium. Regarding the experience to be positive and fruitful, he asked in a text submitted in writing that the council recognize hermits as a normal part of church life. Today, he sees the church's reply in canon 603 of the 1983 code of canon law. It speaks of hermits or anchorites who "withdraw further from the world and devote their lives to the praise of God and the salvation of the world through the silence of solitude and through constant prayer and penance." Historically hermits were associated with monastic life, but De Roo wanted this form of Christian witness to be part of the life of a diocese. The canon now says that "hermits are recognized by law as dedicated to God in consecrated life if, in the hands of the diocesan bishop, they publicly profess, by a vow or some other sacred bond, the three evangelical counsels, and then lead their particular form of life under the guidance of the diocesan bishop." It was therefore on Vancouver Island, De Roo recalls, "that this restoration took place, which has since become rather common in many parts of the world."

Commission work on final texts

The debates ended, the final weeks of the council were devoted to rewriting texts in the various commissions, and voting on final versions in the plenary assembly. Some final comments on the lay apostolate text by Quebec bishops provide an example of the suggestions studied before the lay apostolate decree was promulgated 18 November. Shared with me in an interview, the suggestions came from the members of the French section of the CCC commission for Catholic action and the lay apostolate. Bishop Paul-

Émile Charbonneau, chairman of the section, along with Auxiliary Bishop Gaston Haines of Ste. Hyacinthe, Quebec, and Auxiliary Bishop René Audet of Ottawa, prepared their notes in collaboration with the Montreal national secretariat for L'Action catholique canadienne. One of their aims, Charbonneau explained, was to stress their conviction that "it is by all their 'being' that the laity, living in Christ and acting in the world, must be apostles." They wanted the text to show clearly that the apostolate of the laity "is realized in daily reality, the love of Christ dwelling in them and, through them, transfiguring all things." Within this general framework, they wrote their views on 83 individual points in the draft text. As one example, they suggested a change in the opening paragraph saying that modern times "call for no less lay zeal" than was evident in the early church. For the word "zeal" substitute the word "action," the Canadians suggested, for "in present-day language the term 'action' signifies something more than interior attitude and is more vital than the term 'zeal'; it better describes the total engagement of the laity in the apostolic plan." (The final text, however, was not changed.) On a broader point, in order "better to situate the laity within the church seen as a community of salvation," the Canadian notes wanted the text to speak of "the evident work of the Holy Spirit making lay persons ever more conscious of their own apostolic responsibilities in all fields." This would stress that the laity have responsibilities in the church as such, and also a true and distinctive apostolic role and responsibility in temporal affairs.

They suggested a change to emphasize "the ever-increasing autonomy of the temporal order, in all aspects of human life, has contributed, more than any other factor, to bringing out the urgency and proper field of the apostolate of the laity." They also wanted the text to say that the laity exercise their apostolate of evangelizing and sanctifying "chiefly by penetrating the spirit of the gospel into the temporal order, by perfecting it, in such a way that in this field their action bears witness to Christ and serves the salvation of mankind." They objected to a phrase saying that the laity are called to exercise their apostolate in the world "by the fervor of their Christian spirit," calling the expression too general. It could be interpreted as not calling for a total conversion of life itself, but rather for an "intention" or a voluntary kind of arousement. It would be better, the Canadian notes said, to declare simply that the laity exercise their apostolate in the world "as witnesses of Christ." They had similar comments about a passage dealing with lay spirituality. The draft text said that the apostolate of the laity depends completely on their living union with Christ, and that this union is nourished by spiritual aids, especially active participation in the liturgy. These spiritual aids, it added, are "to be used by the laity in such a way that, while they fulfill their duties in the ordinary conditions of life, they do not separate union with Christ from the active life, but perform their duties in this union." The Canadians thought that "in this passage (as in others) the text does not appear to be based on a sufficiently consistent and dynamic conception of man and of the world." Consequently, they added, "the spirituality proposed appears to refer more to an 'intention' or even to a union but one that is a little artificial, rather than to a transfiguration of the whole being of man and of the whole world. It is impossible to elaborate, even briefly, a lay spirituality without integrating into it participation in creation and the search for God in things and other people. Laity not only 'perform' their duties in this union but also, and even more so, they realize union with Christ in their world."

The group therefore proposed that the text should say that spiritual aids such as the liturgy are to be used by the laity "in such a way that, while they fulfill their duties in the ordinary conditions of life, they unite themselves at the same time to Christ's plan of love and to the new people of whom he is the head." Similarly, the Canadian notes questioned a phrase saying that the laity "mutually help one another in fraternal charity, as regards both the temporal life and the spiritual life." This was unclear, the Canadians said. "The 'spiritual life' of the laity having to develop and grow 'in the temporal,' it is obscure to say that they must mutually help one another 'in the temporal life' *and* "in the spiritual life', as if there are, in some way, 'two lives'." Point by point in this detailed way, the bishops, priests and lay leaders of Canadian Catholic Action suggested changes in the lay apostolate text. They concluded by suggesting that an article in the text on the church in the modern world should "express in a much more complete and profound way the sense and dimensions of the friendship that the laity must arouse among all people."[2]

The work of a Quebec theologian

When the Quebec bishops suggested such an item about the laity in the text on the church in the modern world, they did not know that a Quebec theologian would have a major role in drafting a relevant chapter of that text. As noted earlier, Roy brought Bernard Lambert and Charles De Koninck to Rome to help him in the study of the church in the world. (De Koninck's work on points about marriage was reviewed earlier.) Lambert helped Roy with the section about human activity in the world (Chapter III of Part I of *The Pastoral Constitution on the Modern World*.) As the council entered its final weeks, Lambert ended up as the main drafter of this section. As noted earlier, Lambert brought to this work the fruit of study by the consultative committee in Quebec, set up by Roy and headed by Lambert himself. Recent research shows[3] that, a month before the final council session, Lambert sent some comments on the text to the mixed commission then studying it. His judgment was positive, but he proposed some changes along the same lines as what he suggested the year before. He was most critical of the text's anthropological guidelines. The first chapter was too disconnected from what the introductory said about the signs of the times. Its style was too much like older theological manuals. It missed the central problem of modern people, which was not the relation between the natural and supernatural dimensions, but rather the relation of humanity itself to nature and history. Lambert wrote:

> The problem of humanity today is not about man's vocation as such, but about man situated *today* in *history*, in *the material world*, that is, faced with a new order of nature for which he is in part responsible. The man-nature relationship is no longer what it used to be. Primitive man was *immersed* in nature. Classical man *confronted* nature. Today's man (as fashioned by science and technology) is involved with nature (matter and time) in a network of relations (tensions, dialectic relations, synergies) that result in one totality, an outcome that comes both from humanity

and from nature in an indivisible way. The result is a new way of seeing truth, beauty and goodness. They no longer appear in the perspective of timeless thought as for mediaeval man, or as an idea developed historically as for Hegel, or as a point of converging awareness as in existentialism, but as something transcendental under construction in a globalizing world. The modern mentality is profoundly modified by the idea of the construction of the world. People no longer wish to search for laws by starting from a metaphysical overview of events, but by a reading of the good, the beautiful, the true in the process of building themselves concretely.[4]

For Lambert, then, the main error of the text on the church in the world was its distinction between the human vocation (in the first chapter) and human activity in the universe (in the third). Instead of being distinct, they were two aspects of the same question. The human vocation consisted precisely in the construction of the universe. On 14 October, at a meeting of the central mixed commission, Lambert spoke briefly about the chapter on human activity in the universe, summarizing the arguments of his August document. During this same period, the sub-commission responsible for amending the chapter was working under the direction of Peter Smulders of Holland. His work did not get a positive reception from the mixed commission, so Lambert was asked to get more involved in the sub-commission and replace Smulders in drafting the chapter. During the last part of October and the beginning of November, therefore, Lambert worked intensely on a new draft of the chapter. He had to reconcile four elements: the text discussed by the bishops, that proposed by the sub-commission, Smulders' work, and observations proposed by the mixed commission. Besides continuity in the text, the most important problem was the distinction between earthly history built by human effort and the destiny of the world in heavenly glory. To what point could it be affirmed that the progress of history and of humanity are going in that direction, that they are linked to it, and that the world will not end but be transformed, by human work and the progress of history, in a fulfillment of time?

On the basis of observations by the mixed commission and to strengthen the tone of the text, Lambert changed the structure of the chapter, to correspond to the general intention of the text: to lead humanity "by the hand" to meet Christ. On 10 November, the text with an explanatory note was ready for a council vote. It received a generally favourable welcome and very few final amendments were requested. In the end, the text on which Lambert worked was confirmed in the definitive version of Chapter III, Part I of *The Pastoral Constitution on the Church in the Modern World*.

Reactions by Léger and Roy to Paul VI's amendments

While Lambert was doing work on a chapter that won general approval, Léger and Roy were involved in high drama over some of the hottest questions in the second part of the text on the church in the world. It concerned last-minute changes requested by Paul VI. Léger and Roy intervened very vigorously to resolve a situation that seemed the most critical of the entire drafting process. After the text had been discussed, corrected and submitted for a first approval by the bishops, and during the final phase of evaluating the last requested amendments, Paul VI asked the mixed commission to include some changes in the chapter on marriage. Among them, he wanted to reaffirm the traditional doctrine on the ends of marriage and explicitly condemn the use of all means of contraception, including the new contraceptive drugs. When the papal amendments were sent to the mixed commission, many bishops and experts were dismayed. Paul VI had always asked the bishops in the council not to discuss the question of birth control. He was now asking them to introduce decisive amendments on this subject. It seemed an affront to bishops who had abstained from talking about the subject. Léger reacted against the pope's procedure, not about the content of his request.

During a commission meeting, Léger read a statement underlining the gravity of the pope's request. He questioned the way the amendments had been proposed at the last minute. There would be reactions of great deception among Catholics and even in public opinion. Because of the explicit papal reservation of these topics, Léger stressed, the council had neither the possibility nor the right to examine all the questions related to the doctrine on marriage and birth control. If, at this late stage, the final document of the council said something decisive on this matter, it would be clear that the council had not been free. At the end of this meeting, Léger went immediately to the Vatican to protest personally to the pope. He did not get an audience with Paul VI but he gave the pope's secretariat the text of what he had said in the commission. He wanted clarification on the real authority of the changes, and asked if the commission must simply introduce them as such, or if it could discuss them and eventually adopt them as the commission decided. Léger also noted that the way the changes were introduced had created a very bad impression among the experts and auditors at the commission meeting. He said he was very worried about the possibility of a scandal, if the incident became notoriously public. In other reactions, Ottaviani telephoned to Paul VI's secretariat to tell the pope that the meeting had not gone well and that many disagreeable incidents had developed. Also, Henri De Riedmatten, secretary of the special papal commission on the birth control question, wrote a minute of the meeting for the pope, very critical of the requested changes. Later the same day, it was Roy's turn to try to see the pope. He accompanied the Mexican couple Alvarez, who as lay auditors worked with the sub-commission. They left a petition to the pope from all the lay auditors, asking him not to resolve the marriage questions in an authoritative way "in the form of retouches made at the last minute in a document whose general tone is known in advance in public opinion."

The crisis was resolved by a compromise. Paul VI accepted a rewriting of his suggestions by the mixed commission, but on condition that their fundamental intention be respected. In fact, the mixed commission adapted the changes in a very articulated way and they could be introduced in the text without upsetting the balance of an already complex chapter. The result, accepted by the mixed commission, the council and the pope, can be read today in the constitution. [Footnote 14 in Article 51 of *Gaudium et Spes* recalls teaching on birth control by Pius XI, Pius XII and Paul VI. It then notes "by order of the Holy Father, certain questions requiring further and more careful investigation have been given over to a commission for the study of population, the family, and births, in order that the Holy Father may pass judgment when its

6: The Fourth and Final Session: 1965

task is completed. With the teaching of the magisterium standing as it is, the council has no intention of proposing concrete solutions at this moment."]

Once again, Léger had taken action to bring his views on council business directly to the pope. As usual, he did it in an efficacious and useful way. All during the drafting stage of the text, he was the most influential opponent of Ottaviani on marriage questions. Léger did this with full awareness that he had a personal role to play in relation to the council and the pope. Léger's council record shows he was a man of both word and deed. His 24 oral interventions perhaps overshadow his equally decisive actions. These include his pre-council petition to John XXIII; his meeting with John XXIII about the stalemated text on revelation; his participation in the "*magno cum dolore*" letter about the status of the unity secretariat's work on council texts; his personal appeal to Paul VI at the end of the third session to assure the place of the text on religious freedom; and his direct action regarding Paul VI's last-minute intervention regarding the text on the church in the modern world.

Of the 2,205 oral interventions during the council, 63 were by Canadians: 11 in the first session, 14 in the second, 25 in the third and 13 in the final session. (There were also 4,229 written remarks, an uncounted number of them by Canadians.) Leger spoke 24 times during the four sessions, Hermaniuk eight, Baudoux six, De Roo four, Coderre three, and Roy, Charbonneau and Hacault twice each. Single oral interventions were made by Cabana, Pocock, Flahiff, Jordan, Sanschagrin, A. Carter, Roborecki, Power, Rusnak, Deschatelets, Lalande and Malanchuk. Over the four years, there were 17 Canadian interventions about the church in the world, nine on Christian unity, seven on the nature of the church, five on revelation and on the priesthood, four on each of liturgy, laity, and the pastoral work of bishops. Other topics drew one or two Canadian speeches.

Conclusion

To attempt some evaluation of Canadian participation in Vatican II is to be led into temptation. The mind is tugged toward questions and comments about all that has happened in the church and around it during the 40 years since the council. It is difficult to keep focused on the few years from 1959 to 1965. Regarding the period since the council, a question from Psalm 95 tries to impose itself: Are we a people whose hearts have gone astray? But a prior question arises at once: Astray from what? How well do we know God's ways? Do we really know the council's ways? Within the limits of this project, do we even know enough, have we learned all we can, about what Canadians contributed to the work of Vatican II?

The 63 Canadian oral interventions do not stand out as obviously separate and distinct from the more than 2,200 other 10-minute Latin speeches. However, as a conclusion of this account of what Canadians bishops said and did, some general comments can be made about their work. We have two markers from which to measure progress or retreat. One is the collection of suggestions individual Canadian bishops sent to Rome in 1959. Another is the statement that the CCC, the national association of Canadian bishops, issued in April 1962, nearly six months before the opening of Vatican II.

As the 1959 summer holidays began, Canadian bishops received unexpectedly a request for their ideas for the council's agenda, with a 1 September deadline for replies, just weeks away. In general, they proposed that Vatican II should deal with the pastoral questions they were facing in Canada. Most sent lists of varied suggestions, with little or no attempt to set out an overall plan or vision for the council, or for church renewal and reform. Changes in church discipline for fast and abstinence and work on Sunday came first in Canadian lists. Liturgical changes were listed second. Many made suggestions, somewhat conflicting, about promoting Christian unity. Totally absent, however, was any suggestion that the church should just stand pat, that the council should do no more than reaffirm the practices and teachings of the past. Absent, too, was any call for condemnation of modern ways. Pocock in Winnipeg seemed to sum up the Canadian suggestions. In a few lines, he said there should be some updating of teaching and discipline in language suited to modern pastoral needs, but the council should avoid condemnations and anathemas.

When the Canadian and other bishops wrote their suggestions in 1959, they knew that John XXIII was calling them to a general council. They knew almost nothing of what the pope had in mind for it. For the most part, the pope's ideas about *aggiornamento*, about updating, renewal and reform, were spelled out after the bishops' September 1959 deadline. However, in the 30 months between that date and the April 1962 CCC statement about the council, John XXIII disclosed a great deal of his thinking. Their 1962 statement shows that among the Canadian bishops a majority including the CCC's elected leaders had both assimilated and espoused John XXIII's vision.

What they wrote in April 1962 about the aim of the council anticipated a major point John XXIII made when he opened it six month later. "While clarifying and developing what is fundamental and unalterable in the church," the CCC said, "the council will make opportune changes in certain other aspects. The eternal truths of revelation do not change and can never become antiquated, but their human expression and their concrete presentation must be adapted to the language and customs which change over the years. The church in itself is unchangeable and immutable in its basic constitution founded by Jesus Christ, but in certain details such as liturgical customs or methods of administration there may be elements which are now out of date and which it would be better to change." The CCC members accurately foresaw that at the council "the church will consider its own image, reaffirm its faith, and adapt certain elements of its legislation and sanctifying action to modern circumstances. There will result a better understanding of the place of the church in the world, a more profound and clearer faith in divine revelation, a salutary application of Catholic doctrine to the needs of our times, and a renewal of Christian life." At the council, "it will not be a question of defining a particular point of doctrine; rather, it is the whole approach of life that will be considered." The church, the CCC said, needs to define the attitudes and the means it would use to move people to establish Christian principles in all aspects of life, from family to civic, economic, political and social activities.

Between this CCC statement and the opening of Vatican II, Léger's study of the draft texts was the major development in Canada related to the council. Under his leadership, Montreal theologians wrote a report highly critical of the texts coming from the preparatory commissions in Rome. Léger judged these texts to be too fearful and defensive. To counter their approach, he wrote his September 1962 petition to John XXIII, as reviewed in detail in our first chapter. It is unclear if other Canadian bishops knew of Léger's petition. It provided a framework of ideas for Léger's 24 council interventions. The spirit of his petition also characterized most of the other Canadian interventions.

During the debates of the first session, Léger, Hermaniuk, Baudoux and Sanschagrin argued in favour of adaptability and flexibility, including greater competence for local bishops in such matters as introducing local languages in the liturgy. In particular, they supported and helped to build up the emerging majority view that the texts prepared in advance should be abandoned, and new ones drafted. Only Cabana spoke against this view. Near the end of the session, Léger counseled John XXIII to reject the initial "sources of revelation" text after the majority opposed to it fell just short of the two-thirds vote required to reject it.

The second session opened under Paul VI with study of the nature of the church. Questions about authority in the church, especially about the collegial role of bishops, dominated the debate. Canadian participation began with Hermaniuk's far-reaching plan for renewing a synodal model of governance for the church. Baudoux, Coderre, Roborecki and Malanchuk supported Hermaniuk with various added notes of appreciation for the traditions of eastern Christians. Léger stressed that all the baptized are called to holiness, striking a blow against any notion that Christ's call favours some over others. As study began of a first draft on ecumenism, Léger stressed that Christian relations with Jews should be dealt with in a separate text. Baudoux called for some recognition of other Christian churches. Léger urged deeper study of the Catholic view of church unity, to clarify the importance of diversity. Regarding doctrinal differences, he counseled intellectual humility in exploring what Paul called "the unfathomable riches of Christ." The norm for all Christians should be that of Augustine: "Seek in order to find, and find so that you may continue to seek." Flahiff added that because church divisions arise from sin they are reminders that Christians are not as holy as they should be. The Holy Spirit is truly at work in the ecumenical movement, calling all Christians to renewal, and to new ways of acting and living together in love.

Canadian participation increased during the third and fourth sessions. The council studied two topics never before raised at such a gathering: the role of laity in the church, and how to be church in today's world. Other important points were made: that Catholic language about Mary should be modest, clear, precise and Christ-centred (Léger); that Jews should forever be cleared of the charge of being God-killers (Pocock); that seminary programs should prepare priests for "the real problems, the thoughts and even the language of the real world," and Catholic colleges should coordinate their research, with emphasis on freedom, guided by necessary teaching authority that does not "act hastily or without trust" (Léger). On the two new topics, four Canadians spoke in the third session about the lay apostolate, and a total of 17 Canadian speeches during the two sessions dealt with the church in the world. Though different texts were being discussed, the two topics fitted together. Christ's presence in the world as a human being is carried forward throughout history by members of the church, more than 99.9 percent of them lay people. Christ is always sharing in creation, present to daily life, and redeeming the world through the paschal mystery: crucifixion, death and resurrection. Christ's followers likewise are called to be fully present in the world, involved in building it up according to God's plan for creation, and active in saving it from sin. Lay Christians have a special call to be Christ in the world. Within broad agreement, there were nuance differences in what the Canadians stressed. Léger was concerned that emphasis on temporal activities should not overshadow the importance of the supernatural vocation of Christians. For Hermaniuk, the supernatural transcendence of a Christian's vocation had to assume engagement in building the earthly city. Charbonneau, Coderre, De Roo, Hacault, Power emphasized in various ways the natural aspect of the human vocation, with Christians present in history as leaven in the dough, following Christ already present in the world, starting with the incarnation, even if fully revealed only by the events of Easter. In this context, Léger and De Roo stressed the need for the church to recognize the importance of human love in marriage and family life. Coderre spoke against the scandal of unequal appreciation and mistreatment of women in the church and in the world. Roy, reflecting the study by his Quebec sub-committee headed by Lambert, stressed the church should adopt a language and style suited to the people it addresses. It should be present to people, assume their most common problems including hunger and poverty, injustice and violence, "take them by the hand" to the Lord, expressing the desire of all for development, unity and peace. By assuming these responsibilities day by day, Christians could also respond to their supernatural vocation.

While Léger and his team emphasized new habits for a modern Christian mind, Roy and his team, those working with Baudoux, other Canadian bishops, and theologians such as Baum and Tillard, pointed to new ways of acting, new ways of being church in the world. As Lambert said in his work for Roy, the church's relation to the world should be seen as *presence*, a relationship even closer than that conveyed by ideas such as *dialogue*. Great freedom and openness in meeting others would be the marks of this kind of presence. This involved "restarting evangelization" by looking at what Christians believe in common with other people. It would mean being a church working with the world in seeking a common plan for human existence. A sketch, an outline, of a way to *be* church in the world was perhaps Canada's distinctive contribution to the council.

The high quality of what Canadians said and did at Vatican II is evident. They did good work. Their work continues to produce good in the life of the church. It is, to be sure, unfinished work, work in progress. There was a general unity of mind among the

Canadian participants whose activities are part of the public record so far. Their differences were not basic or glaring, and often had to do with personality or style. While some including McGuigan wanted to keep the liturgy in Latin for the sake of mystery, Sanschagrin's account of his own conversion to the vernacular for the sake of greater participation was typical of most of the Canadians. One major question that persisted at least into the third session was whether to retain or reject the texts drafted before the council by preparatory commissions dominated by Vatican officials. Only Cabana openly argued with the minority in favour of using these texts. Only Rusnak joined another minority during the fourth session in a futile final appeal for a specific condemnation of communism. Future detailed studies, such as analyses of all votes cast, if ever done, might reveal other Canadians who were consistently among the minority. It is to be noted that whereas other Canadians were elected to various council commissions, Pelletier alone was appointed, to the theology commission. He was named by John XXIII, and therefore recommended by Vatican officials whom he may have supported more often than is shown by present research. No thorough study of his personal council papers has been published. This also is true of many other Canadians whose council activities and personal archives remain unexplored. Overall, however, Canada's bishops showed themselves to be supporters of John XXIII's understanding of a church always in need of reform and renewal. To recall their main themes is to be struck by the continuing relevance of their words. Clearly, this Vatican II work by Canadians is an enduring heritage. Besides looking to it for inspiration, today's church members are responsible for keeping it alive and carrying it forward. The Canadian interventions at Vatican II form an important body of pastoral teaching, even taken by themselves. More importantly, their interventions clearly helped to shape the council's final documents. These texts proclaim to the whole world a vision of Christ's church that carries forward into history the many insights and inspirations that were proposed and endorsed by Canadian and other bishops, all solemnly promulgated by Paul VI in his name and that of the bishops.

In one sense, Léger obviously was the leading Canadian at the council. In another sense, the other Canadians were not led by him. Their regard for him was always a mixture of pride along with some measure of reserve, annoyance or regret. On one issue after another, Léger was among the first to voice the opinion that not only rallied the support of other Canadians but also found favour with the entire assembly. What he said about the pastoral office of bishops (21 September 1964) was just one occasion when he "was greeted with applause."[1] Yet, a number of other Canadians pointedly noted that Léger was not a team player. Coderre wrote in his personal journal for 1 December 1963: "Lord, help Cardinal Léger, and help us to understand him and accept him as he is. How strong we would be if we were united."[2] Tillard was the theologian perhaps most involved personally with the Canadian bishops, speaking every week to groups on council themes and helping them to prepare interventions. He wrote later that the other bishops "felt badly that Léger participated in none of our work."[3] Sanschagrin recorded in his journal, as noted earlier, that at their first meeting in Rome the other Canadians declined to let Léger say he spoke in their names without showing them his texts. Pocock's journal shows that a few weeks later during the first session he was pleased that he had not agreed to present a text he thought Léger's team had prepared. However, as Sanschagrin noted, "Léger's interventions drew a lot of attention in the council.... His Latin pronunciation was perfect. His interventions always were heard with interest and attention. There was complete silence in the aula."[4] Coderre's third-session journal entry for 23 September 1964 notes that "for the first time Cardinal Léger said that he spoke in the name of many bishops (*nomine pluribus episcopis*)."[5] Réjean Plamondon, my colleague for the French CCC Information Service, recalls that one day, when the Canadian bishops held their 1964 annual meeting in Rome, he heard Charles-E. Mathieu, the CCC's French general secretary, tell Léger during an animated discussion: "You want to be at the head of the line; but to be there the first condition is that you be in the line, and you never are!"[6] Sanschagrin also recorded a light-hearted moment during a public ceremony for which the cardinals entered in procession. It was after Léger began to let his hair grow longer, in what Sanschagrin called "his patriarchal look." A number of bishops seated close to Sanschagrin tossed some coins on his desk, saying "That's to get your cardinal a haircut."[7]

Personal annoyances and regrets aside, Léger was a towering figure. Only the conservative Italian Cardinal Ruffini spoke more often — 36 times to Léger's 24. Council rules gave cardinals the right to speak whenever they wanted to put their name on the list. By keeping free to act on his own when ready, Léger quickly emerged as a leader within the majority. No other Canadian arrived in Rome for the council's opening as well prepared as Léger. Baudoux's team in St. Boniface also undertook a major preparation, but they were limited to study of the few texts actually circulated before the opening. Roy's team began work after the council was well under way. Léger, as a member of the central co-ordinating committee from the beginning of its work in 1960, had access to all preparatory documents.

Looking back on Léger's work (and therefore some of his own), Naud, one of Léger's council theologians, wrote 30 years later that Léger's contributions could be called an attempt to present a new way of conceiving Christian intelligence — a new mindset for believers. Léger not only evolved a great deal in how he saw things as a result of participation in the central commission before the council opened. His council interventions also reveal a style, a typical way of dealing with problems and questions. This style involved not only a particular idea of what the council should be, but, even more, a certain way of conceiving how the intelligence of a believer should function in the church. Léger saw that a certain spirit, a particular mentality, prevailed during the preparation of many texts for the council. He wanted to counter it with a different mentality and spirit. Léger posited two main reference points for the kind of Christian intelligence he thought was needed. One is fidelity to Christ, the other concern for all humanity. He insisted on the need for openness towards all true human values, no matter where found. Truth must be welcomed if found in new science and technology, all major cultures including non-Christian ones, the Christian values conserved in non-Catholic churches, and the values of the different schools of theology and spirituality within the Catholic church itself. Even those in error must be respected. Léger called for a Christian intelligence that is modest and humble. Naud quoted Léger on this point: "Our teaching should be humble. We must avoid taking up problems for which the church has no competence. With diligence and care we should distinguish sure teaching from theological opinions. We must be careful to avoid anything that makes the people's faith uselessly burdensome. On the contrary, we must learn how to seek with our priests and people an ever deeper knowledge of the Gospel message."[8] In voicing these opinions, Léger clearly was following the lead of John XXIII. While perhaps not as close to Paul VI as to John XXIII, Léger had influence at the highest level until the close of Vatican II. And, while concerned, as Naud says, about the qualities of Christian intelligence, Léger did not remain aloof at the level of ideas. He undertook bold actions when he sent his petition to John XXIII, when he sought a private moment with John XXIII near the end of the first session to urge him to reject the initial text on revelation, when he joined in writing the 1964 "*multo con dolore*" letter to thwart a plan for side-tracking texts on Jews and religious freedom, when he joined Meyer and Ritter to ask Paul VI to allow an initial vote on religious freedom before the end of the third session, and, in the final days of the council, when he and Roy were leaders in pressing Paul VI to modify his suggestions for speaking about birth control in the constitution on the church in the modern world.

During the fourth session, Canada also had a new and different cardinal. Roy was so named in February 1965. Though his profile in the council was lower than Léger's, he was more popular with other Canadian bishops, partly because of his *camaraderie* and quiet sense of humour. He was widely known by Canadians through wartime service as military chaplain and later appointment as bishop for Canadian military personnel wherever they served – doubly appointed as archbishop of Quebec as well. Roy's role, with his team of De Koninck and Lambert, in the final drafting of *The Pastoral Constitution on the Church in the Modern World* was reviewed earlier. I am personally indebted to Roy for help in interpreting one of Paul VI's most puzzling actions as the third session closed. The pope promulgated the *Decree on Ecumenism* and the all-important *Dogmatic Constitution on the Church*, with its final chapter on the Blessed Virgin. Paul VI thus formally expressed his agreement with the council's ecumenically sensitive handling of Mary's role. Immediately after this collegial action, however, he used more exalted language about Mary in his closing talk, and announced a personal pilgrimage to Portugal's shrine of Our Lady of Fatima. A number of non-Catholic observers had a flood of questions. Wasn't the pope contradicting himself and the council? Journalists scrambled to decide what to write about what had happened. After the bishops came out of the closing session, I met Roy by chance at the hotel where both of us stayed. He took time to point out that Paul VI had agreed and in effect voted with the council majority. Then, with that teaching firmly in place, he also offered a personal pastoral gesture to a minority still bitter in defeat. "You have to try to understand how hard they fought for a separate statement on Mary, and how deeply disappointed they are," Roy told me.

He chaired the sub-commission that had handled the comments about a text on Mary, and had full insider's knowledge of the debates and lobbying in the theology commission and other council circles. Neither that afternoon nor later did I question Roy's authority to interpret the mind of Paul VI. Soon after the council, he appointed Roy as first president of new pontifical councils for laity and for justice and peace, two post-council Vatican institutions intended to carry forward what Vatican II taught about the mission of the laity, "to seek the kingdom of God by engaging in temporal affairs and directing them according to God's will."

The heavy cost of secrecy

The more we learn about how the council worked, and about what was said and done at it, the more we should regret the heavy price the church paid for the secrecy that blanketed every stage of Vatican II. Equally important, continuing official secrecy probably has to carry part of the blame for some of the "failures to receive" council teachings, and for some of the post-council divisions of public opinion in the church. Eight hundred million human beings at the time of the council and more than one billion now, the church is the mystical presence of Christ in the world, in the eyes of faith, and also a huge human society. Fewer than half a million of its members make up the ordained and ruling hierarchy. More than 999.5 million other Catholics too often are uninformed "consumers" of official decrees and instructions, for the most part concocted in secret. The Catholic church, as a human society, needs a healthy, well informed public opinion as much as any other community does. Such a public opinion is impossible without full and reliable information. The members of the "people of God" cannot participate fully if they are not fully informed. Secrecy and the attitudes and practices that sustain it – in the Vatican, in the bishops' conferences, dioceses and parishes — are mortal enemies of the full participation that solemn Vatican II documents insist is the right and duty of church members. God works in mysterious ways, but contrived secrecy is the way of the world.

Looking back to Vatican II from a distance of 40 years, I continue to marvel at how much Canadian participants contributed to it. Equally I regret the price paid because the council worked mostly in secret. Following the first session, I was asked to write an evaluation of the council press office. After referring to some technical shortcomings, I especially criticized the way official secrecy prevented journalists from getting a clearer and fuller understanding of the church through the brief but magnificent life of an ecumenical council. Unfettered insight into the council, promised to journalists at the outset by John XXIII, was immediately denied by others. Yet, as more and more information seeped out despite official secrecy, council observers including journalists were edified rather than scandalized.

The church, and especially the council, came to be seen as a living social body that could move from deep divisions to near unanimous agreement by studying, debating, negotiating, praying and voting. That official secrecy impeded nearly 1,000 writers in their work is not the main point. Millions of Christians around the world could have learned much about the church through media reports from the council. The media also could have given a better understanding of Christians to the even larger number of people of other religions. These news media and not church institutions, as Routhier has noted, initially informed the people of the world about John XXIII's plan and vision for Vatican II. The resulting groundswell of anticipation and hope showed that vast numbers were longing for more information, for more good news. If the life of the council could have been fully revealed as it progressed, this pre-existing sense of openness, this widespread attitude of listening and waiting to hear more, might have been nurtured and greatly expanded.

When I wrote my report for the February 1963 meeting of Réunion Internationale des informateurs religieuses (RIIR), I criticized council secrecy. I would have been much more critical if I had known then as much as I do now about the richness of the debates and what Canadians contributed to them. At that time, I had seen only the very short and general summaries of council interventions that we were given during the first session. During later sessions we had more access to details of the debates, but never open access to the thinking of some of the brightest minds in the world, both conservative and liberal. Of course, some writers had special access, despite official secrecy. Francis X. Murphy, who wrote for *The New Yorker* as Xavier Rynne, was an accredited council expert, able to follow all debates with documents in hand.[9] Bob Kaiser (Piser during the first session) covered the council for *Time*. His expense account allowed him and his wife to rent an apartment large enough to host a full time houseguest, the maverick retired archbishop of Bombay, Thomas Roberts. Those who knew of this arrangement wondered little about "special reports" in *Time*. Several European writers, especially for Italian publications, also had "special sources." Fewer than 300 bishops at the council were members of commissions with some direct access to information. Many of the more than 2,000 other bishops, lacking anything like daily "minutes" of the proceedings, were greatly helped by media reports based on "well-informed sources." For the general public, these same reports were the main reason that interest in the council remained fairly high during its four sessions. But everyone could have been so much better informed all the time!

It is not as if nobody thought about greater openness. In his letter to Pocock nearly a year before the council opened, Baum wrote "you may know that a number of bishops have tried to persuade the Holy See to alter the present legislation (about secrecy), so that people and clergy will be able to enter into the anxieties of the church and be more willing intelligently to carry out the decisions of the hierarchy."[10] The 1962 CCC statement noted "this is the first time in the history of the world that it is possible for all Christian people to be fully informed almost instantaneously about the activities and concerns of the council. If the great media of communications rise to the high level of accomplishment of which they have proved themselves capable, it could happen that all the members of the church and indeed all men will feel that they are sharing, really and directly, in the council." John XXIII clearly shared this view, as he indicated in his 13 October audience address to journalists as Vatican II opened. Emmett Carter, interviewed after the first session, said plainly "many of us were not satisfied with the council news service. We felt the secrecy observed at previous councils was no longer necessary, and that newspapermen should be allowed in the sessions."[11] Despite all that, Vatican II proceeded until its conclusion under the tattered rule of "secrecy always and everywhere."

The church should declare a universal policy of getting rid of secrets. In the Catholic tradition, poverty is honoured as one of the evangelical virtues. At the council and during the intervening 40 years, much has been said about the importance of the church embracing poverty, and avoiding attachment to possessions, wealth and power. The church should embrace the poverty of living without secrets. I worked for 33 years as a church "insider" employed by the CCCB in Ottawa, the last six years as an assistant general secretary. My strongest recommendation for the future of the church is that it should rid itself of institutional secrecy as an evil possession, one of the most nefarious trappings of power. The human right to personal privacy in some matters is a different matter than institutional secrecy. God works in mysterious ways, but contrived and enforced secrecy is the way of the world. Institutionalized secrecy becomes a social problem in the church as soon as any group – parish council, school board, diocesan committee, chancery consultants, Vatican congregation, conference of bishops, synod of bishops, ecumenical council – claims and enforces an absolute right to "have" secrets. The worst scandal of recent years, the sexual abuse of children by priests, wormed its way into the church and spread because some people in authority assumed the right to deal in secret with these devastating crimes. Rightly, but so sadly, civil courts are now forcing the church to rid itself of these secrets, which truly can be called social sins in such cases.

It is for more positive reasons, however, that the strongest case can be made for a church cleansed of the scandal of secrets and adorned with the beauty of openness, solidarity and trust. At Vatican II, as non-Catholic observers and journalists learned more about how the Catholic church understands itself and how it functions when at its best, they became increasingly appreciative and understanding. Council secrecy prevented millions from having a greater share in this same enlightening experience. An end to secrecy is of the greatest importance to the church in its relations *ad extra*, with other people outside its membership. Within the church, *ad intra*, a major purpose, perhaps *the* major purpose, of Vatican II was to awaken every church member to a sense of belonging and a lively desire to participate. For many, this is taken to mean greater, more active participation in the liturgy, the church's official public worship of God. However, no Vatican II document limits the right and duty to participate in the life of the church to the liturgy alone. The hesitant beginnings of parish and diocesan pastoral councils show there is some understanding of this. But, as in every social body, church members can participate only if they are first informed.

Secrecy, like fear, kills social involvement. Fear and secrecy feed each other, as when it is argued that only in closed meetings will bishops feel free to speak freely. My last day-to-day work in a major church institution was as a CCCB assistant general secretary. A major duty was taking notes and writing minutes whenever bishops met, whether in small committees or plenary meetings. I never heard a discussion or debate that would not have been instructive and even edifying for all church members and other people if made public as it took place. The same can be said for what I know of the successive meetings of the synod of bishops and, above all, of Vatican II. Great care goes into preventing the news media from covering such events. Then, some time later, precious energy and scarce resources have to be devoted to other efforts to inform church members about decisions or programs that were discussed earlier in secret. This, of course, is how governments and corporations work. More valuable even than wealth, the prized possession of those with power in temporal affairs is secrecy. The church should renounce it. For the sake of participation! In the name of solidarity and trust! To embrace poverty! Stripped of the corruption of secrets, we might have greater hope to enter into God's rest.

Forty years I endured that generation.
I said, "They are a people whose hearts go astray
and they do not know my ways."
So I swore in my anger,
"They shall not enter into my rest."

Psalm 95

Notes

Chapter 1

1. The interest of Canadian Protestants was whetted not only by the work of the Canadian Council of Churches, but also by inter-Christian contacts that followed the Second World War, due to the efforts of the World Council of Churches in Geneva and the subsequent participation of the Eastern Orthodox Churches. However, Catholics were not active in these efforts prior to Vatican II.
2. *History of Vatican II,* Guiseppe Alberigo & Joseph A. Komonchak, editors. Maryknoll/Leuven: Orbis/Peeters, Vol. 1, 1995, p. 28.
3. For more details, see "La couverture de Vatican II dans les quotidiens francophones du Canada (1959-1962)," by Yves Therrier in *L'Église canadienne et Vatican II*, Gilles Routhier, dir., Montreal: Fides, 1996, pp. 145-163.
4. Information Service of the Canadian Catholic Conference (*ISCCC*), Ottawa, 28 January 1959.
5. *ISCCC*, 29 January 1959.
6. "Vatican II remains a work in progress," *The Catholic Register*, Toronto, 15 December 2002, p. 8.
7. The version of Congar's journal quoted here is from Guiseppe Alberigo, *History of Vatican II,* Vol. 1, *op. cit.*, p. 43.
8. Guiseppe Alberigo, *Ibid.*, p. 31.
9. Terence J. Fay, *A History of Canadian Catholics,* Montreal & Kingston: McGill-Queen's University Press, 2002.
10. *Ibid.*, p. 95.
11. Michael A. Fahey, "A Vatican Request for Agenda Items prior to Vatican II: Responses by English-speaking Canadian Bishops," *L'Église canadienne et Vatican II, op. cit.*, p. 63.
12. For the 1943 CCC statement, see Minutes, Vol. 1, pp. 8-9, Quinquennial Plenary Meeting of the Canadian Hierarchy, Quebec, 12-13 October 1943, Item 15. CCCB Archives, Ottawa.
13. *ISCCC*, 14 October 1960.
14. For more details, see Real Charbonneau, "L'Action Catholique et l'apostolat des laics au Canada français," *Laicat et Mission,* Nos 14 et 15, April 1962, Numero special sur Action Catholique et Apostolat Laique, p. 99.

15. Bernard M. Daly, *Remembering for Tomorrow: A History of the Canadian Conference of Catholic Bishops 1943-1993*, Concacan: Ottawa, 1995, pp. 29-31.
16. For more details, see Marc Pelchat, "Les revues canadiennes-françaises de dévotion et le concile Vatican II (1959-1962)", *L'Église canadienne et Vatican II, op. cit.*, pp. 165-188.
17. Jean Hamelin, *Histoire du catholicisme québécois III, Le XX siècle: De 1940 à nos jours*, Boréal, p. 111.
18. Claude Ryan, "L'Église du Québec à la veille de Vatican II et de la Révolution tranquille," *Vatican II au Canada: enracinement et reception,* Gilles Routhier, dir. Montreal: Fides, 2001, p. 172.
19. *ISCCC*, 11 February 1959.
20. *ISCCC*, 06 April 1959.
21. *ISCCC*, 16 June 1959.
22. *ISCCC*, 28 August 1959.
23. *ISCCC*, 09 November 1959.
24. *ISCCC*, 06 November 1959.
25. *ISCCC*, 09 December 1959.
26. *ISCCC*, 05 September 1962.
27. Fahey, *op. cit.*, 66.
28. *ISCCC*, 03 September 1959.
29. *ISCCC*, 16 December 1959.
30. *ISCCC*, 02 September 1960.
31. *ISCCC*, 22 November 1960.
32. *ISCCC*, 09 January 1961.
33. *ISCCC*, 20 April 1961.
34. *ISCCC*, 13 April 1962.
35. *ISCCC*, 02 March 1962.
36. *ISCCC*, 12 March 1962.
37. *ISCCC*, 03 July 1962.
38. *ISCCC*, 25 August 1961.
39. *ISCCC*, 03 January 1962
40. *ISCCC*, 22 December 1961.
41. *ISCCC*, 08 June 1959.
42. *ISCCC*, 30 September 1959.
43. *ISCCC*, 04 May 1960.
44. *ISCCC*, 17 October 1960.
45. *ISCCC*, 08 September 1959. Four Basilian priests of St. Michael's College, Toronto, are credited with drafting the articles that appeared regularly under

McGuigan's name: Elliot Allen, Fred Black, Leo Klem and Lawrence Shook. It is not certain, however, which items each one drafted, or whether some might have been prepared by other priests.

46 *ISCCC*, 08 January 1960.
47 *ISCCC*, 21 September 1960.
48 *ISCCC*, 19 April 1961.
49 For details of the Quebec consultations, see Sylvain Serré, "Les consultations préconciliaires des laics au Québec," *L'Église canadienne et Vatican II*, Gilles Routhier, dir., Montreal:Fides, 1997, pp. 114-141. For pre-council clergy consultations, see Pierre Lafontaine, "L'enquête préconciliaire de l'archidiocèse de Montréal auprès du clergé: portrait d'une Église," *ibid.*, pp. 81-98; and Patrick Allaire, "La consultation du clergé de Québec," *ibid.*, pp. 99-111. See also Patrick Allaire, "La consultation du clergé des diocèses de Rimouski, Saint-Jean-de-Québec, Saint-Jérôme at Sherbrooke," *Cheminements,* Centre interuniversitaire d'études québécoises, 2002, pp. 3-11.
50 *ISCCC*, 23 May 1962.
51 *ISCCC*, 08 August 1962.
52 *ISCCC*, 03 October 1962.
53 *Brief to the Bishops: Canadian Catholic Laymen Speak Their Minds,* Paul Harris, ed. Don Mills:Longmans, 1965.
54 José de Broucker, "Le réveil du Québec," *Informations catholiques internationales*, 170 (1962), p. 9.
55 Sylvain Serré, *L'Église canadienne et Vatican II*, pp. 113-141.
56 *Ibid.*, p. 141.
57 CCC Service d'Information, 175 (1962), p. 7.
58 See "Famille, Mariage et Procréation," Gilles Routhier, in *Cristianismo nella storia*, t. 23 (2002), pp. 367-428.
59 *ISCCC*, 26 September 1962.
60 Detailed analyses of Canadian replies can also be found in Gilles Routhier, "Les vota des évêques des dioceses du Québec," *L'Église canadienne et Vatican II, op. cit.*, pp. 25-59, and in Michael A. Fahey, "A Vatican Request for Agenda Items Prior to Vatican II: Responses by English-Speaking Canadian Bishops," and "A Vatican Request for Agenda Items Prior to Vatican II: Responses from Canadian Faculties of Theology," both in *L'Église canadienne et Vatican II*, pp. 62-71 and pp. 73-80. For my own analysis of replies, I thank Bishop Remi De Roo especially for help with the St. Boniface response which he helped to prepare as one of the 19 priests Baudoux consulted at the time. All translations of the French replies of Blais, Coudert and Léger are my own. Peter Clark OP of the Dominican priory in Grenada translated the fine points of Borecky's reply.
61 Michael Barry in telephone interview with Bernard Daly, 30 October 2002.
62 John A. O'Mara, bishop emeritus of St. Catharines, 02 April 2002 letter to Bernard Daly.

63   MGOS 49.55 in Toronto archdiocesan archives.
64   MGOS 49.61B in Toronto archdiocesan archives.
65   McGuigan to MacDonald, May 16, 1950, MGFA16 31(b) in Toronto archdiocesan archives.
66   Charbonneau to McGuigan, MGFA16.58. Handwritten, St. Joseph's Hospital, Victoria, August 29, 1950. Toronto archdiocesan archives.
67   Gilles Routhier, *op. cit.*, p. 57.
68   Gilles Routhier, *ibid.*, p. 33.
69   For more details, see Roberto Perin, *Rome in Canada: The Vatican and Canadian Affairs in the Late Victorian Age.* Toronto: University of Toronto Press, 1990.
70   Letter from Bishop John A. O'Mara, McGuigan's secretary at Vatican II, to Bernard Daly, 02 April 2002.
71   Attached- PO VA13.05(b) Toronto, November 20, 1961. Toronto archdiocesan archives.
72   Gilles Routhier, "Les réactions du Cardinal Léger à la préparation de Vatican II," *Revue d'histoire de l'Église de France*, LXXX, 201 (juillet-décembre 1994, pp. 281-302.
73   The full text of La Supplique Léger can be found at www.ftsr.ulaval.ca/ftsr/vatican2/supplique.html. This citation appears on page 4 of this text.

Chapter 2

1   Andrea Riccardi, "The Tumultuous Opening Days of the Council," *History of Vatican II*, Guiseppe Alberigo and Joseph A. Komonchak, eds., Maryknoll/Leuven: Orbis/Peeters, Vol. II, 1997, p. 4.
2   From Archives of Mgr A. Sanschagrin, Add. 12-17 October 1962, No. 46.
3   Information Service of the Canadian Catholic Conference (*ISCCC*), CCCB archives, 15 October 1962.
4   See Riccardi, *op. cit.*, fn. 29, p. 15.
5   *ISCCC*, 17 October 1962.
6   Sanschagrin archives, Add 12-17 October 1962, no. 45.
7   Bishop John O'Mara letter to Bernard Daly, 02 April 2002.
8   Sanschagrin council journal, Saturday, 27 October, 1962.
9   Canadian Council of Church 08 November 1962 letter signed by Rev. W. J. Gallagher, general secretary. *ISCCC*, 20 November 1962.
10 Other informal groups listed by council historians include the conservative Coetus internatrionalis patrum, the Church of the Poor group whose members included Dom Helder Camara of Brazil, the Central European bloc, the "Zealot Faction of the Curia," the French group whose lectures were attended by a number of Canadians, the Latin American group, the religious superiors, religious bishops, missionary bishops. Their names suggest the lines of common interest that drew bishops to gather at times according to these groupings.

[11] Jan Grootaers of Louvain has done extensive research on the inter-conference group. See, Jan Grootaers, "Une forme de concertation épiscopale au Concile Vatican II: La Conference des Vingt-Deux (1962 and 1963)," *Revue d'Histoire Ecclesiastique*, 91 (1996), pp. 66-112; and "Le catholicisme du Québec et son insertion dans le melieu conciliare," *L'Église canadienne et Vatican II, op.cit.*, pp. 454-457.

[12] Philip Pocock's first session journal, POAA13.003 in Toronto archdiocesan archives.

[13] For this summary, I draw from Mathijs Lamberigts, "The Liturgy Debate," *History of Vatican II*, Vol II, *op. cit.*, pp. 107-166.

[14] Guiseppe Ruggieri, "The First Doctrinal Clash," *History of Vatican II*, Vol. II, *op.cit.*, p. 233.

[15] Ruggieri, *op.cit.*, pp. 247-248.

[16] John A. O'Mara letter to Bernard Daly, *op.cit.*

[17] Ruggieri, *op. cit.*, p. 256.

[18] *Ibid.*, p. 264, and fn. 83.

[19] Mathijs Lamberigts, "The Discussion of the Modern Media," *History of Vatican II*, Vol. II, *op.cit.*, p. 275.

[20] For a fuller account of the debate on revelation, see Ruggieri, *op.cit.*, especially pp. 347-357.

Chapter 3

[1] *ISCCC*, 04 January 1963.

[2] *ISCCC*, 21 January 1963.

[3] *ISCCC*, 04 January 1963.

[4] *ISCCC*, 04 January 1963.

[5] *ISCCC*, 14 January 1963.

[6] *ISCCC*, 07 January 1963.

[7] *ISCCC*, 08 January 1963

[8] *ISCCC*, 29 January 1963.

[9] *ISCCC*, 15 February 1963.

[10] *ISCCC*, 11 January 1963.

[11] *ISCCC*, 20 February 1963.

[12] *ISCCC*, 31 January 1963.

[13] *ISCCC*, 04 January 1963.

[14] *ISCCC*, 12 December 1962. Translation by B. Daly.

[15] *ISCCC*, 15 January 1963.

[16] Jan Grootaers, "The Drama Continues between the Acts: The "Second Preparation" and its Opponents," *History of Vatican II*, Guiseppe Alberigo and Joseph A. Komonchak, eds., Maryknoll/Leuven: Orbis/Peeters, Vol. II, 1997, p. 385.

17   *ISCCC*, 23 January 1963.

18   For details of the first intersession, I supplement my own files with notes from Grootaers, *op. cit.*, as well as Giovanni Turbanti, "La contribution canadienne à l'élaboration de *Gaudium et spes*," *Vatican II au Canada: enracinement et réception*, Gilles Routhier, dir., Montreal:Fides, 2001, pp. 387-426; and Pierre C. Noël, "Le Cardinal Paul-Émile Léger et le *De Ecclesia*," *Cheminements*, Gilles Routhier, dir., *Évêques du Québec (1962–1965): entre Révolultion tranquille et aggiornamento conciliaire*, Ste. Foy: CIEQ, 2002, pp. 29-65.

19   Jan Grootaers, *op. cit.*, pp. 387-391.

20   *Ibid.*, p. 398.

21   Giovanni Turbanti, *op.cit.*, p. 398. Turbanti records a note by theologian Charles Moeller that Léger read his text at 16h30 on 23 May 1963. Congar, in turn, wrote in his journal for that day: "Very remarkable interventions by Cardinal Léger and Père de Riedmatten." (Mon journal du concile, 23 May 1963).

22   Report No. 5 in the RIIR file for the meeting in Geneva, 2 February 1963. See also *History of Vatican II, op.cit.*, Vol. II, footnote 119, p. 553, and footnote 132, p. 558.

23   Baum to Pocock, 30 May 1963. PO VA13.04.13 in Toronto archdiocesan archives.

24   PO VA13.04(b) in Toronto archdiocesan archives.

25   PO VA13.04(c) in Toronto archdiocesan archives.

26   PO VA13.04(d) in Toronto archdiocesan archives.

27   PO VA10.05 in Toronto archdiocesan archives.

28   *ISCCC*, 05 September 1963.

29   *ISCCC*, 07 October 1963.

30   For a personal account by Tillard of his work with the Canadian bishops at the council, see J.M.R. Tillard, "L'épiscopat canadien francophone au concile," *l'Église canadienne et Vatican II, op. cit.*, pp. 291-301.

31   *ISCCC*, 01 March 1963.

32   *ISCCC*, 14 March 1963.

33   *ISCCC*, 15 March 1963.

34   *ISCCC*, 26 April 1963.

35   *ISCCC*, 06 May 1963.

36   *ISCCC*, 08 May 1963.

Chapter 4

1   Carlo Falconi, *I Perché del concilio*, Milan, 1962, p. 174. Cited in *History of Vatican II, op. cit.*, Vol. II, pp. 209-210.

2   Hilari Raguer, "An Initial Profile of the Assembly," *History of Vatican II, op.cit.*, Vol. II, pp. 210-211.

3   *ISCCC*, 07 October 1963. See also Bernard M. Daly, "Maxim Hermaniuk: Canadian Father of collegiality at Vatican II … and after," *Vatican II au Canada: enracinement et réception, op. cit.*, pp. 427-439.

4   Xavier Rynne, *The Second Session*, New York: Farrar, Straus & Giroux, 1964, p. 163.
5   *ISCCC*, 21 October 1963.
6   Hilari Raguer, "An Initial Profile of the Assembly," *History of Vatican II*, Vol. II, *op. cit.*, p. 182.
7   *ISCCC*, 05 November 1963.
8   *Idem*.
9   I am endebted to Aloysius Kedl, archivist at the Oblate general house in Rome, for this summary of the Deschatelets intervention.
10 See "Vatican II remains a work in progress," *The Catholic Register*, 15 December 2002, p. 15.
11 *ISCCC*, 20 November 1963.
12 Jan Grootaers, "Le catholicisme du Québec et son insertion dans le milieu conciliaire," *L'Église canadienne et Vatican II*, *op. cit.*, p. 448.
13 Jan Grootaers, *idem*, p. 451.
14 *ISCCC*, 13 December 1963.
15 Reiner Kaczynski, "Toward the Reform of the Liturgy," *History of Vatican II*, Vol. III, 2000, *op. cit.*, p. 219.

Chapter 5

1   Remi De Roo interview with Bernard Daly, Toronto, 23 July 2002.
2   BC1304 in Baudoux council archives at St. Boniface.
3   *ISCCC*, 27 August 1964.
4   For details of this process, see Giovanni Turbanti, "La contribution canadienne à la élaboration de *Gaudium et spes*," *Vatican II au Canada: enracinement et réception, op. cit.*, pp. 398–420.
5   PO VA13.04(d) in Toronto archdiocesan archives.
6   Gregory Baum, *That They May Be One*, London: Bloomsbury, 1958.
7   Westminster, MD: Newman Press, 1961.
8   Gregory Baum, "Un Souvenir de *Nostra Aetate*," *Vatican II au Canada: enracinement et réception, op. cit.*, pp. 449–460. For more details on the evolution of the council text on Jews, see John Österreicher, "On the Declaration on the Relationship of the Church to Non-Christian Religions," in H. Vorgrimmler (dir.), *Commentaries on the Documents of Vatican II*, vol. III, Freiburg/Montreal:Herder/Palm Publishers, 1968, pp. 1–136.
9   Pocock, handwritten, to Sergio Pignedoli, 27 September 1964. PO VA04.18(c) in Toronto archdiocesan archives.
10 A copy of Carter's letter to Pignedoli is PO VA04.18(9) in the Toronto archdiocesan archives.
11 Bernard Daly telephone interview with Bishop Borecky, Toronto, 30 October 2002.

12. *Basilian Newsletter*, 3 November 1964, 5; cited by P. Wallace Platt, *Gentle Eminence: A Life of Cardinal Flahiff*, McGill-Queen's University Press, 1999, p. 103.
13. See Decree on The Means of Social Communication, Decree on Ecumenism, Decree on the Pastoral Office of Bishops, Declaration on Christian Education.
14. Personal conversation between Bernard Daly and Bishop Carter, December 1996. See also Bernard M. Daly, "Four Canadian Interventions Helped to Shape Vatican II Decree on the Lay Apostolate," *L'Église canadienne et Vatican II, op. cit.*, pp. 277-290.
15. Denise Robillard, "Mgr Gérard-Marie Coderre: consultation et concertation," *L'Église canadienne et Vatican II, op.cit.*, p. 273.
16. Flahiff letter to Laurence Shook, cited by P. Wallace Platt, *op. cit.*, pp. 99-100. Flahiff referred to Pocock's July 1963 confidential letter to Toronto priests about giving advice in the confessional about birth control. The book mentioned is *Contraception and Holiness: The Catholic Predicament*, New York: Herder and Herder, 1964, a collection of essays by moral theologians arguing for a reconsideration of Catholic teaching on the morality of artificial contraceptives.
17. Also cited by P. Wallace Platt, *op. cit.*, p. 99.
18. Giovanni Turbanti, *op. cit.*, p. 409, quotes an entry in Yves Congar's council journal for 11 September 1964: "Delhaye tells me that Archbishop Roy not only has Fr. Lambert and a layman (De Koninck) as theologians but has a report by the latter in favour of the contraceptive pill…."
19. C. De Koninck and Maurice Dionne, "Le Problème de l'infécondité," *Perspectives sociales*, Vol. 20, No. 1, 1965, pp. 10-16.
20. Xavier Rynne, *The Third Session*, New York: Farrar, Straus & Giroux, 1965, p. 258.
21. *Ibid.*, p. 260.

Chapter 6

1. Xavier Rynne, *The Fourth Session*, New York: Farrar, Straus & Giroux, 1966, p. 208.
2. *ISCCC*, 25 October 1965.
3. In this account I depend on Giovanni Turbanti, "La contribution canadienne à l'élaboration de *Gaudium et spes*," *Vatican II au Camada: enracinement et reception, op. cit.*, pp. 398-426.
4. *Ibid*, footnote 79, p. 417.

Conclusion

1. Xavier Rynne, *The Third Session, op. cit.*, p. 16.
2. Denise Robillard, "Mgr Gérard-Marie Coderre: consultation et concertation," *L'Église canadienne et Vatican II, op. cit.*, p. 267.
3. J.M.R. Tillard, "L'épiscopat canadien francophone au concile," *L'Église canadienne et Vatican II*, p. 292.

4   Sanschagrin archives, Add 12-17 October 1962, No. 45.
5   Denise Robillard, *op. cit.*, p. 276.
6   Réjean Plamondon, "Le service d'information de la CCC à Vatican II," *L'Église canadienne et Vatican II, op. cit.,* pp. 218-219.
7   Sanschagrin archives, *op. cit.*
8   André Naud, "Le cardinal Léger au concile et la conduite de l'intelligence chrétienne," *L'Église canadienne et Vatican II, op. cit.*, p..263. My summary of Naud's views is drawn from this same article.
9   Xavier Rynne may be a pseudonym for co-authors, with Murphy the man with access to the council. The whole story may not be known until some forensic accountant "follows the money" to verify who was paid for the articles and books by *The New Yorker* and Farrar, Straus & Giroux.
10 Baum to Pocock, 20 November 1961. PO VA13.05(a) in Toronto archdiocesan archives.
11 *ISCCC*, 08 January 1963.

Index of Names

Agagianian, P.G. 126
Ahern, Barnabas 31, 91
Alfrink, B.J. 64, 67, 91, 182
Allen, Francis V. 112
Alvarez, Mr. J. and Mrs. L. 216
Antoniutti, Ildabrando 42
Audet, Lionel 54
Audet, René 211-213

Bader, Edward 144, 145, 176
Baggio, Sebastiano 24, 75, 133, 162
Baillargeon, Hélène and Jacques 183
Barry, Michael J. 41, 77
Baudoux, Maurice 41, 52, 53-54, 66, 70, 76, 78, 84, 85, 86, 87, 90, 102-103, 106, 114, 119, 124-125, 133, 134, 140, 149-151, 173, 174, 200, 218, 221, 222, 223, 226
Baum, Gregory 10, 33, 55, 56-61, 78, 93, 103-104, 111-114, 158-159, 223, 230
Bea, A. 56, 60, 91, 93, 98, 107, 113, 158, 172-173
Bélanger, Marcel 54, 114
Bélanger, V. 78
Belleville, Jean-Paul 144, 145, 160
Bernier, Paul 54, 61, 83
Bissonnette, Romuald 160
Blais, Leo 43, 45-46
Borecky, Isidore 50-52, 162, 173, 200
Bourgeois, G.E. 55
Breault, Rita and Gilles 183

Brennan, Bonnie 144, 145, 175-177
Brisbois, G.M. 54
Brodeur, Rosario 76
Browne, Michael 110, 120, 182
Bruchesi, Jean 74-75
Budka, Nicetas 49

Cabana, Georges 36, 41, 44, 54-55, 79, 92, 218, 221, 224
Cardijn, Joseph 171
Carley, John 77, 119, 151
Carisse, Colette 184
Carter, Alexander 36, 41, 55, 103, 113, 114, 116, 164-166, 167, 168, 171, 218
Carter, G. Emmett 102, 137, 162, 194, 231
Caza, Percival 145
Charbonneau, Joseph 28, 29, 42, 43, 113, 114, 145, 165, 166
Charbonneau, Paul-Émile 164, 167, 168, 169, 170-172, 208-209, 210-213, 218, 223
Cicognani, A.G. 112, 127
Clark, Howard H. 32
Clusiau, Marie 77, 151
Cochran, Gerald J. 103
Coderre, Gérard-Marie 36, 53, 95, 135-136, 145, 179-180, 204-205, 218, 221, 223, 225
Cody, John C. 41, 78, 133
Congar, Yves 13, 19

Contant, Cyrille 76
Coudert, J.L. 43, 45, 46, 83
Couture, Cyrille 77

Danielou, J. 13, 108
Davidson, Richard H. 132
de Broucker, José 36
De Koninck, Charles 152, 153, 183, 185-188, 213, 227
De Margarie, Bernard 35, 77
De Riedmatten, Henri 216
De Roo, Remi 53, 164, 166-168, 170-172, 175, 176, 178-179, 202-203, 208, 209-210, 218, 223
de Smedt, E.J. 58, 61
Delhaye, Philippe 61
Deschatelets, Léo 78, 134, 218
Descorcy, Jean 207
Desmarais, Joseph A. 41
Desrochers, Bruno 36
Desrosiers, Yvon 144
Diefenbaker, John 15
Diekmann, Godfrey 31, 148
Dionne, Maurice 185-186, 188
Doepfner, J. 64, 67, 126, 176
Douville, Arthur 44, 54
Doyle, Emmett 102
Duke, William 41, 115
Dunn, Bernie 196
Duplessis, Maurice 15, 27, 29
Dwyer, Paul 207

Etchegaray, Roger 85
Ewen, John 133

Fahey, Michael 21, 32
Fairweather, Eugene 132
Fay, Terence 21
Felici, Pericles 120, 172-173
Fitzpatrick, Robert G. 103
Flahiff, George Bernard 54, 78, 84, 102, 139, 141-142, 162-164, 182-183, 218, 222

Forest, Pierre 144, 145
Fortin, Robert 83
Foucreault, Lucien 114
Frenette, Émelien 36, 55, 145
Frings, J. 64, 67, 71, 91
Furlong, Monica 72-73

Gallagher, Norman 159-160
Gallagher, W.J. 16-17
Garant, Charles Omer 83
Garvey, Edward 115
George, Gordon 77
Gervais, Jacques 115
Gregory VII 130
Grootaers, Jan 85
Grossman, Allan 158
Guay, André 54

Hacault, Antoine 114, 203-204, 223
Haering, Bernard 188
Haines, Gaston 211-213
Hamelin, Jean 28-29
Harrington, Michael A. 41
Haubtmann, Pierre 188
Haucault, Antoine 53, 178, 179, 218
Hayes, James M. 77
Henripin, Jacques 184
Hermaniuk, Maxim 54, 55, 78, 94, 95-96, 103, 121-124, 134, 142, 145, 149-150, 173, 175, 200, 218, 221, 223
Heston, Edward 117, 119
Howell, Clifford 148
Hrnchyshyn, Michael 115

Jaeger, L. 58
Jette, Edouard 36, 41
John Paul II 162
John XXIII 10, 11, 12, 15, 16, 17, 18, 19, 20, 24, 30, 32, 34, 38, 39, 40, 42, 45, 49, 56, 61, 62, 64, 65-67, 69, 74, 75-76, 78, 83, 85, 86, 88, 91, 93, 94, 95, 97, 98, 101, 103,

104, 105-106, 108, 116, 121, 128, 129, 137, 143, 150, 158, 180, 199, 217, 220, 221, 224, 227, 229, 231
Johnson, Martin 41
Jordan, Anthony 101, 198-199, 200, 218

Kaiser, Bob 230
Karsh, Yousef 20
Keirans, Hugh P. 35
Klein, F.J. 31, 196
Koenig, F. 64, 67, 91
Krol, J. 176
Küng, Hans 13
Kutarna, Emil 35
Kutz, Stan 103

Labelle, Lucien 95
Laberge, Léo 54. 114-115
Labourdette, Michel 108
Lafortune, Pierre 61, 109, 146
Lalande, Germain-Marie 190-191, 218
Lambert, Bernard 115, 152-153, 177, 185-186, 198, 213-215, 223, 227
Landazuri-Ricketts, J. 163
Langlois, Joseph A. 52
LeBlanc, Camille 44
Leclaire, J.C. 25
Leddy, John Francis 162
Legault, Émile 144
Léger, Jules 72, 75,
Léger, Paul-Émile 13, 18, 29-30, 35, 36, 38-39, 43, 47-48, 53, 54, 61, 62-67, 69, 71, 72, 75, 78, 79-83, 87, 88, 90-91, 93, 94, 95, 97-98, 104-105, 107, 108-110, 120, 125-126, 130-131, 132, 139-141, 146, 147, 152, 153-157, 158, 161, 162-163, 172-173, 174-175, 176, 178, 181-182, 183, 188-190, 191-194, 198, 201-202, 205-208, 215-217, 218, 221-223, 225-227

Lemieux, Gerard 144
Lemieux, Marie-Joseph 29, 36-37, 41, 44, 78, 81
Leo XIII 25, 26, 44, 137
Lercaro, G. 126, 176
Lesage, Jean 27
Leverman, Alfred B. 44, 102
Liénart, A. 64, 67, 71, 91, 176
Limoges, Raymond 77, 119, 151
Lio, Ermenegildo 108
Littell, F.H. 115-116
Lonergan, Bernard 115
Lussier, Philippe 101

MacDonald, John Hugh 33
MacGillivray, Don 196
Machado, Adelmo 196
MacIsaac, J.K. 207
Mackenzie, R.A.F. 91, 115
MacNeil, Marie 77
Maddocks, Edward H. 133
Malanchuk, Vladimir 142, 173, 218, 221
Marrocco, Francis A. 112
Marsolais, L.J.M. 159
Martin, Albertus 36, 41, 50, 52-53, 58, 78, 81, 87-88, 136-137
Masson, Hélène 77
Mathieu, Charles-É. 77, 151, 225
Maximos IV 150, 182
McCarthy, Thomas J. 31
McDonald, Donald E. 103
McGuigan, James 18, 31, 32, 35, 41, 42-43, 44, 54, 55, 61, 72, 75, 80-81, 91, 132, 224
McManus, Fred 148
Melançon, Georges 41
Meyer, A. G. 163, 195, 227
Moeller, C. 109
Monnet, Marie-Louise 176
Montini, G.B. 42, 64, 98, 106
Morisset, Bernard 114
Moss, John E. 103

Murphy, Francis X. 230
Mutchmore, James R. 132-133

Naud, André 61, 146, 226-227
Newman, J.H. 155

O'Connor, M. 111
O'Donovan, Patrick 72
Ogle, Bob 196
O'Leary, William J. 103
O'Mara, John A. 42, 91, 176
O'Neill, J.M. 115, 132, 146
O'Reilly, Michael 44
O'Sullivan, Joseph A. 41
Ottaviani, A. 78, 90, 91, 98, 107, 109, 110, 176, 182, 216-217

Papineau, J.A. 41
Paré, Marius 78
Parent, C.E. 36, 41,
Parente, P. 109
Paul VI 13, 52, 85, 86, 110, 113, 116, 118, 121, 122, 126, 127-128, 137, 138, 140, 142, 147, 149, 150, 161, 173, 180-181, 184, 188, 189, 194-195, 197-198, 215-217, 216-217, 221, 224, 227-228
Pelletier, Georges-L. 44, 54, 78, 88, 93, 107, 108, 152, 224
Pelletier-Baillargeon, Hélène 52
Philips, G. 97, 109
Pignedoli, Sergio 161, 162
Piser, Bob (*see* Kaiser, Bob)
Pius XI 25, 26, 137, 187, 216-217
Pius XII 18, 21, 23, 26, 27, 30, 31, 44, 59, 88, 187-188, 194, 216-217
Plamondon, Réjean 110, 128, 143, 144, 225
Plaskett, Charles R. 132-133
Pocock, Philip 31, 32, 36, 41-42, 43, 54, 55, 56, 78, 79, 87, 103, 111-114, 157-158, 161-162, 182, 218, 220, 222, 225, 230

Poilievre, Cecile 196
Potvin, Laurent and Colette 184
Poitevin, J.M. 55, 95, 144
Power, William 164, 166-167, 170-172, 218, 223

Quiriga y Palacios, F. 91

Rahner, Karl 13, 21, 90, 97
Raiche, Ida 196
Rainville, Thérèse 77
Ratzinger, Joseph 13, 90
Raymond, Gilles 77
Rioux, Bertrand 184
Ritter, J. 91, 195, 227
Roberts, Thomas 230
Roborecki, Andrew 50, 102, 142-143, 173, 218, 221
Rock, John 187
Roman, Stephen 161-162, 201
Rousseau, Joseph 54
Routhier, Gilles 18, 27, 28, 44, 61, 138, 229
Routhier, Henri 79, 101-102
Roy, Maurice 29, 36, 37, 41, 53, 54, 78, 81, 88, 93, 106, 107, 108, 131, 150, 152, 153, 154, 159, 160, 177, 183, 185, 188, 198, 208, 213, 215-217, 216, 218, 226, 227, 228
Ruffini, E. 91, 176, 182, 194, 226
Ruggieri, Giuseppe 93
Rusnak, Michael 173, 200-201, 218, 224
Ryan, Claude 29, 36, 41, 104, 143
Ryan, Joseph R. 41
Rynne, Xavier (*see* Murphy, Francis X.)

Sanschagrin, Albert 24, 36, 70, 76, 79, 82, 94-95, 218, 221, 224, 225
Savaryn, N. 173
Schillebeeckx, Edward 90, 97
Shea, John 77

Silva, F. da 176
Siri, G. 91
Skinner, Patrick I. 31, 44
Slipyi, J. 145
Smith, Nora 77, 151,
Smith, William 41
Smulders, Peter 214
Somerville, Henry 25
Spellman, F. 176
Suenens, L. 64, 67, 91, 97, 98, 106,
    109, 126, 128, 129, 152, 180, 182,
    183

Tardini, D. 39-40, 41, 43, 50, 82
Thérrien, Jean M. 207
Tillard, Jean-Marie 115, 223, 225
Tisserant, E. 195
Turbanti, G. 153, 188

Van Den Broeck, Gommar 54
Vanier, Georges 138, 139
Veuillot, Pierre 85
Villeneuve, Jean-Marie-Rodrique 22
Visser't Hooft, W.A. 17

Weigel, Gustave 32
Wheeler, G.W.B. 133
Wilhelm, Joseph 132
Wojtyla, Karol 175

MEMBER OF SCABRINI MEDIA
Quebec, Canada
2003